VIETNAM REVISITED

Vietnam Revisited

From Covert Action
to Invasion
to Reconstruction

David Dellinger

South End Press   **Boston**

Design, typesetting and layout by South End Press
Manufactured in the U.S.A.
Cover by Todd Jailer

Library of Congress Cataloging-in-Publication Data

Dellinger, David, 1915-
    Vietnam revisited.

    1. Vietnam—History—1945-1975.   2. Vietnam—
History—1975-   .   I. Title.
DS 556.8.D45   1986   959.704   86-6631
ISBN 0-89608-320-9
ISBN 0-89608-319-5 (pbk.)

South End Press
116 St. Botolph St.
Boston, MA 02115

Dedication

To six friends who fought in Vietnam:

Eddie Wright, John Watson, Louis Pulver,
John Sheehan, Ron Kovic and Barry Romo;

And to All Veterans of the Vietnam War:

Those Who Fought In It
and
Those Who Fought Against It

Acknowledgements

We all need each other, and there were a lot of people whose help I particularly needed in order to write this book. Some made it possible for me to travel to Vietnam. Others helped by reading all or parts of the evolving text and making it more readable and free of factual errors than it otherwise would have been. I want to express my especial thanks and appreciation to some of them here.

In alphabetical order, let me mention Mike Albert, Peter Biskind, Noam Chomsky, Dan Dellinger, W.H. and Carol B. Ferry, Mitchell Goodman, Betsy Hess, Scott Hines, Todd Jailer, Arthur Kinoy, Berta Langston, John McAuliff, Elizabeth Peterson, Barbara Webster, Dan Weiner and Nancy Wiegersma. There is no way I can adequately thank these people, but I do want to absolve them of any weaknesses or errors that remain. As a couple of them know, their interpretations sometimes differed from my own. Although I benefitted greatly from their help, here and there I stuck to views that preserve the difference.

For those readers who might not know, Todd Jailer was my long suffering and skilled editor at South End Press. Elizabeth Peterson is my even longer suffering wife and "best friend." Elizabeth not only encouraged and supported me but did a sterling job of simplifying innumerable sentences that were originally too complex and confusing to stand the test of her common sense and high standards for written communication.

In addition to the above, I want to thank some others who are too numerous to name personally. I read parts of the book to four groups that provided support and stimulating comments. These were: 1) my fifteen-member nonviolent affinity group, Northern Lights; 2) a group of friends and neighbors in Peacham, Vermont; 3) students and faculty attending a summer session of the Social Ecology Institute; and 4) students, faculty and staff of the Adult Degree Program at Vermont College who were in my residency group or who attended a weekend conference of the ADP faculty.

Finally, I want to thank a lot of Vietnamese people, a few of whose names appear in the text. I am speaking in particular of: 1) ardent supporters of the current regime who spoke honestly of its (and their) shortcomings and mistakes; and 2) more severe critics of the regime who honestly expressed their respect for those things in it that they found valuable.

Table of Contents

Introduction

I began this book to report on a visit I made to Vietnam in April-May, 1985, on the tenth anniversary of the end of the U.S.-Vietnam war. But a strange thing happened when I sat down to write. I found myself writing about events that began forty years earlier, in 1945. Why?

In August and September of 1945 the Western Allies did something in Vietnam that most Americans would consider almost impossible to believe. What they did and why helps to explain the subsequent history of U.S.-Vietnamese relations. And the history of U.S.-Vietnam relations from 1945 to the present helps to explain what the U.S. is doing in other countries today—in Southeast Asia of course, but also in Central America, the Middle East, Southern Africa, etc.—all around the globe.

In Part One I present some highlights (really lowpoints) of a mostly unknown history, from 1945 to 1965, that had catastrophic results for millions of Vietnamese and hundreds of thousands of young Americans and their families, lovers, neighbors and friends. The events and attitudes described are not ancient history. They reveal patterns that persist today and are harmful to the legitimate aspirations and inalienable rights of millions of people. The earlier policies climaxed in a tragic war. Today's policies threaten to culminate in an even greater catastrophe for all of us, Americans and non-Americans alike.

In Vietnam the human losses were horrendous, but did not lead to nuclear war. We were saved by some not completely understood combination of luck and the restraining hand of a finally aroused and rebellious American people. Several times the U.S. stopped short of using The Bomb. Now, under a right-wing Reaganite regime, a psychology has developed which makes it less likely that our government would accept defeat in a new Vietnam anywhere in the world, no matter what the consequences of that refusal. If a newly aroused and rebellious public does not reverse the present trend, the next climax may provide the answer to the debate about whether anyone or anything will survive nuclear war.

The purpose of my early chapters, then, is not simply to provide a clearer picture of Vietnam today by showing some of the internal and external forces which have formed it. Indeed, this is an important task, which I try to accomplish. But much of the information I discuss tells us more about the United States than about Vietnam. It tells us about the United States in the Fifties, Sixties, Seventies and Eighties—and as it will be in the Nineties and into the Twenty-first Century (if we survive that long), if we fail to face up to these realities and change them.

In 1945, the U.S. government decided to violate its anti-colonialist promises of World War II and suppress the Vietnamese independence movement. At the time, most Americans didn't even know Vietnam existed, let alone worry about its independence. But if the methods it used to suppress Vietnam's independence had been made public, they would have shocked the American people. Even General Douglas MacArthur was horrified (see Chapter One).

From that time on, in one form or another, the U.S. opposed Vietnamese independence through twenty years of covert warfare. Even publicly proclaimed policies, such as supporting the cruel and repressive Diem regime in South Vietnam (see Chapter Five) had their real character and purpose camouflaged by a tissue of disinformation and lies. Contrary to a popular misconception, we did not stumble into the Vietnam War by mistake. U.S. actions from 1945 to 1965, laid the groundwork for the next ten years of full-scale warfare from which neither Vietnam nor the United States has recovered to this day—Vietnam physically and politically, the United States spiritually and politically.

A veteran anti-war activist to whom I sent the early chapters phoned long-distance to say that he was shocked by things he had not known during his anti-war days. Two Vietnam veterans who had willingly fought in the war responded similarly. If people as directly involved at the time as these three knew only a small part of the background to the war that has forever changed their lives, what can we expect of the generations who have grown up in the intervening years? For them, the public focus has shifted from Vietnam, except for the efforts of partisan propagandists to falsify that history to justify current U.S. interventions in other countries.

One of the continuing realities, from 1945 to the present, is this huge gap between governmental policy and public knowledge. Sometimes the gap results from the inability of the media to penetrate a screen of governmental secrecy and lies. Sometimes it is caused by a form of self-censorship in response to two realities of our technically free press. The first reality is the business needs of the gigantic corporations that dominate the public's normal access to the news. They depend on corporate advertisers for profits and on governmental "information" for a substantial portion of what is presented as news. The second reality is the belief of most large publishers and TV executives that their own self-interest and that of the country require a perpetuation of the status quo.

Most honest journalists who have been around for a while will say privately—to someone they trust—that these considerations have a profound effect on the views of editors and publishers in determining what is proper for the American people to know. After a while, smart reporters learn what kind of stories their editors and publishers want them to file. They learn what kind of material will be censored at the editor's desk or in the cutting room. If they want to work their way up the corporate ladder—or simply to remain in good standing—they must play down certain items or present them in a context that "balances" them. A lot of important information appears briefly and then is left to die, not followed up on.

An example of the latter is the media's handling of former Senator J. William Fulbright's statement in 1985 that he believes that the Korean Air Liner 007 was on a governmental spy mission when it was shot down (see Chapter Six). If U.S. intelligence services did indeed "kidnap" an airliner loaded with civilians and divert it to a dangerous spy mission, in which they all died, thanks in part to Soviet paranoia, the implications are far reaching and frightening. And Fulbright is not someone whose views on such subjects can be dismissed lightly—except by the mass media. He was chairman of the Senate Foreign Relations Committee at the time of the 1964 Gulf of Tonkin incident (discussed in Chapter Six). He was told, like everyone else and contrary to the truth, that the North Vietnamese had launched an unprovoked attack on the U.S. destroyer Maddox. Supposedly it was "peacefully minding its own business" in the Gulf of Tonkin. From a series of such experiences, he now says that

> "The biggest lesson I learned from Vietnam is not to trust Government statements... They fit the facts to fit the policy," he said of officials' statements on Vietnam and Central America.[1]

Senator Fulbright looked beneath the government's claims that the 007, "accidentally" off course for 5 hours and 26 minutes and with its lights out, was "peacefully minding its own business" over sensitive Soviet military installations.[2]

Senator Fulbright concluded that the government was lying to us—and said so. The story appeared once in the inside pages of the *New*

York Times and then was left by the *Times* and the rest of the media to die, suffocated by a lack of public airing.

Actually the failings of the press are probably somewhat worse now than they were during the Vietnam War. While a certain amount of attention has been paid by the peace-and-justice movement to what the government learned from its Vietnam failure, not enough is paid to what the major publishers and TV producers learned. While they learned to distrust government news and information, they also learned to fear the growth of a massive public resistance movement similar to the one that so thoroughly frightened them in the late Sixties. So they are discreet in the extent to which they reveal their suspicions. They concentrate on minor details and safe areas rather than on fundamental or dangerous questions that might arouse or inflame the public. And they downplay a domestic resistance movement that is far more extensive than one could possibly realize by reading the daily papers or listening to the TV news. The movement that they report on as if it were insignificant and impotent is potentially both contagious and explosive. This is what they are guarding against.

Finally, in Part One we see the underlying continuity in the government's activities and deceptions through a series of supposedly contrasting Democratic and Republican administrations—those of Truman, Eisenhower, Kennedy and the early Johnson administration—right up to the time when the war burst suddenly and unexpectedly upon the public consciousness and began, step by painful step, to produce the massive anti-war movement of the late Sixties and early Seventies. This continuity tells us something about the limitations of working for peace and justice by exclusively electoral means. It reminds us of the importance of building an informed and active mass resistance movement, such as the one that lost the 1968 and 1972 elections but made it impossible for the winning administration of Nixon and Kissinger to continue the war. In my view, that need not mean withdrawing entirely from electoral politics and lobbying, flawed as they are in a society dominated by money and the power of a mass media whose in-house censors are part of and committed to the status quo. But it means not allowing such activities to crowd out more basic forms of grassroots and national protest and affirmation.

In Part Two, I concentrate on the present situation in Vietnam. There is a tendency for people to want simple answers to complex problems. Over and over, I found people wanting me to tell them in a few unequivocal words whether Vietnam is a good society or a bad one, totalitarian or free. But my 1985 visit convinced me that the positive and negative factors are far too diverse and transitional to justify simplistic answers. I found some aspects of Vietnam disappointing and frightening. I found other aspects encouraging and superior to the way we go about things in the United States.

Which of these aspects will triumph is hard to tell. Vietnam's forms and traditions are different than ours. Moreover, the direction in which their society moves is heavily influenced by the direction in which our society moves. Will the U.S. continue in its efforts to punish the Vietnamese for their insolent rejection of our domination, their insistence on wanting to be independent and to develop their society in accord with their own traditions and views? Will the U.S. continue to drive them into the arms of the Soviet Union in order to prove that developing countries cannot be independent and non-aligned but must accept a subservient relationship to one or the other superpower? For all these reasons, I began by describing what I had seen, experienced or heard. Sometimes I contrasted this with examples of the flagrantly distorted U.S. reportage that came out of Vietnam during this period. Perhaps inevitably, I occasionally departed from this discipline and offered some personal speculations on the directions in which Vietnam seems to be moving and the strength of the forces that may carry it in one direction or another.

I have also tried to guard against responding to the U.S. media and government caricatures of Vietnam by overemphasizing the positive side of what I observed. My aim at all times was to avoid double standards: the one by which Americans condemn in Vietnam things that they support in the United States; or, alternatively, any tendency to make excuses for negative features of Vietnam that I do not accept when they occur in slightly different form here.

Finally, as I wrote I kept wishing that I could be miraculously transported back to Vietnam to ask follow-up questions or conduct further research. I longed to be able to provide more complete information on most of the subjects I discuss. My visit was shorter than I wish it had been and as a result some of my information is too fragmentary to provide as conclusive an indication of the current Vietnamese reality and trends as I would like to provide an open-minded reader. My hope is that other visitors will take the process of investigation further and that they will be helped in doing so by what I have written. Meanwhile, I have tried to make clear both the strengths and the limitations of the knowledge that I do have.

Another aim, of course, is to provide some useful first-hand information about the nature of a society that has played such an important role in our recent history, has suffered—and is still suffering—so much at our hands. I hope that in doing so I will help counteract the misinformation and disinformation that dominate our media and permeate the propaganda of those who are determined to prove that in Vietnam "there is nothing good under the sun," only evil so bad that in retrospect the American war was justified. Obviously, a second, ongoing purpose of such propaganda is to justify the current

U.S. interventions in Central America and elsewhere—and to pave the way, "if necessary," for future Vietnam wars.

Beyond this, I hope that the following pages will provide information of a different kind of political usefulness. I hope they will add to our knowledge of the efforts of a courageous people to build a non-capitalist, non-totalitarian society that will provide its own forms of justice and fulfillment for all its members. Despite the differences between their culture and problems and ours, we have a lot to learn from their experiments under extraordinarily difficult conditions.

Part I

The Long Road to Independence

Vietnam Emerges from World War II: Early Betrayals by the U.S.

> If there is anything that makes my blood boil, it is to see our allies in Indochina and Java deploying Japanese troops to reconquer the little people we promised to liberate.
> —General Douglas MacArthur
> In Tokyo, shortly after the end of World War II.[1]

When World War II ended on August 15, 1945, Vietnam erupted in favor of the independence that it had long struggled for and that had been promised by the Allies. By August 17, the Viet Minh, or League for the Independence of Vietnam,[2] had taken power in Hanoi. On August 26, the Viet Minh People's Committee took power in Saigon. On September 2, with the Viet Minh "solidly in power in the north and the south,"[3] half a million Vietnamese gathered peacefully in Hanoi's Ba Dinh Square and Ho Chi Minh read Vietnam's Declaration of Independence.

The document was modelled in form and content on the U.S. Declaration of Independence, beginning with the opening words:

> "All men are created equal. They are endowed by their Creator with certain inalienable rights; among these are Life, Liberty and the pursuit of Happiness."

> This immortal statement appeared in the Declaration of Independence of the United States of America in 1776. In a broader sense, it means: All the peoples on the earth are equal

1

from birth, all the peoples have a right to live, to be happy and free...

Nevertheless, for more than eighty years, the French imperialists, abusing the standard of Liberty, Equality and Fraternity, have violated our Fatherland and oppressed our fellow citizens... They have deprived our people of every democratic liberty.

The document then enumerates a long list of abuses suffered under the French, similar to the listing of abuses the American colonists suffered under King George the Third. A couple of them give the flavor:

They have built more prisons than schools. They have mercilessly slain our patriots...

They have robbed us of our rice fields, our mines, our forests and our raw materials. They have monopolized the issuing of bank notes and the export trade.

They have invented numerous unjustifiable taxes...

Yet, despite the atrocities suffered by the Vietnamese during nearly a century of white, Western imperialism, there are no traces of racism in the Declaration, nothing similar to those which demean the otherwise noble American document, with its reference to "the merciless Indian savages." Instead, the Vietnamese conclude their list with a massacre of six months earlier and cite their response as an example of their positive attitude toward the French people.

After four-and-a-half years of French collaboration with the Japanese, they say, with "our people subjected to the double yoke of the French and the Japanese," on March 9, 1945 the Japanese attacked the French and the French "either fled or surrendered." When this happened,

The French colonialists so intensified their terrorist activities against the Viet Minh members that before fleeing they massacred a great number of our political prisoners detained at Yen Bay and Caobang.

In spite of all this, our fellow citizens have always manifested a tolerant and humane attitude towards the French people. After the Japanese putsch of March 9, 1945, the Viet Minh helped many Frenchmen to cross the frontier, rescued others from Japanese jails and protected French lives and property...

The French have fled, the Japanese have capitulated, Emperor Bao Dai has abdicated. Our people have broken the chains which have fettered them for nearly a century and have won independence for Vietnam...and established a democratic, republican regime.

We are convinced that the Allies who at the Teheran and San Francisco conferences upheld the principle of equality among the nations cannot fail to recognize the right of the Vietnamese people to independence.[4]

A people who have courageously opposed French enslavement for more than eighty years, a people who have courageously sided with the Allies against the fascists during these last years, such a people must be free, such a people must be independent...

When these events were taking place, only a handful of Americans had ever heard of Vietnam, let alone knew anything about it. But significant contacts between the U. S. government and those who were to become the government of Vietnam had been taking place for some time. The U. S. Army had made parachute drops of arms and supplies to the Vietnamese anti-fascist underground, headed by Ho Chi Minh, and, beginning in March 1945, O.S.S. teams (Office of Strategic Services, the forerunner of the C.I.A.) had worked inside Vietnam with Ho and the partisans. Influenced by this cooperation as well as by the U.S. Declaration of Independence and the oft repeated wartime goal of putting an end to colonialism, Ho and the Vietnamese were probably at least as shocked as General MacArthur when the Allies launched their violent and bloody suppression of the new Vietnamese government.

The Potsdam Conference (July 17-August 2, 1945) had assigned Britain the responsibility for "restoring law and order" in Southeast Asia whenever the Allies would decide to act on the persistent messages from Japan that it was ready to surrender.[5] But by then the United States was the dominant force in the alliance with war-exhausted Britain, and American military teams were present in Vietnam, both the O.S.S forces and new teams sent in to take charge of Americans who had been captured by the Japanese and held prisoner in Vietnam. As the quotation from General MacArthur indicates, the U.S. was fully aware of what was happening and never indicated any disapproval or made any attempt to stop it.

The Allies freed and rearmed their Japanese prisoners, rearmed five thousand French troops (who had been disarmed in March by the Japanese) and brought in fresh "British" troops (mostly Indians under English command). The combined forces brutally assaulted the Vietnamese and step by step restored a violent, unstable and ultimately doomed Western control of the Southern half of Vietnam.

"Law and order" was not the issue, but rather a restoration of Western colonial dominance. Harold Isaacs, an American journalist who was in Vietnam at the time, reported on the situation in August and September, 1945:

The Republic of Vietnam came into being while...thousands of unmolested but unarmed Frenchmen looked helplessly on. The new regime took swift hold. In the cities and countryside there was order. Markets thrived, utilities and public services continued to function. In government bureaus, Annamites[6] set about the exciting business of creating a government of their own. There were scarcely any incidents. In all the month of August, by subsequent official French acknowledgment, only one Frenchman was killed in a street clash.

During an early morning Allied coup in Saigon, on September 23, troops attacked the various buildings that lodged members of the Vietnamese government:

> Sentries were shot down. Occupants...were either killed or taken prisoner... Foreign eyewitnesses saw the blood flow and bound men beaten...
>
> On October 12 the British and French, with Japanese troops assisting, opened a formal campaign to widen the perimeter around Saigon...
>
> There was no secret about the use of Japanese troops against the Annamites [although] the British command... forbade Japanese officers to talk to newsmen... The British spokesman announced on October 18 that the headquarters had thanked General Terauchi, the Japanese commander, "with highest praise"... The British were delighted with the discipline shown by the late enemy and were...warmly admiring...of their fine military qualities.

Sometime in October, Ho Chi Minh sent the first of eight letters to President Truman and the U.S. Secretary of State, expressing Vietnamese dedication to the ideals of the American revolution and friendship with the United States. He proposed a peaceful solution under which Vietnam would undergo a period of international trusteeship prior to independence. The United States declined to dignify his request with a reply but cabled the U.S. representative in Hanoi that Ho had "a clear record as an agent of international communism" and that the diplomat should work to prevent "establishment of a Communist-dominated, Moscow-oriented state [in] Indochina." [7]

In the midst of this one-way correspondence and the bloody struggle that denied Vietnam both trusteeship and independence, Washington announced a deal with France to sell it a hundred and sixty million dollars worth of "vehicles and miscellaneous industrial equipment" for use in Indochina. The description sounds like an early version of the "non-military," "humanitarian" aid that a bi-partisan Congress voted for the Nicaraguan Contras in April, 1985.

By mid-December, there were about fifty thousand French troops in the Southern zone and the British began to withdraw. As the commanding British General, General Gracey, commented at the time,

We have discharged our obligation to them [the French]. Now it's up to them to carry on.[8]

In the northern half, the Allies assigned control to China, and a hundred and twenty thousand Nationalist troops were brought in. Unlike the British—and probably because Chiang Kai-shek was preoccupied with his struggle for control of China against the Communist insurgency led by Mao Tse Tung—China technically (and temporarily) recognized the Vietnamese government rather than attempting to crush it. But for more than four months Chinese troops looted and seized stockpiles of minerals and other natural wealth for shipment to China. Then they withdrew, ending months of tension and conflict. On February 26 1946, Chiang signed an accord with the French, which allowed them to take over the northern half of Vietnam. Like the British, China left the future of Vietnam to be fought out between the country's inhabitants on one side, and the French and France's eager ally, the United States, on the other.

Until the Chinese invasion of Vietnam in 1979, these were the only Chinese troops to enter Vietnam in the twentieth century. In 1945, they invaded as allies of the United States and very few Americans knew, let alone cared, what they did to the Vietnamese. By the time of China's 1979 invasion, the U.S. and China had become friends again, with the U.S. selling arms to China and both countries working actively against Vietnam. But in the early Sixties, when the U.S. made its big push to maintain and expand its shaky control of South Vietnam, the supposed presence of Chinese troops supposedly aiding the supposed invasion of South Vietnam from the North was used as a major justification for a very real invasion by the United States. Early opponents of the U.S. invasion were asked: "Would you rather fight them (the "little yellow hordes" of decades of racist paranoia) in Vietnam or in the streets of San Francisco?" For the most part this propaganda lie has been dropped down the Orwellian memory hole, but it was discreetly (though only partially) noted in passing on an ABC Nightline broadcast on the tenth anniversary of the end of the (overt) U.S. war against Vietnam:

> KOPPEL: Let me just turn to General Haig for a moment... During the early years of our involvement...the fear was Chinese expansion. Were we wrong about that?
>
> GEN. ALEXANDER HAIG: Well, clearly we were, Ted.[9]

In addition to its earlier political and financial contributions to the French cause, between 1950 and 1954 (when the French war ended), the U.S. spent 2.6 billion dollars in support of the French effort. In the closing years of this "First Indochina War," the U.S. provided 80% of the costs and supplied combat personnel. French military historian

Bernard Fall has written that *in 1953*

> I flew with some of the Americans who were flying with the
> French at the time. They were from Civil Air Transport of
> General Chenault [a C.I.A. front]... We went into a shallow dive
> to dump our six-ton load of ammunition over a French
> encircled outpost...and all of a sudden there was Communist
> flak fire... Earthquake McGoon [nickname for Earl McGovern,
> Fall's pilot in 1953] was shot down just about a year later...over
> Dien Bien Phu [with "six tons of ammunition aboard again."][10]

The American public didn't know about U.S. participation in
these combat missions, any more than it knows now about most of the
United States's similar activities in various parts of the globe today.
Earl McGovern's name is not listed on the War Memorial in Washington, with the names of *all* those who died in Vietnam. I wonder how
many others who fall into this category of MIAs are missing from the
memorial—and how their deaths were explained to their families at the
time. In the 1980s U.S. servicemen killed in similar missions in Central
America are reported as having been killed in one kind of an accident or
another, usually far from where they served. As one largely ignored
news story reports,

> Members of a secret U.S. Army helicopter unit, wearing civilian
> clothes and flying at night, have entered into hostile territory in
> Central America to aid pro-American forces, according to
> relatives of unit members.
> "Don told me that if he ever failed to return from one of
> those missions, the Army already had a story to make up for his
> crew's disappearance and nobody would ever know the differ-
> ence," said William Donald Alvey of Morganfield, Kentucky.
> According to the Army, Alvey's son, Warrant Officer Donald R.
> Alvey, 26, was killed on March 20, 1983, when a Chinook
> helicopter he was piloting crashed 23 miles offshore of Norfolk,
> Virginia.[11]

Undoubtedly, the French public didn't know about these U.S.
missions, either. But the French government knew and always suspected that the United States was using France to gain later control of
the area for itself. And so did the Vietnamese. In 1950, Ho Chi Minh was
asked at a press conference about the U.S.'s "interventionist policy in
Indochina." Ho's reply was

> The U.S. imperialists have long since openly intervened in
> Indochina. It is with their money and weapons and on their
> instructions that the French colonialists have been waging war
> in Vietnam, Cambodia and Laos.
> However, the U.S. imperialists are seeking more and more
> to oust the French colonialists and gain complete control over

Indochina. They intervene ever more directly and actively in every field—military, political and economic. For this reason, contradictions have multiplied between them and the French colonialists.[12]

Despite the French government's suspicion of U.S. motives and the tensions this caused, their needs were great and they accepted the aid. Similarly, the Vietnamese have always suspected the aims of the Soviet Union and China, but their needs have been (and are) great. So they too have accepted the aid when it has been available—and have consistently expressed their gratitude for it.

Perhaps the Vietnam position in this respect can be best illustrated by a story Staughton and Alice Lynd brought back from Nicaragua in the fall of 1985. Someone asked a group of Nicaraguan Christians why Nicaragua continues to accept Soviet aid, even though the U.S. uses the aid as an excuse for trying to overthrow the Sandinista government, and the Soviet Union might seek to use it as a means of unduly influencing Nicaraguan policy. Tomas Tellez of the Baptist Convention of Nicaragua replied by asking what the Jew in the story of the Good Samaritan should have done, when he lay by the side of the road, beaten by robbers and half dead. First a priest came by and did not help him. Then a Levite came, looked at him and passed by. When finally the Samaritan came and offered to help, should the wounded man have asked if he was a Jew? And when he found out that he was a Samaritan, should he have refused the aid?

But, some may say, this is more than a question of Vietnam accepting aid from the Soviet Union. Are not the Vietnamese leaders themselves Marxist-Leninists? Do they not stress their international solidarity with their "Communist brothers"? Have they not entered into a number of treaties and other agreements and exchanges with the Soviet Union?

The answer to all these questions is yes. But this does not give the United States the right to intervene against the Vietnamese "in every field—military, political and economic," from 1945 to the present. Its military assaults have included covert action, massive invasion and the dropping of over seven million tons of bombs, nearly three times the 2.5 million tons it dropped in Europe and the Pacific during World War Two.

Nor does it mean that there have not always been major contradictions and serious disagreements between Vietnam and the Soviet Union.

Finally, even if there were no such strains and differences, this would be no justification for the U.S. crimes in Vietnam.

Ironically, it seems that the most distressing thing about Vietnam to the United States power elite is that it *does* have serious differences with the Soviet Union and, in any case, wishes to be an independent, non-aligned nation, working with all countries and developing its own indigenous form of "Communism with a human face." The United States, having failed to establish its own dominance in Vietnam, is anxious to drive Vietnam a lot further into the Soviet Camp than the Vietnamese want to go. That would, in the U.S. mind, provide retroactive justification for the Vietnam war. It would help justify its current policies, not only against Vietnam but against other governments and movements in Third World countries that want to develop their own systems, free from the economic injustices and corporate rule in the United States, free from the bureaucratic rigidities and statist tyrannies of the Soviet Union, and free from the control of either of them. It would "prove" that there is no viable alternative to the distressing models championed by the two superpowers, no alternative models that will be allowed to experiment, make their own mistakes, adjust, develop and grow.

Understanding this explains the logic of the so-called domino theory under which the United States clung so desperately to the war in Indochina, long after it was a losing cause and was threatening the internal stability of the United States. As Noam Chomsky has explained,

> The concern is that if some region, however insignificant, undertakes social and economic development in terms that might be meaningful to oppressed and impoverished people elsewhere, then "the rot will spread"—to use the terminology of the planners—and others may seek to do likewise. The demonstration effect of successful development outside of the framework of U.S. domination is the major concern. This explains why tiny and insignificant countries such as Laos or Grenada have been the victims of such extraordinary U.S. hostility... In fact, as the documentary record shows, the major motive for the 25-year U.S. war against Vietnam was the fear that the rot of successful development in terms that might be meaningful for the Asian poor might spread, so that the whole U.S.-dominated system in Asia might ultimately unravel... Suppose that subversion or aggression do not succeed... Then the fall-back position is to drive it into the hands of the Russians... A further benefit is that Soviet influence is certain to strengthen the more brutal and repressive elements that will be found in any revolutionary movement or regime, and that come to the fore in the course of violence and aggression... The next step is for the intellectuals in the U.S. and its client states to shed crocodile tears over the betrayal of the revolutionary promise, thus contributing further to the attacks that have exactly this as their intent...It is easy for us to sit back and give advice, but things look different at the wrong end of the guns.[13]

...And by the Russians

The Russians refused to recognize the new Democratic Republic of Vietnam—and its President, Ho Chi Minh—until 1950. So much for the American claims that Ho was a Moscow-oriented "agent of international communism." In fact, Ho learned relatively early not to trust the Russians, and their failure to support the new Vietnamese government was probably less of a surprise to him than the complicity of the Americans in the efforts to crush it.

Historian Gabriel Kolko says that

> Ho was surely aware of his disagreements with the Comintern in both substance and emphasis by no later than 1931... [He] organized the founding meeting of the Vietnamese Communist Party in February 1930, bringing three disunited factions together and writing its first statement of tactics and its appeal... [T]he statement...emphasized the need to rally the peasantry by means of a land revolution coming at the expense of big landlords, feudalists and imperialists and explicitly exempting rich peasants, middle and small landlords, and that all encompassing but elusive...class—the national bourgeoisie... [T]he Party's future program was enunciated, but within months the Comintern denounced it as unprincipled and the following October ...a Comintern-approved program was imposed along with selected leaders... For at least three more years, Ho was reviled for alleged reformism.[1]

Kolko also points out that "after 1945, Stalin's suspicion of Ho was certainly open knowledge among leading world Communists." And

Harold Isaac's first-hand report of Vietnam in 1945 states

> From the small handful of French Communists in Indochina, the Annamite comrades learned a remarkable lesson in their kind of politics. There were only twenty in the French Communist group in Saigon. "Of these only one," said my Annamite Communist companion, "*Only one* solidarized with us. The rest stood aside." [Emphasis in original]
>
> The French group prepared a document for the Indochinese Communist Party which bore the date of September 25—two days after the French seized power in the city. I was able to read the document... It advised the Annamite Communists to be sure before they acted too rashly that their struggle "meets the requirements of Soviet policy." It warned that any "premature adventures" in Annamite independence might "not be in line with Soviet perspectives." These perspectives might well include France as a firm ally of the USSR in Europe, in which case the Annamite independence movement would be an embarrassment.

The "French group" turned out to be prescient. France and the Soviet Union did become allies and, as Bernard Fall wrote later,

> [In 1946] Vietnam...was totally isolated from any major source of Communist power. He [Ho] had access to nobody until December, 1949 [the year Mao Tse Tung and the Chinese Communists came to power]. Yet he fought on, and against a French Communist-backed government, for nothing else but purely Vietnamese national objectives, and that fact is terribly important *to this very day*. [Written in 1967.][2]

Isaacs' report continues with a discussion of the Vietnamese nationalists' waning hope that the United States would honor its wartime commitments.

> Annamite nationalists spoke of the United States as men speak of a hope they know is forlorn but to which they desperately cling all the same. Could all the fine phrases of the Atlantic Charter, of the United Nations pact, of President Roosevelt and his successor, really have meant nothing at all? Nothing? All right, let us make allowances for expediency, for big power politics... Would not the United States still find it wiser for the sake of its position in the Far East to win support among the people rather than to cling to the rotten imperial system of the past?

Finally, after mentioning the "American deal" to sell $160,000,000 worth of equipment for French use in Indochina, Isaacs concludes:

> To the Annamites this looked like American underwriting of

the French reconquest. The Americans were democrats in words but no help in fact, just as the Russians were communists in words but no help in fact.

"We apparently stand quite alone," said Ho Chi Minh simply. We shall have to depend on ourselves."³

These were lessons Ho remembered and acted on until his death on September 3, 1969. But despite the early attacks on him personally, it was less a matter of personal offense than of the very substantial differences between the Soviet manner of operating and that of the Vietnamese Workers (Communist) Party and government.

From the beginning, Ho stressed that "To make the revolution, one must first and foremost remold oneself"⁴ and he set the example by his own modesty and simple life-style. Typically, he told me in Hanoi in 1966 that in the Twenties he had worked as a "houseboy" for a family in Brooklyn, and instead of narrow-mindedly condemning them as "bourgeois" or "class enemies," he said that

> They were very nice people and they treated me very well. When you go back to the United States you can tell your friends that when I worked as a domestic servant in Brooklyn I earned $40 a month and now that I am President of Vietnam, I get paid $44 a month.

"Egoism," "bureaucracy" and both personal and Party privilege were "prime villains, from 1945 on," according to Kolko. It wasn't that they didn't have to fight constantly against these abuses; Ho's speeches and the Party's resolutions are full of complaints about them and campaigns against them:

> Our Party has brought up a revolutionary young generation of boys and girls full of zeal and courage...
> These are beautiful flowers of revolutionary heroism...
> However, besides these good comrades, there are still a few cadres and Party members whose morality and quality are still low... Their motto is not "each for all" but "all for me." They sink into corruption...waste and luxury. They are proud and conceited...hold the masses in contempt, act arbitrarily and tyranically. They...are affected by bureaucracy and com-mandism... Criticism and self-criticism should be seriously practised in the Party. Frank criticism of cadres and Party members *by the people* should be welcomed and encouraged.⁵
> [Emphasis added]

The campaigns were unflinching and constant. Besides helping weed out members "whose morality and quality" were low, they succeeded in developing a leadership whose life styles and attitude toward power were very different than that of the Soviet leaders.

The constraints on Ho applied to [other Party leaders] also. With a few exceptions, they were extremely modest men, many were proud of their anonymity, and none ever took the personal privileges commonly taken by their peers in the USSR and China.

Their second dominant characteristic was a strong tendency after 1941 to compromise their differences as long as possible for the sake of policies that often were eclectic and at times at odds with each other. They would often test credible options and experiment, the results often proving decisive to a debate, and they tried to avoid closing doors behind themselves.[6]

This description sounds like a description of the early New Left in this country, roughly from 1962 to 1967 or 1968, before it was significantly corrupted by "scientific" Marxists who had a different conception of science than Ho and the Vietnamese.

One approach to scientific Marxism is to believe that there is a "single correct line" which has been revealed by science to a "single correct vanguard." Usually those who hold this view ascertain, "scientifically," that they are the Vanguard. They are the true (fundamentalist) followers of their scientific predecessors in nineteenth-century England (Marx) and early twentieth-century Russia (Lenin).

But to the Vietnamese Party, even though they sometimes refer to themselves as a vanguard—and on occasion have acted as one, in the narrow, dogmatic sense—for the most part science has meant experimenting and engaging in an open-minded, good-faith exploration of paradoxical and sometimes even contradictory hypotheses. Meanwhile they embrace policies and tactics that, from a narrower perspective, appear to be "at odds with each other." To them, true science's chief enemies are the rigidity and dogmatism that produce—and are produced by—egoistic self-righteousness and sectarianism.

From this, there has always followed another contrast—and another source of tension with Moscow—the Vietnamese insistence that

Communists of various countries must put Marxism-Leninism in concrete form proper to circumstances of the given time and of the given place... We do not...apply the experience of brother countries in a mechanical way...

Our country has its own peculiarities. Disregard for the peculiarities of one's nation while learning from the experiences of the brother countries is a serious mistake, is dogmatism.[7]

There has never been any question in either Vietnam or the Soviet Union that repeated statements of this kind have been aimed at the Soviet Union as well as at Vietnam's own zealots. Vietnam's dedication to "learning from the experiences" of the Soviet Union clearly applies to the USSR's mistakes and crimes as well as its accomplishments. This is not to say that the Vietnamese have been flawless in applying their principles, given the pressures of their need for aid, or have been incapable of error.

When the Soviet Union and its Warsaw Pact forces invaded Czechoslovakia in August 1968 to destroy the Czech party's independent initiatives to create "socialism with a human face," Vietnam initially issued a statement supporting the invasion. This disappointed me, as I had met with a number of Vietnamese officials from both the NLF and the North in Czechoslovakia in 1967, a year before the invasion. They had made clear their disrespect for the old-line Party officials, because of their dogmatism, elitism and isolation from the common people, and their enthusiasm for the more democratic and humane policies of Dubcek and his associates. It wasn't until a few months later that Vietnam issued a statement cautiously expressing its reservations. In personal conversations with Vietnamese officials shortly after the invasion, I found them much more blunt in their criticisms.

My own impression is that for delicate diplomatic reasons the Vietnamese have tried to avoid public criticism of Soviet policies that they differ with, but have enunciated and carried out their own quite different policies in an independent fashion. In all my visits and contacts, they have found ways of making clear their differences with the Russians, while expressing their gratitude for Russian assistance and identifying Vietnam as a Marxist-Leninist country.

Vietnamese Successes and Failures and American Propaganda

One of the unusual characteristics of the Vietnamese Communists has been their abililty to apply their common-sense approach to the "circumstances of the given time and of the given place" not only in their relations with the Soviet Union, China, *et. al.*, but also inside Vietnam. In particular, they have usually been good about recognizing and respecting the differing situations and dynamics between the North and the South and, country-wide, between urban and peasant areas.

During the years in which the South was run by foreign-dominated, dictatorial regimes, the Workers Party leaders in both the North and the South made great efforts not to let the better established and more stable leadership in the North impose its views on members in the South. Those in the North bent over backwards to let those who were best acquainted with the local dynamics—and were on the front lines of danger—dominate the decision-making in their area. And those in the South, who were subject to the danger, developed a self-reliance that was not about to take orders from those who were not. To use a term much in use in certain U.S. circles today, the Southerners were "empowered" by the encounters brought about by their lives of struggle. In the U.S., the term is often applied to what happens in largely personal encounters (with the self, with others) in workshops and meditation centers. Valuable as these activities often are, they rarely extend outward as well as inward, to embrace the political as well as the personal. But the empowerment the Southerners achieved led them to do battle against both personal and social indignity and oppression. It won (and sometimes compelled) the respect of the Northerners.

Concerning urban-peasant relationships, the Party has suc-cumbed from time to time to repeating "in a mechanical way" a Marxist-Leninist cant that, fortunately, has not dominated its practice. Vietnam's current constitution, for example, solemnly—and, to me, ridiculously—proclaims that the Communist Party of Vietnam "con-solidated the worker-peasant alliance *led by the working class.*" [emphasis added.] Yet the peasants have always formed the bulk of the population, were the prime victims of colonial rule and generally have taken the lead in the struggle against both foreign and indigenous oppression—and usually the Party has recognized this. In the words of Ho:

> Ours is an agricultural country. More than nine-tenths of our people are peasants. The National Defense Army, the regional forces, the militia and guerilla units are mostly made up of peasants. For the war of resistance and national construction to be successful...reliance should be placed on the peasant forces."[1]

Vietnam never did fit into the economic pattern of nineteenth-century industrial Europe that produced some of the rhetoric:

> The main economic impact of the French was on the land system... Their nonagrarian activities...affected only a small percentage of the workforce after 1918... Land was the most important resource the French had for funding a colonial administration and exploiting the nation... Land became capital for France's consolidating of colonial power.[2]

> The French colonial system acted to destroy the village as a social and economic unit producing security for the poor.[3]

In practice the Party has usually been more sensible than its occasional obeissance to a fundamentalist foreign shibboleth might suggest. They can be compared in this respect to some of the Christian base communities in Central America (pragmmatic practitioners of liberation theology) who render occasional ritualistic homage to the Pope, in all his reactionary pomp and politics, but humbly devote their own lives to the poor. The Workers Party has both encouraged and responded to local peasant initiatives (both Party and non-Party) and have for the most part adjusted their program and tactics, in a remarkably sensitive and democratic way, to peasant understandings of their own experience and situation.

This sensitivity has been made easier by the Party's emphasis on "simple living" in the midst of the poor, and on refusing to seek or accept the "personal privileges commonly taken by their peers in the USSR and China." During the war-time years, before any important policy debate in the North, a representative always spent at least six months in the South, with all the sharing of risks, privations and other learning experiences that involved. And similarly, in both North and South, a number of Party leaders and cadres (most of whom came from privileged urban backgrounds, a fact not mentioned in the rhetoric about "working-class leadership") have lived for months and years in peasant villages. There, they have been enjoined by Party morality to practice the "Three Withs"—

> Eat with the peasants, live with the peasants and work with the peasants.[4]

In both instances, they kept in touch with Hanoi as best they could, to facilitate a two-way process, or genuine dialectic. Besides learning from the peasants, they played an important role, also as best they could, in educating and guiding them in line with the Party's overall goals and principles.

Some of the Party's respect for local initiatives was a pragmatic necessity, at least in the beginning stages. The periodic "spontaneous" outbursts of energy from the peasants in response to the crudely repressive measures, first of the French and later of the U.S. and Saigon regimes, sometimes gave the Party no alternative, if it did not want to be left behind and isolated from the struggle.

A second reason was the technological state of the country, which was primitive enough to begin with and even more limited after the U.S. bombings began in 1962.

> In a nation more than 3,000 kilometers long with poor, or often no, system of rapid communications and contact, the existence of effective, adaptive local organs of authority and power became crucial to the Revolution's ongoing efforts.[5]

For the most part, the Party leaders responded positively to these necessities, learned from the experience and made what began as a necessity a key part of their philosophy and practice. For whatever Ho and the others learned from their "brother countries"—and one should not minimize Ho's emphasis on learning from both Marx and Lenin—it was always emphasized that the major source of learning was "from the people."

This required living one's life as a "servant of the people," meeting their needs, loving and being "loved, trusted and admired" by them[6]—the only organic way in which a valid, two-way learning process could take place over a period of time. It also required establishing forms through which the people could speak formally as well as informally:

> Mobilizing the masses into networks was a crucial part of that process...but so, equally, was learning from, listening to, and even...following them... [A]fter the August [1945] Revolution... the new government organized people's councils. These coun-

cils were direct representative bodies based on universal suffrage and a means of obtaining the participation of the host of people on the scene and of channeling them. The councils also elected administrative committees, which were really executive organs representing the masses, the Party, and the government; resolving the function and role of this structure...sometimes became inefficient or pro forma, or had to be modified during the war with France... Still, as a means of transcending the limits of relying exclusively on the Party, the assets of the council system far outweighed its liabilities.[7]

By the time of the American war, the Party had succeeded in establishing relatively democratic rule in most of the villages, with provisions for input and influence by the local Workers Party providing a link to national policy. In doing this, the Party was building on the pre-colonial, collective nature of the traditional Vietnamese village before it was disrupted by the introduction of competitive private ownership under the French. Nancy Wiegersma describes the decision-making administration of a typical Northern village:

> There were three levels of administration in the nineteen sixties northern village. In a sense, the General Assembly of Villagers ruled, because they selected the Administrative Committee. This committee was quite large. For example, in one co-operative it included sixty-five members or one tenth of the total co-op membership. The day-to-day decisions were made by a smaller group, the executive organ of the Administrative Committee, called the Management Committee. This Management Committee was made up of the Collective's President and General Secretary, who were elected by the General Assembly, and the Heads of Production Brigades, who were selected by the Administrative Committee.
>
> The Workers Party leadership was interconnected with collective leadership at the village level. There was a controlling commission in the village which was invested with permanent overseeing responsibilities. The Workers Party cell secretary generally headed this commission. The party cell nominated the President of the collective but this nomination had to be approved by the members of the collective in its General Assembly...
>
> In the early sixties, women were a small minority of officials...but toward the late sixties women's leadership increased... Affirmative action regulations were set down to encourage women's participation.[8]

A Serious Breakdown: The Land Reform Program

The most serious breakdown in the relationship between the central Party leadership in Hanoi and the rural peasantry (including many of the Party's own cadres) occurred in the North in the early days after the defeat of the French. As early as November 1945, the new government had instituted a program of land reform that included both drastic reductions in rent and distribution to the peasants of the lands of the French and of landlords who had collaborated with them. In 1953, they had adopted a policy of coordinating and regularizing further distributions in response to widespread initiatives by the peasants, who in many instances were seizing the land of collaborators and of particularly cruel, especially rich landlords. But until the defeat of the French in the spring of 1954, land policy was erratically implemented and secondary to the war effort, serving as much as anything as a method of giving the peasants something more tangible to be fighting for than abstract patriotism.

By late 1954, early 1955, the rural dynamics had gotten thoroughly out of hand. Angry peasants seized the occasion to ignore the Party's guidelines and wreak vengeance both on landlords and on Party members who tried to restrain them. And contrary to the Party's policies, they ignored the distinction between "patriotic landlords," who had supported the independence struggle, and collaborators with the French. Among scholars, Kolko presents one of the more severe estimates of the events that rocked the countryside for a year or more:

> The toll on wealthy landlords and *on many party members* alike...was substantial in terms of people executed and imprisoned. Anywhere from five thousand to fifteen thousand landowners were killed by local peasant courts, probably closer to the latter figure, and twenty thousand persons were imprisoned, the majority of whom were released [after a campaign by the Party] demanding an end to excesses, particularly against middle and rich peasants.[Emphasis added][9]

(In explanation of the reference to middle and rich peasants, the Party had classified the rural farm population into the following categories: Landless peasants; poor peasants (tenant farmers); middle peasants (small landholders); rich peasants (large landholders) and landlords.)

Wiegersma, who gives a lower number of executions (5,000), writes:

> What were later to be considered errors in need of rectification, were actions against rich peasants, landlords and sometimes mis-classified middle peasants. Open meetings...were held where poor peasants and landless laborers could bring evidence... Landlords were brought to trial and imprisoned or

killed...for a mixture of reasons. Some landlords were active supporters of the French and some had been responsible for the deaths of supporters of the revolution. In addition, there was class hatred towards many landlords because of their cruelty and acts of beating or rape... The vengeance of former tenants seems to have taken on its own momentum...and the land-reform hierarchy, at least to some extent, lost control of the situation...

Christine White believes that patriarchal behavior was the reason for some of the mistaken categorization... Those who engaged in "feudal" behavior such as wife-beating and gambling were sometimes wrongly classified as "feudal landlords.".... Women were active in the land-reform trials because crimes of "cruel landlord notables" had often been against women.[10]

On the one hand, the excesses accompanying the land reform cannot be passed over lightly. Nor, can they all be attributed to the anger of male and female peasants, even though "many Party members" fell victim to the violence. The Party acknowledged its failures when it dismissed the Party's secretary-general and those in charge of the land reform program, and when Ho "apologized to the nation" for what had happened. Ho did this even though he had warned, early in the program, against those who

> thought it was better to deviate to the "left" than to the "right." That is not so, for left or right, either side is far from reality.[11]

In August 1956, Ho told the peasants and cadres:

> Land reform is a class struggle against the feudalists, an earth shaking, fierce and hard revolution... The leadership of the Party Central Committee and of the Government is sometimes lacking in concreteness and control... All this has caused us to commit errors and meet with shortcomings in carrying out land reform: in realizing the unity of the countryside, in fighting the enemy, in readjusting the organization, in applying the policy of agricultural taxes, etc.
>
> The Party Central Committee and the Government have rigorously reviewed these errors and shortcomings and drawn up plans resolutely to correct them... What can be corrected immediately should be dealt with without delay... It is necessary to further the achievements we have made and at the same time resolutely to right the wrongs committed.[12]

On the other hand, we should take note of the gross distortions in the American propaganda that has attempted to capitalize on these errors and the accompanying tragedies. For years the U.S. has claimed that 700,000 landlords were killed by the communists during the land reform act. It turned out that the figure came from Hoang Van Chi, a Vietnamese refugee who had lived in a village where 10 people had died during the years of the land reform—only one at the hands of angry peasants, the other nine from other causes, including starvation (undoubtedly not landlords). Since ten deaths constituted 5 per cent of the population of Chi's village, he wrote, in a book that is generally believed to have been subsidized by the CIA, of "the massacre of about 5 percent of the total population in North Vietnam," or about seven hundred thousand. This estimate, which bore no relationship to reality, was given wide publicity by the U.S. National Security Council—and later, in even more exaggerated form, by President Nixon.

In 1966, in Hanoi, I met with a group of "leaders of mass organizations"—youth, labor, farmers, women's union, Buddhists, etc. and confronted them with these "facts" and Ho's supposed confirmation of them, which I had picked up from Bernard Fall's *The Two Vietnams*. I have to say that as I strongly raised these charges, I half expected my Vietnamese hosts to bring the meeting to an abrupt end—or at least to break off relationships after the meeting and never invite me back. Instead they said that there had indeed been murders of particularly oppressive landlords by angry peasants, but on nowhere near the scale I had mentioned. They said that the Party had been partly at fault, and had taken vigorous steps to rectify its errors. And they added that Ho had vigorously condemned the abuses and had headed a campaign to eliminate them.

The next day I had an unexpected meeting with Ho, who quickly informed me that he had heard a tape recording of our whole discussion the previous day. Having other matters to deal with, such as my pleas for humane treatment of the American POW's, with no war crimes trials, neither he nor I referred to the part about abuses under the land reform. But as I left he gave me his *Collected Works*. When I got on my plane a few hours later, the book mysteriously opened to the section on land reform, and a quite different version of events than I had seen in the United States. Besides his criticisms of the Party Central Committee and of the Government, he noted that

> Nearly ten million peasants have received land, tens of thou-
> sands of new cadres have been trained in the countryside...
> This...opens the way for our peasants to build a life with
> enough food and clothing, and brings a valuable contribution
> to the economic rehabilitation and development, and the
> consolidation of the North into a solid base to reunify the
> country.[13]

The accuracy of Ho's appraisal of the successes of the land-reform program is testified to by the fact that Bernard Fall, the leading specialist on the country's agricultural situation, had predicted that the North would either suffer certain famine or be forcibly ingetrated into China if it was cut off from the rice-producing regions in the South.[14] The North was cut off from the South's rice, but its agriculture flourished and neither dire consequence ensued.

Did The North Invade Or Follow The South?

The most significant instance of the Party's having to adapt to local and regional initiatives or be left behind occurred between 1958 and 1960. This was the critical period when the all-out war between the U.S. and Vietnam began to take shape, the period when, according to U.S. propaganda, the North invaded the peaceful, democratic South, thereby requiring (and justifying) all subsequent U.S. interventions. Most Americans still believe this, but the exact opposite is true. As Phillipe Devillers, an independent, non-communist French historian who had lived in Indochina during the French war, wrote in 1962,

> The point of view of most foreign governments, in the West especially, is that the fighting going on in South Vietnam is simply a subversive campaign directed from Hanoi... [This] leaves out of account the fact that the insurrection existed before the Communists decided to take part, and that they were simply forced to join in. And even among the Communists, the initiative did not originate in Hanoi, but from the grass roots, where the people were literally driven by Diem to take up arms in self-defense.
>
> As early as 1958...the Communists [in the South] finding themselves hunted down, began to fight back. Informers were sought out and shot... Diem's police...resorted to worse barbarity... And in that fateful year of 1958 they overstepped all bounds.[15]

This picture of local resistance to U.S.-Diem atrocities starting the war in the South, rather than "invasion" from the North, has recently been supported by a former Assistant Secretary of State for Far Eastern Affairs, Roger Hilsman. Hilsman has written that

> It would be nice to believe that the North Vietnamese were the ones to escalate the war and that the war was being won before they did so. The historical record indicates the opposite.
> ...[T]here is no evidence of infiltration of significant numbers of individual North Vietnamese, much less of regular troops, before December 1964.[16]

During the fall of 1960, the Party's southern affiliate, the Revolutionary Peoples Party, joined with a broad assortment of Southern resisters, Party and non-Party, in forming the National Liberation Front. Its formation was completed and announced in December. Wiegersma describes the setting and groups:

> The United States sponsored leader, Ngo Dinh Diem, attempted to repress former Viet Minh sympathizers by killing 90,000 of them and imprisoning another 800,000, many of whom were tortured... Massive resistance developed... By 1958, [villagers] were defending themselves with homemade shotguns and

crossbows... Tens of thousands of peasant women descended on towns which were district or provincial administrative head-quarters and protested the conduct of the government troops.

After the 1960 uprisings, local and regional groups which had been fighting against Diem saw the advantages of unifi-cation. The formation of the National Liberation Front was the crystallization of the struggle which had been waged in all parts of South Vietnam for years. The groups forming the Front included Cao Dai and Hoa Hao religious sects [later alienated from it], Cambodian and Montagnard minority group mem-bers, representatives of farmers organizations from the Mekong Delta, students and intellectuals. There were three political parties in the Front, the Radical Socialist Party, the Democratic Party and the Revolutionary Peoples Party [affiliated with the Workers Party of the North]. The Front group chose as its president Nguyen Huu Tho, an intellectual without party affiliation, who was a leader of the Saigon-Cholon Peace Group.[17]

Kolko writes that

The Party made the National Liberation Front...the vehicle for realizing its southern strategy. It was totally candid about its purposes, and...it never sought to conceal the relationship of the Party to the NLF... The Front was a logical context for the party. It served to inhibit any impulses to take power in the party's name alone—impulses that had existed earlier...but that the Party's leaders deemed sectarian... *such a policy in the South was paralleled in the DRV by greater reliance on mass organi-zations than on the local parties.* [Emphasis added][18]

Alliances Of Convenience—Vietnam-Soviet And U.S.-Soviet

All these differences between the practice of "Marxism-Leninism" in Vietnam and in the Soviet Union did not prevent Vietnam from entering into various accommodations and friendly agreements with the Russians. One can gain a perspective on this by considering some of the shifting relationships between the U.S. and the Soviet Union. Clearly the virulent hostility of the U.S. toward the Soviet Union goes far beyond Vietnam's principled reservations about the Soviet model's bureaucracy, "new class" elitism and authoritarian *modus operandi*. But this has not prevented the U.S. from entering into periodic accommodations. One has only to remember the close U.S.-Soviet alliance of World War II, which took place under circumstances that were no more threatening to the United States than the U.S. bombing raids and its 550,000 troops were to Vietnam in the 1960s. Certainly this war-time alliance did not mean that the U.S. had abandoned its own political or economic system in favor of the Soviet model. Then there is the more recent, on-again, off-again practice of "detente." Significantly, detente was not ended by either country during the U.S.-Vietnam War but by President Carter in 1979, in an attempt to reverse his declining popularity by taking a stand against the Soviet's 1979 invasion of Afghanistan, an invasion that in many ways parallels the U.S. invasion of Vietnam—even to getting bogged down in a quagmire of native resistance. And President Reagan, for all his hostility to the Soviet Union, lifted Carter's embargo on wheat sales to Russia in the interest of boosting the sagging U.S. economy.

As we have seen, none of the differences between the Vietnamese and Soviet communists disappeared between 1930 and 1945, and they publicly surfaced again at the 1954 Geneva Conference that formally ended the French War. In Geneva, both the Soviet Union and China sided with France and the United States against Vietnam's hopes for a reunified and united country. And, drawing both on known historical events and on my own numerous contacts with the Vietnamese Communists—in Vietnam, Cambodia, Laos, Peking, Moscow, Czechoslovakia, Paris and New York—I will attempt to show that the same basic differences have persisted to this day. The same independence of thought and action still exists in Vietnam, even though U.S. (and Chinese) policies force Vietnam to turn to the Soviet Union once again for support and survival. The inevitable result is a complex mix of agreement and disagreement, accommodation and resistance.

In its own relationships with a wide range of Third World countries, the United States has had significant success at being able to purchase the "loyalty" of non-Communist governments, with military and economic "aid" programs that provide both the power base and an added source of enrichment for the local elite. So Washington, based on its own experience, finds it hard to believe that Vietnam, a small, poor, besieged Third World country, can stand up as much as it does to the Soviet superpower that is supplying it with so many things it desperately needs.

This skepticism exists today, when Vietnam's needs are mostly economic, as it struggles to deal with the aftermath of years of devastation and the impact of the current U.S. trade embargo. And it existed during the years when the U.S. was waging open, military war against Vietnam. Not surprisingly, then, Henry Kissinger and Richard Nixon thought that the way to gain the victory the United States couldn't win on the battlefield was to work out deals with the Soviet Union that would grant it enough concessions elsewhere in the world to cause it to tell its dependent, Vietnam, to stop the nonsense and end the war on

Nixon's and Kissinger's terms. Kissinger describes this approach in his book, *White House Years*:

> My approach was...geopolitical. I attempted...to create incentives or pressures in one part of the world to influence events in another.[19]

So began, in 1969, the tortured diplomacy that, among other things, involved playing the Soviet Union and China off against each other.[20] It culminated in Nixon's trips to Peking and Moscow in 1972, trips that seriously offended the Vietnamese, since both the Chinese and the Russians welcomed Nixon in the midst of brutal U.S. escalations of the war. Just before Nixon was scheduled to leave for Moscow, the mining and bombing of Haiphong Harbor sunk Soviet ships and killed Soviet seamen, but the Russians weren't overly concerned. They welcomed Nixon anyway, and Kissinger concluded, with some justification, that his efforts were succeeding.

> Conscious of its own vulnerabilities, the Kremlin therefore cut loose from its obstreperous small ally on the other side of the globe. By proceeding with the Summit, Moscow helped neutralize our domestic opposition, which gave us freedom to break the back of the Vietnamese offensive. Our strategy of detente—posing risks and dangling benefits before the Soviets—made possible an unfettered attempt to bring our involvement in the Vietnam war to an honorable close.[21]

The only problem was that the attempt failed—except for its temporary effect on sections of the U.S. public. The Vietnamese, as usual, refused to take orders from Moscow.

World Policeman for God, Justice, etc.

> The whole picture is one of an enormously equipped and self-complacent white civilization in combat with a huge, sprawling colored and mestizo world (a majority) armed with anything they can get their hands on. And the implicit assumption behind it all...is that *we* are the injured ones, we are trying to keep peace and order, and *they* (abetted by communist demons) are simply causing confusion and chaos, with no reasonable motives whatever. Hence *we*, being attacked, have to defend ourselves, God, justice, etc. Dealing with these "inferior" people becomes a technical problem, something like pest extermination. In a word, the psychology of the Alabama police becomes in fact the psychology of America as a world policeman.
>
> —Thomas Merton.[1]

Merton wrote this in 1965, after seeing a copy of Life magazine "full of helicopters in Vietnam, white mercenaries in the Congo, (U.S.) marines in Santo Domingo"—and with images of the police attacks on the Selma, Alabama civil-rights marchers fresh in his mind.

If he was right—and who can study the record and doubt it?—it didn't make a lot of difference to the United States what the state of affairs in Vietnam was, or the actual relationship between Vietnam and the Soviet Union or between Vietnam and China. The U.S. was determined to slay the Communist demons—and as many "inferior" people as that required—for the sake of God, justice, etc.

And "to defend ourselves!" True, *they* hadn't attacked *us* yet, but they would if we didn't wipe them out over there. And how much better for the inevitable war to be fought sanitarily half way around the globe rather than on our own shores.

Better for most of us, that is, but not for all of us. Not for those who had to fight it. And even that burden fell unequally:

* Even though blacks made up only 11% of the population, by the start of the Vietnam war they comprised 31% of the combat troops. From 1961 to 1968, blacks accounted for 16% of the combat deaths in Vietnam. In the year 1965, 23.5% of all enlisted men killed in action were black.

* To an administration trying to fight both a ground war in Asia and a war on poverty at home, it must have seemed a stroke of genius to fight one war with the other. A program known as "Project 100,000" was developed. It was designed to lower the minimum entry level requirements for the army so that more bodies of the poor would be available for duty in Vietnam...

* Pentagon studies indicate that about ten percent of the men never finished their service because they were either killed, disabled or released with bad discharges. The proportion who received training in a skill transferable to civilian life was small.[2]

As early as the spring of 1954, when the Geneva conference was gathering to act on the French defeat and bring peace to Vietnam, Richard Nixon, Vice President of the United States, had publicly declared

> The Vietnamese lack the ability to conduct a war by themselves or govern themselves... The United States as a leader of the free world cannot afford further retreat in Asia. It is hoped the United States will not have to send troops there, but if this government cannot avoid it, the Administration must face up to the situation and dispatch forces... This nation is the only nation politically strong enough at home to take a position that will save Asia.[3]

"The Vietnamese" Nixon was referring to, who could neither conduct a war nor govern themselves, were "our" Vietnamese, a handful of opportunist collaborators with whomever the occupying colonial power was at the time—France, Japan, France again, and soon the United States. The other Vietnamese were within days of the final defeat of the French, despite France's massive assistance from the United States. The reference to the U. S. as "the only nation politically strong enough at home" to take on the task is ironic, given the later (if much too long delayed) emergence of a huge domestic protest movement.

It didn't make any difference that the Geneva Agreements had said that the division of Vietnam into two zones was strictly temporary, pending national elections two years later, in July 1956:

> The military demarcation line is provisional and should not in any way be interpreted as constituting a political or territorial boundary.[4]

As President Eisenhower explained later, in his book, *Mandate for Change*, the U.S. could not—and did not—permit the scheduled elections to take place because

> I have never talked or corresponded with a person knowledgeable in Indochinese affairs who did not agree that had elections been held as of the time of the fighting, possibly 80% of the populace would have voted for the Communist Ho Chi Minh.

The reference to "at the time of the fighting" should not mislead us. The fighting ended in May, 1954, with the fall of Dienbienphu; the Geneva Agreements, with their guarantee of elections, were completed in July. By then the U.S. had already decided not to permit the elections. Moreover, all studies indicate that *after* the end of the fighting, Ho and his colleagues had even more popular support, since they had presided over a victorious war that promised reunification of an independent, non-aligned Vietnam.

The U.S. had already decided to do a lot more than prevent the elections from taking place. According to the *Pentagon Papers*,

> The [U.S.'s] Saigon Military Mission [SMM] was born in a Washington policy meeting early in 1954, when Dien Bien Phu was holding out against the encircling Viet Minh. The SMM was to enter into Vietnam quietly and assist the Vietnamese [our Vietnamese], rather than the French, in unconventional warfare. The French were to be kept as friendly allies...as far as possible.

These instructions are significant in view of the long-term French suspicion—and charges by Ho—that the U.S. was aiding it in order to gain control of Vietnam for itself.

The first covert-action team arrived in Saigon on June 1, 1954, during the Peace Talks. Soon there was a team in Hanoi as well, headed by long-time C.I.A. operative Col. Edward Lansdale, fresh from a similar campaign in the Philippines. Lansdale's report on the evacuation of the French from Hanoi states that

> The northern SMM team...[was] disturbed by...the contrast between the silent march of the victorious Vietminh troops in their tennis shoes and the clanking armor of the well-equipped French whose Western tactics and equipment had failed against the Communist military-political-economic campaign.

How many lives might have been saved, how much pain, anguish and trauma avoided, if the C.I.A., supposedly an "intelligence" agency—or the politicians and experts from Harvard, Yale, etc. who received its reports—had analyzed this piece of incidental information and headed off the coming disaster.

But Lansdale and his sponsors were preoccupied with the part of Lansdale's report that dealt with the team's purpose for being there.

> The northern team had spent the last days of Hanoi [*sic*] in contaminating the oil supply of the bus company for a gradual wreckage of the buses, in taking the first actions for a delayed sabotage of the railroads (which required teamwork with a C.I.A. special technical team in Japan who had performed their part brilliantly), and in writing detailed notes of potential targets for future paramilitary operations.

Lansdale also reported that

> Towards the end of the month [September, 1954] it was learned that the largest printing establishment in the north intended to...do business with the Vietminh. An attempt was made by SMM to destroy the modern printing presses, but Vietminh security agents already had moved into the plant and frustrated the attempt.
>
> Earlier in the month [we] had engineered a black psywar strike in Hanoi: leaflets signed by the Vietminh...about property, money reform... The day following the distribution of these leaflets, refugee registration tripled. Two days later, Vietminh currency was worth half the value prior to the leaflet. The Vietminh took to the radio to denounce the leaflets; the leaflets were so authentic that even most of the rank and file Vietminh were sure that the radio denunciations were a French trick.[5]

Meanwhile, the Saigon team, "working in close cooperation with George Hellyer, USIS [United States Information Service] Chief," was engaging in its own psychological warfare campaign:

> The first rumor campaign was...a carefully planted story of a Chinese Communist regiment in Tonkin taking reprisals against a Vietminh village whose girls the Chinese had raped, recalling Chinese Nationalist troop behavior in 1945 and confirming Vietnamese fears of Chinese occupation under Vietminh rule.[6]

These and other revelations in the *Pentagon Papers* of the secret world of the U.S. government may be shocking to most Americans, if they ever learn of them. But they were taken for granted by their sponsors as "honorable," "legal," and well established, "normal" methods by which the U. S. advances its "vital interests" around the globe:

> This world has a set of values, a dynamic, a language and a perspective quite distinct from the public world of the ordinary citizen and of the other two branches of the Republic—Congress and the judiciary. Clandestine warfare against the North Vietnamese, for example, is not seen, either in the written words of the senior decision-makers in the Executive Branch or by the anonymous authors of the study, as violating the Geneva Accords of 1954... Clandestine warfare, because it is covert, does not exist as far as treaties and public posture are concerned. Further, secret commitments to other nations are not sensed as infringing on the treaty-making powers of the Senate, because they are not publicly acknowledged.[7]

There is a lot of evidence that Sheehan was unduly kind to Congress and the judiciary, when he exempted them from this self-justifying mode of thinking and acting. Certainly anyone making a serious study of the role of Congress in recent years in respect to Pentagon, C.I.A. and State Department activities in Central America, the Philippines, the Middle East, Angola, etc., would be hard put to grant them such an exemption. To cite one example, in 1976 the C.I.A. planted a story, similar to the one it had planted in Vietnam in 1945, of the mass rape of Angolan women by Cuban troops. John Stockwell, C.I.A. chief in Angola at the time, testified in a U.S. courtroom that the story got a lot of coverage in the U.S. and Free World media for two or three weeks. When it began to die down, the C.I.A. revived press and public interest by concocting a follow-up story that the Cuban rapists had been tried, convicted and then executed by a firing squad of African women.[8] Even after the information that these events had been fabricated by the C.I.A. was made public, Congress did nothing to stop the covert activities in Angola. Beginning in November 1985, Congress and the White House were *openly* discussing the sending of 28 million dollars to Angolan forces linked to South African attempts to overthrow the government.

Humanitarian Aid

The very existence of the Saigon Military Mission in 1954 was a closely held secret. But there were other groups whose existence and arrival in Hanoi were heavily publicized, because of their ostensibly humanitarion reason for being there. What was not known, until the release of the *Pentagon Papers* in 1971, was the range of destructive activities they carried on under that cover.

The Geneva Accords had specified that for a 300-day period

any civilians...who wish to go and live in the zone of the other party shall be permitted and helped to do so.

Good-hearted Americans—and the somewhat less compassionate U.S. government—sent a variety of operatives to help rescue North Vietnamese who desired to move to the South. Those desiring to do so included a large number of Catholics.

The Catholics were a by-product of the French rule, members of a minority religion which had been brought by Portugese and French missionaries into a predominantly Buddhist population. The Catholic communities in the North had enjoyed a protected status under the French and they had raised militia units that fought beside the French against the Viet Minh. With the collapse of the French, these communities feared reprisals, or at least grave restrictions on their activities.[9]

In case this wasn't enough of an incentive, or didn't extend to enough Catholics, the C.I.A. invented a story that the Virgin Mary had appeared to a devout Catholic in North Vietnam, announced that she was going South and said that all true Catholics would follow her. The story spread like wildfire, as the appearance of the Virgin Mary to a peasant woman in Lourdes, France, had done a century earlier, especially since the C.I.A. deluged the countryside with leaflets telling of the Virgin's new appearance and her message to the faithful.

Among those who came to help the faithful was a young doctor, Tom Dooley, who had volunteered to serve in the U.S. Navy's program of helping transport refugees to the South. After the completion of this initial mission, Dooley, a devout Catholic, settled in Southeast Asia (off and on) as a medical missionary. Whether he was a self-sacrificing idealist or a self-promoting egotist who allowed the medical services under his care to deteriorate—as was charged at the time by other medical missionaries in Asia—is a matter of historical controversy. Perhaps he was a little of both. What is not controversial is that he was a fanatical anti-Communist who believed in the "white man's burden" and thought that France (and now the United States) was selflessly civilizing Vietnam. The terms he chose with which to condemn the Vietminh give us a clue as to his attitude:

They preached hatred against the institutions, traditions, and customs of colonial Vietnam. Everything "feudal" or "reactionary" was to be destroyed.[10]

Whether naive to the core or a wily opportunist, Dooley made a powerful appeal to the best instincts of the American people and served as a convincing cover for the United States real interests and activities in Vietnam:

We [the United States] had come late to Vietnam, but we had

come. And we brought not bombs and guns but help and love.

At the same time,

> No act attributed to the Communists was dismissed as un-
> believable or as requiring factual substantiation. All of them
> fitted [his] "devil theory" and were passed on to the millions
> who read his book [*Deliver Us From Evil*, 1956], heard his
> lectures [two tours in the U.S.] and saw the film based on *Deliver
> Us From Evil...*
>
> The 17th Parallel that divided the refugees from the free
> world was "the rim of Hell" with "the demons of Communism
> stalking outside and now holding the upper half of the country
> in their strangling grip."[11]

Apparently Dooley believed in the warning message from the
Virgin Mary, along with a number of other rumors the C.I.A. fed to him
and the Vietnamese Catholics. One that he promoted with an effec-
tiveness that no one else could have achieved was a claim that

> Ho Chi Minh had begun his war against the French ..."by
> disembowelling more than 1,000 native women in Hanoi" who
> were associated with the French.[12]

It didn't matter that knowledgeable people, including Paul Mus, a
French scholar who at the time was probably France's most authori-
tative expert on Vietnam, exposed the falsity of this and other stories. It
was believed by hundreds of thousands in Vietnam and by millions in
the United States.

In 1960, Dooley was named, in a Gallup Poll, as one of the ten
most admired Americans. If Tom Dooley hadn't existed and hadn't
gone to Vietnam in 1954, the government would have been hard put to
invent anyone half so helpful to its purposes.

In 1961, he died of cancer. After his death it was revealed that he
had been in the employ of the C.I.A. It wasn't made clear whether this
was true when he first arrived in Vietnam, or came about shortly after
his arrival as a result of his eager collaboration with the C.I.A.'s secret
operatives in the North during that period.

One of the teams operating in the North under a humanitarian
cover at that time was headed by a Major Conein. The *Pentagon Papers*
tell us that

> Major Conein was given responsibility for developing a para-
> military organization in the north, to be in position when the
> Vietminh took over... [His] team was moved north immediately
> as part of the MAAG [Military Assistance Advisory Group]
> staff working on the refugee problem. The team had head-
> quarters in Hanoi, with a branch in Haiphong. Among cover
> duties, this team supervised the refugee flow for the Hanoi
> airlift.

The team's qualifications for this sensitive relief operation may be judged by the following story.

> One day, as a CAT C-46 finished loading, they saw a small child standing on the ground below the loading door. They shouted for the pilot to wait, picked the child up, and shoved him into the aircraft, which then taxied out for its takeoff... A Vietnamese man and woman ran up to the team, asking what they had done with their small boy... The...team finally talked the parents into going south to Free Vietnam, put them into the next aircraft to catch up with their son in Saigon.[13]

An estimated 850,000 Vietnamese moved south during the 300-day period alloted for such migrations. Approximately 200,000 of them were members of the French colonial armed forces and most of the rest were Catholics. By contrast, only about 150,000 Southerners moved North. This 700,000 discrepancy in favor of those "fleeing totalitarianism" was trumpeted by the U.S. government and media as proof that the Vietnamese people had "voted with their feet" for the U.S.-sponsored regime and against Ho and the Communists. But in addition to the reasons we have seen for the size of the migration southward, there were solid human and political reasons why those who supported Ho and the Vietminh did not move north.

Because they believed, naively, that the promised elections would take place, and were confident that the South and the North would soon be unified under the freely elected government that they supported, they saw no reason to uproot themselves and make the long trek northward. For non-Catholic Vietnamese, with their emphasis on tending the graves of their ancestors, the religious factor weighed heavily in favor of staying in or near their ancestral village. Moreover, if they feared persecution in the South and were therefore tempted to break this tie, they would have had to travel without the assistance of the U.S. Seventh Fleet, the French Navy, CAT-46 aircraft and the more than a dozen private U.S. and French agencies that provided free travel and resettlement assistance for those moving to the South. Finally, for those who were most active in support of the Vietminh, there were strong political reasons for staying; namely, that the South was the place where pre-electoral work would be the most useful. An overwhelming electoral victory in the area temporarily governed by the U.S. puppet, Ngo Dinh Diem, would strengthen the new government's international prestige. For all these reasons, the Vietminh urged the bulk of its followers in the South to stay there. It did ask for some volunteers to move north temporarily, in order to be trained in the kind of society that existed there and would be installed in the South after the elections.

These circumstances were never explained to more than a tiny minority of the American people—and it was nine years before Eisenhower made his statement that "possibly 80 per cent" of the populace would have voted for the Communist Ho Chi Minh." So, along with rumors invented by the C.I.A., spread by Tom Dooley and others, and highlighted in the American press, the discrepancy between the numbers who travelled South and the numbers who travelled North was used as final proof that the Vietnamese people were justifiably terrified at the prospect of a Vietminh victory.

Clearly the good offices of the United States were needed to protect them—"to defend ourselves, God, justice, etc."

The C.I.A. Finds a Catholic Ruler for South Vietnam (and What We Don't Know Does Hurt Us)

The passage in Eisenhower's memoirs giving the reasons for deciding not to permit the internationally supervised elections promised by France, England, China, the Soviet Union and (supposedly) the United States, reveals the alternative our "democratic" government had in mind:

> As one Frenchman said to me, "What Vietnam needs is another Syngman Rhee [U.S. backed dictator in South Korea], regardless of all the difficulties the presence of such a personality would entail."

The United States found such a man in the person of Ngo Dinh Diem, a World War II collaborator with the Japanese who was living in Princeton, N.J. His American backers included Cardinal Spellman, Joseph P. Kennedy, Joe's son Senator John F. Kennedy, (Democratic) Senate Majority Leader Mike Mansfield—and Colonel Lansdale. Washington installed Diem as Prime Minister in Saigon, supplied him with military equipment and advisors, and used him to prevent the elections from taking place

> American opponents to a reunification election in any form included the *New York Times*, Senator John F. Kennedy, and many others, and neither Diem nor the United States ever consented to repeated requests by the DRV and Geneva Conference Co-chairmen to meet to discuss modalities of an election.[1]

When the members of the International Commission entrusted

with supervising the elections gathered in Saigon for its first meeting,

> the Diem regime staged an attack on the hotel where the
> Commission members were staying. The Vietminh regime in
> the North, for its part, eagerly welcomed the Commission, and
> as the documents...show, generally cooperated... The story
> became newsworthy in the U.S., partly because the American
> hostess, Perle Mesta and other American dignitaries were turned
> out of the hotels by the rioters.[2]

Robert Scheer says that

> from the very beginning Diem displayed that tendency toward
> autocracy and family rule for which the mass media would
> belatedly condemn his administration eight years later.

Diem's "tendency toward autocracy" led to the formation of a
private political party, the Can Lao, which was the only legal party.

> The Can Lao also served as a secret police, modeled after the
> system the Japanese used in Vietnam during World War Two—
> which Diem had studied in detail.[3]

It also produced, as we have seen, the death of 90,000 opponents
and the imprisonment of another 800,000, with many of them tortured.
But thanks to the planted stories of the C.I.A. and of the prestigious
Oram public-relations firm, which had been hired by some of Diem's
U.S. supporters, Diem was hailed in the U.S. media for having created
the "Miracle of Vietnam." The "miracle," of course was to have
"defeated" the Communists and introduced a "success story" of Free
World, capitalist rejuvenation. When Diem came to the United States
in 1957 for an official visit, he was flown in on President Eisenhower's
personal plane, the "Columbine," and the President met him at the
airport.

However, Diem's "success" in the United States did not help him
solve the economic or political problems in South Vietnam. And
although his American backers succeeded in winning the hearts and
minds of the American public for him, it was a different story in South
Vietnam. Gradually, bits and pieces of the real story began seeping into
the United States, climaxing when a succession of Buddhist monks
immolated themselves in the street. As Scheer puts it,

> The "miracle" thesis formulated by the lobby was accepted by
> most of the mass media during the first five years of Diem's
> regime... [Then] the "miracle" bubble of Vietnam burst; it had
> been nothing more than a miracle of public relations.

When Diem first arrived in Vietnam in 1954, a Catholic coming to
rule at the behest of a foreign power in a country whose population was
80% Buddhhist, the C.I.A. had hired a crowd of several hundred

"welcomers" to greet him at the dock. But not even the C.I.A. and Diem's more respectable U.S. backers could permanently counteract his lack of an indigenous base, his bloody suppression of all opposition, from Buddhist monks and members of the Hoa Hao and Cao Dai indigenous religions to peasant patriots, bourgeois devotees of law, order and a modicum of justice, and rival generals—"all the difficulties the presence of such a personality would [and did] entail."

Finally, having become a liability to the United States and its plan to get Vietnam firmly under its control, Diem was assassinated, with C.I.A complicity, on November 2, 1963. A key C.I.A. operative in this complicated, on-again, off-again and finally on-again plot, was the same Major Lucien Conein (now a Lieutenant Colonel) who first appeared in Hanoi in 1954. At that time he was a "humanitarian" relief worker assisting refugees from Communist violence, but his real job was to develop "a paramilitary organization in the north to be in place when the Vietminh took over."

Three weeks after Diem's assassination, President John F. Kennedy was assassinated in Dallas and Malcolm X horrified the U.S. press and public by declaring that "America's chickens have come home to roost."

By then, the United States had long since forestalled the implementation of the Geneva provisions—which would have permitted the existence of a democratically elected government in a non-aligned, independent and unified Vietnam. Not satisfied, still not in control—and probably feeling on the defensive because of the beginnings of serious domestic opposition—top officials proceeded to lie shamelessly to the American people about the text of the Agreement.

> Secretary of Defense Robert McNamara announced that the Geneva Agreements of 1954 happily provided for the emergence of an "independent entity"—the state of South Vietnam.[4]

And President Johnson told the American Bar Association that the "Agreements guaranteed the independence of South Vietnam." In the same speech, L.B.J. also claimed that

> For ten years, through the Eisenhower administration, the Kennedy administration, and this administration, we have had one consistent aim—observance of the 1954 Agreements.[5]

Quite to the contrary, President Eisenhower sent in 400 U.S. military "advisors," of whom Col. Lansdale's team was an example.

By the time of John Kennedy's assassination in November 1963, [the number] had grown to more than sixteen thousand U.S.

soldiers participating in hundreds of armed confrontations. By the end of 1963, they had flown some seven thousand air missions, lost twenty-three aircraft and suffered 108 deaths.[6]

Here we have another 108 "unknown soldiers," whose identity and cause of death were known to the government but withheld from the American public. From what we know about similar U.S. combat deaths in Nicaragua and El Salvador today, it is probable that the cause of death was never honestly revealed to their families, either.

These violations of international law, public trust and the rights of families are not unique to the Eisenhower, Kennedy, Johnson and Reagan administrations but are part of a long, little known, almost never discussed, tradition of secret wars, unexplained (or dishonestly explained) deaths and the consistent failure of the U.S. Free Press to call more than passing attention to them (if that), even when they know of them. I wonder, for example, how many Americans knew at the time, or even know now, that Winston Churchill informed the British Parliament that President Roosevelt had committed us to war against Japan in August 1941, four months before the Japanese attack on Pearl Harbor. Or that besides the other provocative actions the U.S. took to fulfill that commitment and make it acceptable to the American people,

> Naval officers have admitted that *before Pearl Harbor*, they were sent on secret expeditions with orders to shoot Japanese ships and aircraft—on sight and without warning.[7]

Knowledge of the long history of such activities, along with the more positive aspects of the American reality (about which there is no dearth of governmental and media attention) is a crucial part of the context in which our views about the strengths and weaknesses of our society, its functioning (or malfunctioning) as a democracy and its historic "civilizing" mission should be formed. Without knowledge of this secret governmental "world [that] has a set of values, a dynamic, and a language and a perspective quite distinct from the public world of the ordinary citizen," we are hampered in our national debates about decisions that affect the fate of millions (Vietnam, Central America, Southern Africa, etc.). In the case of Vietnam, besides the death and destruction imposed on the Vietnamese, what are we to say about the 3,700,000 Americans whose lives were disrupted to serve there, the over 58,000 who were killed, the 300,000 who came home wounded, etc. What are we to say about the danger that some such secret war today can escalate not only into a disastrous "conventional" war but into the Final Solution?

Some Commonly Overlooked Causes of the Vietnam War

In 1963, even most members of the anti-war movement of the day did not know that a war was going on in Indochina. Many still think that the first U.S. air attacks against Vietnam took place in August, 1964, under Johnson. That was after an incident in the Gulf of Tonkin in which the United States accused the North Vietnamese of firing on one of its ships but failed to mention that the ship had been involved in a naval attack on Vietnam. (See next chapter for details.)

I. F. Stone summed up the history of that early period in the war as follows:

> Long before the North was accused of interference, its govern-ment was complaining to the [International] Control Commis-sion of "border and air-space violations by the South and infringement of the Geneva Agreements by the introduction of arms and U.S. Servicemen." For four years after Geneva, both North Vietnam and China followed the "peaceful co-existence" policy while the U.S. turned South Vietnam into a military base and a military dictatorship.[8]

Harrison Salisbury suggests one of the motivations for turning South Vietnam into a U.S. military base—and reminds us of the dollar costs, even at that early stage:

> So the forces built up. There were American military men who were eager for a showdown in Indochina. They wanted to finish what they felt had been denied by the truce in Korea—a resound-ing military victory in Asia over the Communists. Some perhaps dreamed of an escalation into China itself. U.S. funds began rolling into Saigon. They hit two billion dollars in 1955-56.[9]

The two billion dollars he mentions came out of the pockets of U.S. taxpayers and created a highly profitable boom in the armaments industry. This economic calculation is a factor in the motivations of only a tiny minority of the population (those who derive the profits and some of those they hire). And it does not receive the attention it deserves from most anti-war organizations. But it plays a powerful role in encouraging the cold war propaganda that makes it appear as if we arm not to make the arms corporations rich (and not to dominate the world ourselves) but to save countries like Vietnam from the Communists— and, of course, to deter war.

There was a third factor as well. The stalemate in Korea had offended not only sections of the military who wanted to "have it out once and for all" with the Communist devil, but also other important sections of the country's power elite. They, too, felt that it was the U.S. mission to convert the heathen, hold onto the wavering, and preside over a world of Free Enterprise and U.S. style "democracy." But, if possible, they wanted to avoid a full scale showdown with China, the Soviet Union or both—at least for now. Their chosen method was a combination of "covert action" and discreet "counter-insurgency warfare."

After the Korean failure, the United States had succeeded by this method in overthrowing the democratically elected governments of Iran—right on the Soviet border—in 1953 and Guatemala in 1954. It had failed in Cuba, at the Bay of Pigs (1961), but this was attributed to faulty planning and the last minute failure to send in additional air cover. The Kennedy administration decided that this could and must be remedied:

> The day after the Bay of Pigs, it created a special task force on Vietnam with the mandate "to grasp the new concepts, the new tools"...that might defeat "subversion" everywhere in the world.[10]

But it would be wrong to think that these were the only motivations for the U.S. war against Vietnam. There was another, more "idealistic" side as well. At least on the part of the American people, including most of the first couple of million G.I.s who went to Vietnam to fight that war.

The Gulf of Tonkin and the U.S. Burden

In October 1966, in Hanoi, Ho Chi Minh told me that he felt sorry for the American G.I.s because they came to Vietnam thinking they were helping the Vietnamese people and found out, after they had been there a while, that this was not the case:

> I don't have to tell you the terrible things they have done; you have seen them with your own eyes... But we feel sorry for them because they have come here thinking they are helping the Vietnamese people, saving them from some terrible thing called communism... After they have been here a while, they find out that even the anti-communist Vietnamese don't want them here.

I discuss this interview more fully in Chapter Eighteen ("Treatment of U.S. and Vietnamese P.O.W.s"), where I point out the failure of some of the Vietnamese to live up to Ho's sentiments. But Ho's words are relevant here because they affirm from an unexpected source the idealistic sentiments that led many Americans to support the war effort, particularly in the early years.

It is my belief that Ho also understood the "terrible things" that some countries had done in the name of communism, the most obvious example being the Soviet Union under Stalin, both internally and in Eastern Europe. I gathered this from the context of some of the things he said at the time, and from some of his gestures when he said them, though I can't prove it with direct quotes. But whatever Ho intended to communicate about the historic crimes of some communists, these atrocities were only part of the background to the misguided and patronizing idealism with which so many Americans endorsed or fought in the U.S. war "to make the world safe for democracy"—for U.S.-style democracy, power and profits, that is. The more contemporary background was the lies of the U.S. government and media. They lied to us about the true situation in both North and South Vietnam, about the hidden goals and objectives of the U.S. intervention, and about the years of vicious, secret warfare carried out by the United States before the conflict finally began to attract public attention in August 1964 with the Gulf of Tonkin incident.

Typically, the government lied to us about the Gulf of Tonkin incident, too. The first episode took place on August 2, when the American public was told that North Vietnamese had made unprovoked attacks on a U.S. destroyer, the Maddox, minding its own business in international waters. For months, U.S. destroyers had been aiding South Vietnamese commandos in the bombing and shelling of oil depots, offshore islands and crowded North Vietnamese ports. On this occasion, the Maddox was engaged in such an action, was approached by North Vietnamese patrol boats and attacked them, sinking one and crippling two others. It received return fire but suffered no casualties or damage.

The second episode, which was manipulated to arouse the most public indignation, was mostly a matter of nervousness in the sonar room of the Maddox and nerviness in Washington, which had wanted for months to get Congressional endorsement for bombings and other actions that it was finding increasingly difficult to keep secret. A report that the North Vietnamese had fired torpedos at the Maddox was used to whip up a frenzy of self-righteous indignation and justify a series of bombing raids on North Vietnam (sixty-four sorties). The most serious consequence, however, was to rush through Congress a Gulf of Tonkin Resolution that served for the next six years as an unofficial Declaration of War.

But there had been no North Vietnamese boats in the area and no torpedoes fired.

> Not a single sailor on either vessel [the Maddox and the aircraft carrier Ticonderoga] had seen or heard Communist gunfire... The Crusader pilots detected no enemy craft during their forty minutes of flying over the area.

As Captain Herrick of the Maddox tried to tell Washington,

> The Maddox had not made any "actual visual sightings" of Communist patrol boats. The radarscope blips apparently showing the enemy had been due to "freak weather effects," and an "overeager" young sonar operator was responsible for recording the torpedoes.[1]

Lyndon Johnson had his own contemptuous explanation of the

incident that he and his aides used to the hilt for their own purposes. He confided his understanding to one of the aides, but not to the public.

> Hell, those dumb stupid sailors were just shooting at flying fish.

The administration's chief ally in getting the Gulf of Tonkin resolution through the Senate was Senator J. William Fulbright of Arkansas, chairman of the Foreign Relations Committee. After Fulbright found out how the government had lied, even to him, he gradually became a cautious opponent, within the Congress, of the war. In April, 1985, on the tenth anniversary of the end of the war, he was less cautious:

> "The biggest lesson I learned from Vietnam," he said, "is not to trust Government statements... They fit the facts to fit the policy," he said of officials' statements on Vietnam and Central America.[2]

Significantly, the brief article in the *Times* indicates that the government's lies were not limited to Vietnam, even then:

> Mr. Fulbright's disillusion with Mr. Johnson's policies began in 1965 after the President sent American troops to the Dominican Republic. The Senator began to believe, as the result of his committee's hearings, that Mr. Johnson had deceived the public about his reasons for sending the troops... Mr. Fulbright did not seem interested in discussing Vietnam so much as the current situation in Central America. He contended that...the Reagan Administration was hiding the facts about what is happening there.
>
> "The American people don't have any idea of what is going on in Central America," Mr. Fulbright said... "We made a great mistake in Vietnam and are making another one in Central America."

I give the *Times* credit for including still another excerpt from Mr. Fulbright's observation, even though the item was somewhat buried in the story, without a headline and, so far as I have been able to ascertain, without any follow-up, despite its explosive implications:

> He said he had also been convinced by a book he had just read that the South Korean airliner that was shot down in September 1983 by the Soviet Union was on a spy mission, even though that view is not widely shared.

Perhaps the Senator's view would be more widely shared by now if the *Times* had printed the title of the book. (I think he was referring to Alexander Dallin's *Black Box: KAL 007 and the Superpowers*.)

After the first public indignation at Vietnam's "attack" had settled down—and Lyndon Johnson had won the election as a peace candidate against the "pro-war" Barry Goldwater—a consensus emerged. It was that the United States, acting with commendable restraint, was serving as an international policeman in Vietnam, upholding law and order against the unprovoked violence of North Vietnam.

Those who supported the activities carried out in the name of this seemingly selfless role, an overwhelming majority at first, honestly believed, then, that the U.S. was responding to illegal interventions from the North into the South by hard-line Communists beholden to, and directed by, the International Communist Conspiracy. Besides the cold war paranoia about the Soviet Union, it was thought—and flamboyantly proclaimed by the government—that Chinese expansionism was the driving factor behind North Vietnamese actions, with Chinese troops already in Vietnam. Not one of these supposed facts was true. But for years even many opponents of the war accepted some or all of these premises. Their argument was that it was neither proper nor safe for any country, not even the United States, to play policeman half way around the globe from its own soil, an argument that was valid enough but not complete.

By now, the best one can say in favor of the policeman theory is that Thomas Merton's analysis was correct. The U.S. was acting in the tradition of the Alabama police at the bridge in Selma, trying to suppress the efforts of a "racially inferior" subject population to gain freedom, justice and dignity. But the vast majority of the "ordinary" G.I.s sent to Vietnam between June 1965 and the signing of the U.S-Vietnam peace treaty in January 1973, had no idea, not even more than a handful of the blacks at first, that this was the reason they were there. They accepted with little or no serious questioning the lies and idealistic pretenses put forward by Washington. And whatever some of them may have done under the inhuman pressures that they were subjected to in Vietnam, they were, for the most part, relatively innocent and terribly vulnerable armed intruders who had been trapped into the service of the U.S. power elite, who had lied to them and, in the end, conscripted most of them.

No wonder Ho Chi Minh said he felt sorry for them.

Before we leave the policeman analogy, it is worth pointing out that there were other, "special" forces in Vietnam who acted completely contrary to almost anyone's positive conception of the policeman's role. Some of them, such as those in Colonel Lansdale's crews, acted as saboteurs and terrorists (the C.I.A.'s usual euphemism is that it "destabilizes" non-democratic governments). Others, who worked in the C.I.A.'s Phoenix program, acted as hired assassins, with a goal of "winning the hearts and minds" of the Vietnamese people by assassinating members of the National Liberation Front's "infrastructure." The number it succeeded in killing is shrowded in mystery; official estimates today say a "mere" six to eight thousand. Others put the figure as high as thirty to fifty thousand South Vietnamese, with thousands of others tortured. Whatever the true number, it seems clear that, inevitably, many of the victims were not even members of the NLF.

Whatever the strengths and weaknesses of the policeman analogy, however defined, I find another description of the U.S. role more accurate. Behind all the rationalizations and camouflages—even the anti-communism—there was something else involved. I think it came closest to an updated, strictly American version of what the English used to call the "white man's burden." When I spent a year at Oxford in 1936-7 and mingled with England's "best and brightest," I was amazed to see how sincerely they believed in the idealism of their mission of civilizing the backward peoples of the world. They spoke of bringing the benefits of medicine, education, technology—and of course Christianity (as they understood it)—to the natives of Africa, India and other faraway places. The only trouble was, as black civil rights leader James Farmer once said to me, that

> Before the English came, the Blacks had the land and the Englishman had the Bible. After the English had been there a while, the Englishman had the land and the Blacks had the Bible.

World War II basically put an end to the Englishman's "burden" and passed it on to the United States, with its new power and newly intensified sense of righteousness in international affairs. But the U.S. took up its civilizing mission with enough sense not to call it by a discredited name with racial overtones. "We" were bringing "democracy" (or what passes for democracy in this country) to the unenlightened. We were picking up "the democratic man's burden"—and millions of Americans sincerely believed it, even though the U.S. began (unbeknownst to most) by preventing elections and installing its own man, Diem, to take charge, at least until "we" could be sure (we thought) that the elections would turn out the way we wanted instead of the way the Vietnamese would have voted.

The trouble was that there was an underside to our mission, too. In June of 1965, Lyndon Johnson blurted it out when he addressed the U.S. troops at Cam Ranh Bay:

> You know, the trouble is that there are only two hundred million of us and there are nearly three billion of them, and they want what we've got and we're not going to give it to them.[3]

Not that this "bottom-line" sentiment was prominent in many people's consciousness—probably it was not even uppermost in the thoughts of our own "best and brightest" who were the prime architects of the Vietnam war. They were following, rather, in the tradition of the founders of the Republic, who had combined an eager idealism and an emphasis on "democracy," "equality" and "freedom" with the practice of slavery and a genocidal destruction of the Indians whose lands they coveted in behalf of their own "life, liberty and the pursuit of happiness." Ironically, even the ships used to carry the kidnapped Africans to our shores bore idealistic, "Christian" names:

> The slave ships were called "Brotherhood," "Justice," "Integrity," "Gift of God,"..."Liberty," "Jesus," "Mary," and "Morning Star."[4]

So the contradiction has been with us from the beginning—and it was primary in Vietnam. What began on the East Coast with blacks and Indians moved erratically southward, into Puerto Rico, Cuba, Nicaragua, large hunks of Mexico, etc. and westward across the continent and into the Philippines, Micronesia, etc. Finally, it hit Indochina.

William Appleman Williams says that we have always thought of ourselves as "The City on a Hill on an Errand into the Wilderness." The reference, I believe, is to the "shining city on a hill" of Biblical lore. He says that the doctrine of containment of communism, which is the flip side of our democratic errand into the wilderness, is

> the modern version of the traditional American dogma that ultimately sermonized, cost-accounted, and marched America and Americans—in the name of duty and immortality—into the graveyard of Vietnam...
>
> [John Quincy] Adams understood that the theology of The City on a Hill contains a demonology and a thirst for immortality that are inherently, inevitably destructive...
>
> [F]rom the beginning, the dogma contained a strong and persistent determination to control the economic benefits of transforming the Wilderness into a suburb of the City...
>
> So economics and theology and secular ideology converged in Vietnam.[5]

Let us look for a moment into the "secular ideology" part of this unholy trinity.

If the containment of communism has become the necessary precondition for fulfilling the errand into the wilderness in behalf of the white man's democratic mission, this is because of the widespread fear that the "international communist conspiracy" will abort the mission by taking over new areas of the world for a non-democratic, non-capitalist alternative.

It is undeniably true that the Soviet society is undemocratic. After more than sixty years, one can sum up the history of the Soviet experiment by saying that, whether consciously or not, it has been an experiment to see whether it is possible to establish economic democracy without political democracy (including civil liberties and the right of independent political organizing)—and the answer is overwhelmingly negative. Without political democracy, even economic democracy is impossible. This lends a semblance of reality to the U.S. fear, a fear that is periodically whipped up into a paranoia by means of distorted and exaggerated U.S. versions of the Soviet society and its drives and expansionist capabilities.

On the other hand, it can be said with equal justice that the United States from the beginning has been an experiment, whether conscious or not, to see if it is possible to have political democracy without economic democracy (that is, under capitalism)—and that once again the answer is overwhelmingly negative. One has only to observe the ability of corporations (including banks and the multi-million-dollar media agencies), and those who draw income and power from them, to violate the democratic process through their influence both on elections and on the policies (both secret and public) of whatever government is elected. Only today, I read of a man in California who spent $1.1 million dollars, successfully, to defeat a Senatorial candidate in Illinois.[6] And no one should overlook the influence of huge corporations and the wealthy on the courts, universities, religious institutions, the medical profession and, above all, the workplace, in producing a lack of democracy in the daily life of the country's citizens. So even if the United States did not customarily install or support dictatorial regimes in the countries in which it intervenes, thereby denying the residents most of the civil liberties and human rights that do exist inside the United States, the "democratic" model it claims to be promoting in these countries is not genuinely democratic.

The consequences of the lack of democracy in both the capitalist and the "socialist" countries—and therefore in their foreign policies—are serious for Third World countries like Vietnam.

On the one hand, Vietnam (and also Nicaragua, Cuba, Zimbabwe, Angola, Guinea-Bissau, etc.) must struggle against attempts of the big-power communist countries (the Soviet Union, China or both) to use the Trojan horse of military and economic aid to exert undemocratic influence or control. Given the needs of Vietnam and other transitional societies—and the refusal of the United States to interact positively with them—they will sometimes be forced to yield. Sometimes they will yield a little; sometimes a lot. But, besides the strength of these countries' indigenous drives for independence and justice, there are two important limitations on the ability of the Soviet Union (the U.S.'s current "focus of evil in the world") to either insinuate or impose its flawed system on them, limitations that U.S. cold war propaganda has consistently failed to acknowledge.

First, the days when the 1917 Revolution and some of its early drives and accomplishments could serve as an exciting model for other countries are largely past, erased by decades of disillusioning internal and external Soviet actions. Besides the history of the Vietnamese communists' experience of the Soviet reality that we have seen in previous chapters, Americans can draw a lesson from the contrast between the the powerful role the American Communist Party played, and the loyalties it inspired, in the Twenties and Thirties and its inability to win any significant support or influence in American anti-war or pro-justice forces today. Second is the equally obvious fact that the Soviet Union has its hands full closer to home, in Eastern Europe, Afghanistan and (to a lesser extent, for now, but always a threat) internally.

Beginning in 1859 (long before there was a Soviet Union) and continuing today, Vietnam has had to contend with the profit and power drives of the capitalist countries, most notably France, Japan and the United States. For, despite all the emphasis within the United States on the Soviet conspiracy to dominate the world, the United States has its own drives to run the world, not only in the interests of expanding its profits and gaining or maintaining access to scarce raw materials, but also in fulfillment of its sense of an historic civilizing mission. On top of these drives, are widespread American yearnings to taste the joys of being Number One in the world. These yearnings are a logical by-product of the capitalist ethos, both in those who achieve great power and become intoxicated with it, and in those who are relatively powerless in their daily lives and long for a vicarious exercise of power through a strong, confident and seemingly virtuous leadership in Washington.

Gabriel Kolko offers a description, if anything, understated, of the American psychology that produced its aggression in Vietnam and continues to dominate its foreign policy today—except as it is erratically and partially restrained by the ambivalent, uneasy conscience of the American people and the popular resistance movements this produces:

> The hallmark of American foreign policy after 1945 was the universality of its intense commitment to create an integrated, essentially capitalist world order out of the chaos of World War Two and the remnants of the colonial systems. The United States was the major inheritor of the mantle of imperialism in modern history, acting not out of a desire to defend the nation against some tangible threat to its physical welfare but because it sought to create a controllable, responsive order elsewhere, one that would permit the political destinies of distant places to evolve in a manner beneficial to American goals and interests far surpassing the immediate needs of its domestic order.
>
> The regulation of the world was at once the luxury and the necessity it believed its power afforded, and...its inevitable costs were justified, as all earlier imperialist powers had also done, as a fulfillment of an international responsibility and mission.[7]

7

"Only a Little War"

A lot of the information I have been presenting was available in the early Sixties. But to find it, one had to do a lot of digging, or, more likely, be present at the early teach-ins and anti-war demonstrations at which some of those who did the digging presented their findings. But these activities were slow in getting started and had to go on for years before they finally reached more than a minute percentage of the population.

Even the traditional anti-war movement was slow to pick up on Vietnam, preferring (like the Freeze movement of the Eighties) to concentrate on the "ultimate" question of The Bomb. To paraphrase the poet Kenneth Patchen, they thought they could get rid of The Bomb without getting rid of the reasons for The Bomb. They thought it would confuse people, reduce their numbers, and alienate their Congressional supporters if they concerned themselves with the "little" undeclared war in faraway Indochina. But such wars are never little for those who die in them. And if left unchallenged, they can grow and fester into the Final Big War.

Because of this one-sided focus, well into the Sixties most people in the anti-war movement knew little or nothing about how Diem had become the ruler of South Vietnam, how the U.S. had used him to frustrate the Geneva Peace Accords, or how the population of South Vietnam had been driven to revolt against Diem and his U.S. sponsors. Too often they accepted the government's explanation that the conflict was not indigenous to Vietnam but resulted from the expansionist drives of "Red" China and the Soviet Union. When the American protests did grow in size and frequency, the impetus came primarily from:

* Young, mostly Southern, blacks in the Student Nonviolent Coordinating Committee (SNCC), which had been realistically confronting the "little," non-nuclear question of black oppression in the South. SNCC attracted both white and black co-workers from all over the country and inspired and energized them and others to new insights and efforts, including some of the first efforts to put the Vietnam War on the national agenda.

* Northern campuses that held teach-ins and spawned the Students for a Democratic Society (SDS), which initiated the first large-scale national demonstration against the Vietnam War.

* The hard-core Left, which had very limited public outreach but provided a lot of necessary information and initial organizing energy.

* A minority of radical pacifists and other, mostly lower-echelon members of the anti-war organizations who viewed the struggles for justice and for peace as inseparable and were strengthened by the activities of SNCC and SDS.

Although I was a member of this last group, typically, I knew very little about the Vietnamese reality as late as the spring of 1963. The following excerpt from something I wrote a little later tells the story of what happened at an anti-war rally in New York City and, *two long years of Vietnamese deaths later*, in connection with the first large "national" anti-Vietnam-War protest:

> [A]t the Easter 1963 protests...signs had appeared demanding withdrawal of American military "advisers," Special Forces and weaponry from a little-known "civil war" in Vietnam. I happened to be a speaker...and was relatively uninformed on the extent of America's illicit and largely secretive involvement in Vietnam. To the best of my recollection, I had not even planned to mention it in my speech. But I was shocked—and intervened—when the rally chairman ordered the signs about Vietnam removed... As a result of my intervention and the hasty addition of a few words about Vietnam to my remarks, the executive secretary of [the largest anti-war organization of the day]...told me that I would never again be allowed to speak at a coalition anti-war rally.
>
> In this particular instance, an additional factor was at work: the anti-communism of some of the anti-war leaders... Not only was the war in Vietnam considered by them to be an act of "communist aggression," but they were offended because some at least of the offending signs were carried by Trotskyists...
>
> In April 1965, twenty-two prominent anti-war leaders... issued a public statement opposing a protest in Washington

that had been initiated by Students for a Democratic Society because SDS refused to condemn Moscow and Peking equally with Washington. U.S. bombing of North Vietnam had begun in earnest in February, and the protest drew by far the largest number of demonstrators of any protest up until that time [about fifteen thousand].[1]

When the protests finally did grow in size and frequency, the media mostly ignored any revelations in the printed literature or speeches that contradicted the government's version of events, whether the revelations came from distinguished scholars, energetic students who had done their homework, or (later) visitors to Vietnam or disillusioned veterans of the conflict. If the press took notice of the information at all, they presented it in the back pages and in contexts that indicated that it was not to be taken seriously. The media focused instead on the beards and hair lengths of some of the participants, and on any acts of petty violence that occurred around the peripheries of major events. In the early days the violence consisted of attacks by anti-communist refugee groups subsidized by the C.I.A. and by other Right Wingers. They usually carried signs saying "Bomb Hanoi" or "Go Back to Russia." Later, these attacks were less frequent but better organized and more vicious when they did take place. More common then, in addition to the regular attacks by police, were frequent "trashings" by understandably angry or impatient students around the edges of major demonstrations. They broke the nonviolent discipline by turning over trash cans or breaking the windows of a particularly offensive bank or corporate headquarters. Trashing almost never involved more than a few dozen of the tens of thousands of protestors (or, later, perhaps as many as a hundred of several hundred thousand protestors). But it usually appeared in the headlines and first paragraph of the story, or was featured on TV. In my view, these acts of petty violence were almost always counterproductive. They intimidated or otherwise alienated potential recruits who were beginning to turn against the war but didn't want to be involved in (or identified with) such scenes. By now it is undeniable that trashings (and later, some even more counter-productive bombings) were *always* encouraged, and usually organized by, agents provocateurs who knew (or at least their government paymasters did) that, with an assist from the media, they would hamper the growth of a disciplined nonviolent movement with wide public appeal.

Once in a while, bits and pieces of reality did appear in the media, but for years they were outnumbered by stories about unprovoked atrocities by the NLF or North Vietnamese and by the official briefings by government officials on the nobility of U.S. efforts to bring democracy and freedom to Vietnam. The occasional publication of information or viewpoints that challenged the official version (except for those that argued that the U.S. should be doing *more* rather than less in Vietnam) had about as much standing and impact as a sentence in a sensationalized account of a brutal mass murder that the man who was obviously guilty had pleaded innocent. In the murder story, if the arrested man was indeed innocent, it might be months or years before anyone would find out, possibly not until after he had been executed. In the case of Vietnam, the "guilt" of the demonstrators was to indulge in the "unAmerican" act of violating the democratic (electoral) process by going into the streets in opposition to the policies of "our" "democratically elected" government and calling for an end to the slaughter. It took years and perhaps three quarters of a million deaths before more than a handful of Americans knew even a few of the facts that suggested that it was the government that was guilty of the "unAmerican" violation of our professed ideals.

Some of the media coverage began to change a little after the first publicly announced arrival of U.S. combat Marines in South Vietnam in June 1965, and the subsequent, also public, disclosures of the sending of more and more troops, until the total there at any one time leveled off at 550,000. Then the anti-war protestors were accused of "stabbing our boys in the back." But reporters flocked to the scene and some of them, especially some of the TV crews, began to communicate an occasional bit of the day-to-day reality, such as the torching or bulldozing of a peasant village, or the ghastly results of using napalm. These were the eminently photographic episodes that "brought the war into our living rooms." They had a powerful impact on the public, comparable in their way to the heartrending images of starving Ethiopians that TV showed in 1984. They were always accompanied, as they should have been, by images of battle-weary or wounded G.I.s, images which initially rallied support for the war and then gradually began to serve as an argument against it.

In 1967, I spoke in Phnom Penh, Cambodia with members of a network TV crew who had just arrived from South Vietnam after capturing on film a scene in which human error or a sudden shift of wind had caused the napalm to fall on U.S. troops, with terrible results. They were simultaneously horrified by what they had witnessed and exhilirated by the scoop they had stumbled upon and the effect it would have on the American public. Two days later, they informed me that the package had been intercepted in Tokyo—by U.S. authorities, they presumed—and the damning segment removed before it could be transmitted to the United States to be shown to the public.

In 1969, shortly after Vice President Spiro Agnew's series of attacks on the media (written by William Safire, now a columnist for the *New York Times*), a reporter for *Newsweek* showed me some photographs of a group of G.I.s posing on a hillside with the severed heads of Vietnamese impaled on their bayonets. He said that a few months earlier they would have been published but not anymore. His boss had informed him that the major media had yielded to governmental criticism and pressure and had adopted a more stringent policy of withholding from the public anything that would inflame public opinion and add to the alarming civilian *and military* unrest. Most of the incidents of army revolt were withheld from the public, at least to the extent possible. But in June, 1966, three soldiers at Fort Hood, Texas publicly announced their refusal to obey army orders to go to Vietnam. And gradually, after that, news of other anti-war activities by G.I.s began to leak out: desertions to Canada and Sweden, a refusal by several dozen soldiers at Fort Hood to be shipped to Chicago to prevent anti-war demonstrations at the 1968 Democratic Convention, etc.

Coverage was also influenced by the fact that reporters were dependent on the military for transportation to the areas where the most visible of the unsettling acts were being carried out. They soon learned that unfavorable stories resulted in their being denied the necessary travel permits, as well as access to the privileged interviews with an unidentified "senior official" that were demanded by their editors and formed the bulk of the front-page news. And whether favored with passes and high-level interviews or not, they were flooded with official briefings and "information," most of which they dutifully passed on to the public—as their counterparts in Central America and other trouble spots still do today. But some of the continuing TV footage and print photographs dramatized the use of napalm and other atrocities and contributed, along with the anti-war movement, to a growing change in public attitudes and a concern to find out more. This and the increasing disillusionment of many of the on-the-spot reporters encouraged them to indicate more and more of the discrepencies between what they were told at the daily news briefings in Saigon, which they now labelled the "Five o'Clock Follies," and what they saw and heard with their own eyes and ears.

The government's political rationalizations and lies dominated the media accounts until the early Seventies, except for an increasing number of stories skeptical of U.S. claims that it was winning the war—"could see the light at the end of the tunnel." All in all, support for the war eroded more at a gut level than from widespread public understanding that the political realities were the opposite of those so sanctimoniously proclaimed by the government. A significant percentage of those in the media, the public and even in the active anti-war movement never did conclude that the basic drives and purposes of the government in Vietnam were similar to those of most international aggressors—in this case expressions of the U.S.'s historic "civilizing" mission, our own romanticized brand of Western imperialism. It was more comforting to believe, at least as long as possible, that the country's concerns were basically democratic, even though subject to occasional excesses and honest mistakes of judgment and tactics. Many people turned against the war not because it was a dishonest and immoral war of aggression but for the reason (also valid) that the costs in American lives and domestic disorder were too great to bear.

In 1983, at a Vietnam Reconsidered conference, Seymour Hersh, a former reporter for the *New York Times* who broke the story of the My Lai Massacre (years after such massacres had been commonplace and ignored by the media), looked back and separated himself from those of his Vietnam War colleagues who had been busily explaining that they really had been "patriotic" and careful but couldn't help noting some of the more obvious discrepancies between government briefings and the reality all around them. He told a stunned and uneasy audience that:

> I do not think the press is very relevant at all. I think that the *Pentagon Papers* and the Vietnam War showed us that there is not much the press can do when the government decides to lie... The history of Vietnam is a history of lies, a history of evasions. And even though the press is doing a great job of reporting in Central America, we just do not know what is going on... I think a lot of us try hard and want to do well, but the fact that the government has such awesome power renders the press powerless.
>
> For...all the wonderful reporting that has been done, these things happened; they can still happen ... At some very basic level, nothing we have done in Vietnam or in Watergate has really changed the attitude of the people running the government, the absolute certitude they have that a lie they tell can go down, the absolute ability they have to look at a foreign policy event and commit our children to it without ever once saying: Who is going to die? How many people are going to die because of this?

News Of The North Was Even More Scanty

For all this ability of the government to lie and to get away with it, bit by bit the American public learned certain crucial facts about what was happening in South Vietnam. But as late as 1966, almost nothing was known about the extent, nature and effects of the bombing of the North. On the one hand, the government described its bombing raids as "surgical" operations that were carried out with great precision and care. Their purpose was to prevent the cancer cells of a violent, foreign-dominated communism from spreading to South Vietnam. It was claimed—and widely believed—that "we" were bombing only "steel and concrete," not civilian areas; destroying the bridges, roads and military installations that were used by the North Vietnamese to supply manpower and weapons to the "terrorists" in the South.

Of course the North Vietnamese made contrary claims, but this was rarely noted, and when it was their claims were presented much as the pronouncements of the anti-war movement were—as anti-American propaganda. If there were a few civilian casualties, they were thought to be few indeed and unavoidable.

At the other extreme, by the spring of 1966 China was claiming that Hanoi had been almost completely destroyed. If this were the case, the Vietnamese were strangely silent about it—or so it seemed, since one rarely got a chance to hear or see what it was that the North Vietnamese were saying. All in all, it was almost impossible to know who or what to believe. As an American active in the anti-war movement, I felt it important that we find out what the reality was. With a lot of effort and even more luck, I was able to visit North Vietnam in October 1966, after first visiting the South. As a result, I learned that neither the Chinese nor the Americans were telling the truth. And of course I learned much more.

I have decided to include here the report that I made at the time, in *Liberation* magazine. I do so in part because current discussions of Vietnam's post-war difficulties almost completely ignore the devastation created by the war and its inevitable effects on the economy to this day (See Chapter Eighteen). This immense destruction is a subject that was prominent in the minds of all the Vietnamese I spoke with during my visit in April of 1985. Yet it was almost completely ignored by almost all the American reporters who visited Vietnam at the same time, as I discovered in my conversations with them and in their published reports. Yet the tonnage of bombs the U.S. dropped on Vietnam, Laos and Cambodia was more than double the combined totals of the tonnage it dropped on Europe and in the Pacific during World War II. And,

> Between the Second World War and the Korean War, the tons of munitions per man increased eight times, but during the Vietnam War it was twenty-six times greater than in 1941-45.[2]

No wonder Ho Chi Minh told me in 1966 that if Vietnam had been an urbanized, industrial country, like the countries of Europe, it would have been forced to surrender in the first few months of the bombing.

But there was much more involved than the tonnages dropped and the terrible consequences for the Vietnamese. There were terrible consequences for young Americans as well. After the above passage, Kolko goes on to point out something that indicates the calloused disregard of the U.S. planners for their own troops, caught up as the planners were in their insane pride in their historically unprecedented technological power. He says

> In [South] Vietnam, the combat soldier was primarily a bait for
> the techological colossus behind him.

I shuddered when I read this, but it wasn't until I read *Dear
America,* a collection of letters written from Vietnam by American
servicemen and letters to them by friends and families, that I felt the full
impact of this statement. The letters were collected by the New York
Vietnam Veterans Memorial Commission for the purpose of including
excerpts on the Memorial erected in Vietnam Veterans Plaza in New
York City. The last letter in the book is written by the mother of
William R. Stocks to her dead son, fifteen years after he was killed in
Vietnam. She writes of having been told by one of her son's friends, a
man in his outfit, how her son had died.

> He said how your jobs were like sitting ducks. They would send
> you men out to draw the enemy into the open and then they
> would send in the big guns and planes to take over. Meantime,
> death would come to so many of you.[3]

This was one terrible side of the U.S. war that anyone who was in
South Vietnam during the war had to feel and observe, especially those
who had to go through it in ways that I didn't, in my brief, relatively
safe visits. The other terrible side, of course, was the tragedy of what I
saw happening to the Vietnamese, their punishment, as it were, for
having had the insolence to challenge our right to control their country
in the interests of our type of democracy and freedom.

Eighty percent of the victims of the bombings were civilians, and
the report helps explain why. It also conveys some of the impact of the
war on the psychologies of the grass-roots people who survived, people
whom the United States claimed it was saving from communism. In
that respect, it says something about the idea that the U.S. can win
friends and influence people in El Salvador and Nicaragua today by
supplying the planes, bombs guns, "intelligence" coordination (and
sometimes the pilots or other crew members) that bomb and strafe
them.

A Contrast Of Views

Two nights before I left for Vietnam, I spoke at an anti-war rally at
Rutgers University. Hardly had the meeting begun before the police
arrived and cleared the auditorium, because of a reported bomb threat.
A half hour later, no bomb had been found and we went back into the
auditorium. To my surprise, the first few rows were now occupied by
ROTC students in uniform. My first thought was that perhaps they had
called in the threat in order to gain this advantageous position for
launching an attack on the platform—a not uncommon occurence in

those days. But as I looked out at their young, eager faces, I thought more about the promise in life that should be theirs at this stage of their lives and about the fate that probably awaited them instead. As ROTC students they were prime candidates to be sent to Vietnam.

I began to think about how I could speak to them with a message of human solidarity that would transcend our immediate conflict of views and open up the possibility that we could share our feelings and together activate the best instincts and impulses that motivated them in their readiness to "defend their country" militarily, and that motivated us in opposition to the war. Suddenly I was startled out of my revery by hearing the strident voice of the first speaker, my "colleague" in the anti-war movement, in the middle of an attack on them as "fascists in the service of capitalist oppression." By now, I cannot remember what I said in my efforts to undo his tirade and accomplish my purpose, but I do remember seeing some positive responses in the faces of some of the ROTC members. And the meeting ended without any attack from the front rows. Probably there had been no plans for one.

When I left for Vietnam, this troubling episode was strong in my consciousness. It was strong during my time in Saigon, where I spent some friendly moments visiting with G.I.s, in the airport and in a bar in Saigon. But perhaps my strongest memory now is of having it prominent in my thoughts when I heard Ho Chi Minh express his positive attitude toward the G.I.s who had come to Vietnam thinking they were helping the Vietnamese people by saving them from some terrible thing called Communism.

Ho Chi Minh and David Samas, James Johnson and Denis Mora, three soldiers at Fort Hood who refused to be sent to Vietnam, helped me to understand that we must *never* allow our positions on opposite sides of any conflict to interfere with our sensitivity to the human qualities that unite us far more than any of our differences. These are qualities of humanity that all of us, on both sides of any conflict, are always tempted to lose sight of in the ardor of our commitments. But they are always there, however hidden or forgotten. We must always search for them, in ourselves and in those who oppose us. We must always seek out open, unselfrighteous exchanges and communication. As Gandhi and many others have told us, we can be opponents, but we must not be enemies.

The Fort Hood Three helped me because they sought me out, an anti-war activist of whom they had heard but whom they had never met, for help when they had decided to refuse to go to Vietnam. I introduced them to A. J. Muste and to black leaders of the anti-war movement, and we were all inspired by them, not just by their refusal but by their sensitivity toward those in the service who held different views. Together we held a press conference at which they announced their decision and we announced our support.

Next, I include an editorial I wrote in *Liberation*[4] about these three brave soldiers and then I end this section of the book with my "Eyewitness Report from North Vietnam."

The Fort Hood Three

The struggle against the war in Vietnam entered a new phase on June 30, 1966 when three brave soldiers announced their refusal to obey army orders to go to Vietnam. The three men, Private David Samas, Private First Class James Johnson and Private Dennis Mora, were on a thirty-day pre-embarkation leave, after having received their orders.

Significantly, the soldiers made their announcement at a press conference in New York City, called by the Fifth Avenue Vietnam Peace Parade Committee, a coalition of niney-three local and national peace groups, and were supported in person by Stokely Carmichael, chair of S.N.C.C., and Lincoln Lynch, public relations director of C.O.R.E., both of whom expressed their hope that other soldiers and potential draftees would follow the example of the three refusers. Badly needed muscle was added to the peace movement, not only by the soldiers' action but also by this coming together of three important groups: the traditional (if expanded) peace movement, the militant Afro-American movement for civil rights, and the soldiers themselves. In the past, the peace movement has been surprisingly slow to carry its message to soldiers, the men on whose unquestioning obedience the government relies to be able to thwart the democratic will in time of unpopular war. But then, in our lifetime no other war has been so clearly unpopular as the American aggression in Vietnam.

The three soldiers told the press that after seven months in the army it was their opinion that a majority of the soldiers do not believe in the war but feel trapped and helpless. Our democracy is not vital enough for its citizens to believe that they can decide for themselves such an important matter as whether or not to risk their lives killing Vietnamese peasants who are in search of their independence. After the press conference, Michael Armstrong, an ex-Marine who served ten months in Vietnam, told me that in his view as many as eighty percent of the military in Vietnam are disillusioned and disgusted by the war and want out.

These figures may be exaggerated. What is more, soldiers are notoriously brave under combat conditions, even when they are frankly cynical about the motives and trustworthiness of the homefront politicians. But clearly the men in the armed forces must learn that they are not alone, that it is both possible and honorable to resist, and that in the spirit of Nuremburg, large sectors of the American public will support those who refuse to commit atrocities against their fellow human beings.

There is no reason why any Americans, including those in the armed forces, should be cut off from their inalienable human rights. We have assumed too long that draftees and other soldiers can be separated from their constitutional rights of freedom of speech, press, assembly, and meaningful political expression, without harm to them or the democratic process—even as during most of our country's history it has been assumed that people with black skins could be excluded without making democracy a lie.

Today the militant wing of the civil rights movement is moving away from reliance on the inadequate and extremely unreliable charity of the political establishment, as negotiated by well-motivated middlemen who seek to liberalize the status quo without repudiating its main assumptions. Surely this is the major thrust of the emphasis on "black power." It is no accident that an integral part of the new, more revolutionary orientation is a more serious challenging of the war. Most "Gandhians" in the civil rights movement have been handicapped by loyalty to existing institutions, including the primacy of the electoral process.

A similar coming of age is important for the peace movement, which must learn to develop and use its muscle seriously. We must create a power base which is not beholden to the established power structure, mentally, morally, or politically. It may seem odd, but one of the ways for the peace movement to build its own independent constituency is to reach out directly to the soldiers and to other young people who are subject to the draft but presently lack the "religious training and belief" associated with the privilege of exemption as "legitimate" conscientious objectors. Soldiers and young people whose cultural position does not lead to draft deferment should be brought into the dialogue so that a badly needed cross-fertilization can take place between them and the peacemakers. Soldiers ready to take a stand similar to that of Mora, Johnson, and Samas should be given help in finding lawyers and gaining the support of broadly based defense committees.

In part it was coincidence that the three soldiers announced their stand in the same week that the U.S. flyers extended their country's murderous air bombardment into the densely populated industrial complex of the Hanoi-Haiphong area and simultaneously began to nibble away at the life-sustaining, life-protecting dikes of North Vietnam. Even so, the new bombings served to emphasize the logic of the three men's refusal to take part in a war which they characterized as "immoral, illegal, and unjust." In their joint statement they said: "[in the army] we have been told that many times we may face a Vietnamese woman and child and that we will have to kill them." Extending the bombing shocked and horrified most of the world. (Only Americans are sufficiently insulated and blindly enough pro-American to be relatively immune to the horror.) But this new act of terror was only the latest of many immoral escalations in the illegal commitment of more and more American conscripts to the killing of more and more Vietnamese, including women and children, in an unjust war for American domination of Southeast Asia.

A second coincidence took place about a week later when Hanoi began to talk about trying the offending airmen and American military authorities announced that the three soldiers would be brought before military courts-martial. The soldier-prisoners in Hanoi were shot down while raining death on people below, but the three soldier-prisoners at Fort Dix were seized illegally on the streets of New York while on their way to address a peace meeting at the Community Church.

Two days after the press conference, the Pentagon announced, in its best public-relations manner, that the three men "had exercised their right of free speech and had not—as yet—violated military discipline." *(New York Times,* July 3.) But in the same interview there was an ominous note: "A senior legal expert at the Defense Department indicated today that members of the armed forces who refused to fight in Vietnam might be prosecuted under existing laws and regulations and, in extreme cases, might be sentenced to death." As usual, the government gave lip service to America's high ideals but issued a thinly veiled threat to those who might take them seriously. After the men had made clear their refusal to succumb to bribery by retracting their statements and had agreed to speak at a series of public meetings in their remaining days of leave, the government forgot its profound devotion to free speech and kidnapped them.

For humanitarian reasons, the lives of the prisoners in Hanoi should be spared... And we must press for exonerations for James Johnson, David Samas and Dennis Mora. We should hail them as the heroes they are, make it possible for them to put their courage and devotion to humane and humanitarian tasks, and encourage others to follow their example.

The power of their action lies in the possibility that others will take a similar stand. Otherwise it becomes another in a series of isolated, idealistic acts, which typifies the traditional weakness of the peace movement. There can be no beginning without such acts but they must come to fruition in widespread, politically effective actions by "ordinary" people.

Today the peace movement has an historic opportunity to move from its perpetually repeated "beginnings" to a new stage of historic relevance. Close alliance with the black-power militants and the draftees is a necessary prerequisite.

[Note: The following is the text of a telegram sent July 7 to the Attorney General by the coordinators of the Fifth Avenue Peace Parade Committee.]

We strongly condemn harassment by Federal agents of servicemen such as PFC James Johnson, Pvt. Dennis Mora and Pvt. David Samas, who have filed injunction in Federal Court against shipment to Vietnam on grounds of immorality and illegality of the war.

We are reliably informed that on July 4 an officer of the Modesto, California police force visited the parents of Pvt. Samas. The officer said he had been contacted by "higher authorities" and that if Pvt. Samas would rescind his action and his statement against the war, and in effect abandon his fellows, he would not be prosecuted and would receive an Army discharge. The officer obviously acted under instructions of Federal agents in proposing such a bribe.

Such acts show desperation in attempt to stem growing opposition to the war among young men facing the draft or already in military service. The peace movement will continue to aid in every possible lawful way anyone, civilian, soldier, sailor or Marine, who opposes this illegal and immoral war. The young men in the armed services are entitled to know the truth about the war and to engage in discussions about it. Citizens are likewise entitled to communicate the truth about the war to servicemen, and the peace movement is determined to exercise that right.

8

Vietnam: Eyewitness Report, 1966

Tomorrow I leave for Peking and Hanoi. Before I go I want to record some of what I have seen and learned during the past two months in the course of a trip that has already taken me to Saigon, Phnom Penh (Cambodia) and Bangkok, to Tokyo, Hong Kong, Delhi, Cairo and Moscow.[1]

In Phnom Penh and Moscow, I had a series of conferences with spokesmen of the National Liberation Front and with representatives of the Democratic Republic of Vietnam. In Saigon I met with leaders of the opposition to the U.S.-Ky government. These opponents included not only Buddhist monks, students and intellectuals, but also early members of the Diem government who resigned when they became convinced that the United States insists on a policy which is the exact opposite of its public rhetoric of peace, political freedom and social justice.

Let me start in Saigon. At midnight I saw a mother gather four little children around her, one at the breast, to catch what troubled sleep they could on a rain-drenched sidewalk. Nearby a group of eight- to twelve-year-olds, without either homes or parents, tugged at my sleeves for a *piastre*. Some whimpered plaintively while others smiled eagerly and looked up with the irresistible faces of innocence. Most heartrending of all was the fact that the whole performance was obviously rehearsed for maximum impact. Victims of war that do not appear in the statistics or the military reports: children not only orphaned and desolate but progressively hardened and corrupted in order to survive.

A TV man who had been in Saigon for eighteen months told me

that these particular children will not be on the streets for long. There is a constant influx and a high turnover. He said that juvenile delinquency work (and a lot of the other nonmilitary operations in Saigon) is being taken over by West Germany. The Germans are more efficient than the Vietnamese, and besides there is a shortage of reliable Vietnamese collaborators. Periodically the authorities "clean" the streets by having the homeless waifs arrested. Kids as young as ten are given sentences of ten to fifteen years on trumped-up charges, and then trained as suicide squads. They can gain their "freedom" by risking death or mutilation while betraying their countrymen to the hated foreign invader. (Given the depth of that hatred, I wonder how many of them actually carry out their missions. But where do they go, what do they do, if they don't?)

At the entrance to my hotel, a little girl, perhaps eight years old, asks for money. After she gets a little, she runs back a few steps and cries out defiantly: "*Ka Ka Do* Americans; *Ka Ka Do* Americans." ("Cut the Americans' throats.") Just then two American M.P.s ride slowly by in a jeep, chins and guns protruding menacingly. The little girl turns from me and screams at the soldiers: "*Ka Ka Do* M.P.s; *Ka Ka Do* M.P.s." In the background the voice of someone who is obviously half drunk can be heard complaining, "Nobody likes the Americans and I look like an American, but I'm not. I'm a Canadian."

Early in the morning, in the men's room of my Saigon hotel, a boy about ten years old, with a drawn and pinched face, smiles wanly, makes obscene gestures with his hands, and invites me to follow him. It is not clear whether it is he or his mother I am supposed to "enjoy," but that is all that is left obscure as he pushes a finger of one hand back and forth through a hole formed by the thumb and fingers of the other.

I follow the hotel doorman instead. He has offered to "change money." I shall not do it, but I want to find out a little about the black market. He starts by offering me one and a half times the official rate and gradually climbs to more than double, taking my continued refusals and disclaimers as sharp bargaining.

I apologize for having wasted his time and wander into the street. Packages of American cigarettes catch my eye. There are strange white labels under the cellophane wrapping. Looking more closely, I read on a pack of Pall Malls:

For use outside U.S.
Donated by M&O Chevrolet Co.
427 Franklin St.
Fayetteville, N.C.

I decide to buy a pack as a "souvenir" and select a package of Lucky Strike Filters. The label says:

For use outside U.S.

Donated by
Colonia Memorial Post 6061 V.F.W.
606 Inman Ave.
Colonia, N.J. 07067

On the top is printed:

Tax Exempt
Not to be sold

This routine and perhaps minor perversion of the generosity and idealism of the donors back home strikes me as symbolic of the perversion and corruption of all the varied idealism and self-sacrifice which innumerable Americans have poured and are pouring into Vietnam. Most heartbreaking of all, of course, are the sacrifices of those who fight and die there, believing, for a time at least, what the government has told them.

If they arrive in Saigon thinking that they have come to help the Vietnamese, they soon find that the Vietnamese have a different view. Saigon is the heartland of the "pro-American" sector. Besides the hit-and-run attacks of the N.L.F. guerrillas, there is the sullen aloofness and hostility of the general population, which is not above making a fast dollar off the Americans but never really fraternizes with them—and always protects and shelters its own. A bomb explodes, a symbolic assault is made at the very center of Saigon in full view of hundreds of people, and the perpetrators are almost never caught. The population opens up and swallows its own.

The Venerable Thich Thien Hoa, President of the United Buddhist Church, explained the universal hostility toward Americans in the following manner:

> We realize that many Americans want to help us. We thank them for this. But the policy of the United States government is not to help the Vietnamese people but to help a small group which oppresses the people. The American government has been here more than ten years and it has always supported dictator governments, so the Vietnamese people are against the American government.

Similarly, members of an underground student group told me:

> All the present collaborators were collaborators and hirelings (*serviteurs*) of France. During the Japanese occupation they collaborated with the Japanese. This tiny oppressing minority collaborates with whatever foreign power is seeking to rule over us. They profit from colonialism so they don't want independence. They profit from the war, so they don't want peace. But

the people are against the Americans. That is for sure. One hundred percent of the people are against the United States.

Like others I talked with, these students made it clear that it was not Ky but the United States which was responsible for the brutal suppression of last spring's Buddhist demonstrations. They spoke with anguish of the number of people who had been killed or put in jail. They said that the suppressions were so extensive that they were unable to plan and launch an offensive just now. But they emphasized that new uprisings were inevitable.

Despite the persuasiveness of American money and power, the ranks of the collaborators are thinning out. In Phnom Penh I spoke with wealthy and conservative refugees who talked with tears in their eyes of their disillusionment with the United States. One of them had served in the governments of both Bao Dai and Ngo Dinh Diem. In 1951 he was declared by the Viet Minh to be under sentence of death, as a notorious collaborator with the French. In 1955, the Americans sought him out in Paris and made him a member of the Diem government. Still looking and talking like an aristocrat, but obviously a man of both courage and integrity, he said to me:

> No one can accuse me of being anti-American. On the contrary, I collaborated with the Americans under Diem. But I resigned when it became clear that the United States did not want peace. I wanted to collaborate with the Americans, but I wanted to collaborate for peace, not for war. I wanted to work with them for the good of my country, not for its destruction... After the assassination of Diem, your government contacted me again and asked me to serve in the new government. I refused, making clear that I still wanted to follow a policy of peace and would not serve in a government that was set up by the Americans in order to wage war.

A second man had studied at M.I.T. in the early Sixties and looked me up at my hotel in Phnom Penh. He explained that he thought he had heard me speak on the radio in the United States, but as he talked I realized that his real reason was that he needed to work out his ambivalence by discussing it with an American. This man also appeared quite aristocratic in his manner and in general was both so mild and nonpolitical that he took me completely by surprise when he said:

> I hesitate to take up a gun and fight because I know so many Americans. They are my friends. But I am very much opposed to what the Americans are now doing and before long I may decide that I have to join the war against them.

As he spoke I had the feeling that he had just about made up his mind but had needed to "explain" his action to an American first.

In Saigon itself, I spoke at length, behind locked doors and drawn blinds, with an important public official *of the present government*. He also was an aristocrat, one of the "tiny minority" who until recently had no difficulty getting along with the various foreign rulers that have occupied his country. But as he put it to me:

> We have had war since 1939. My hair has become gray. War, always war, and everyone suffers. And since the United States is insistent on continuing the war, I have come to feel that it would be better for us to form a new government, one that will deal with the National Liberation Front. One that would initiate a cease-fire, bring peace, and try to absorb the N.L.F. It would have to be a new nationalist government for peace. Ky is where he is today only because of the Americans. In the end whichever group wins out in the peaceful competition between ourselves and the N.L.F., it will be better than what we have now.

At Tansonnhut Airport in Saigon, youthful Vietnamese are leaving the country to study in France, Canada, and the United States. At the same time youthful Americans are arriving, many of them to die in the paddies and jungles of Vietnam. I had the opportunity to interview a number of the departing students. None of them seemed too troubled over who wins the war. When I asked one of them, as gently as I could, if he felt any hesitation about leaving his country to study in the United States while Americans were coming there to risk mutilation and death, he replied:

> As a human being, yes. But you must remember that it is the United States which insists on continuing the war.

Report from North Vietnam

I hope that I may be forgiven for beginning this report by saying that I recoil from the prospect of writing it, because of the difficulties of communication involved. The problem is partly the superficiality of our most cherished words and concepts before the abrupt finality of premature, man-made death and the lingering horror of dismembered or faceless survivors. But there is a cultural and political problem as well, involving the gap between American experience and Vietnamese experience, American political assumptions and Vietnamese assumptions.

What words are there with which to talk to any young mother who tearfully hands one a snapshot and says: "We Vietnamese do not go to the United States to fight your people. Why have they come over here to kill my children?"

What can one say to a twenty-year-old girl, swathed in bandages and still in a state of shock because her mother, father, three brothers and sisters were all killed at their noonday meal when American bombers attacked the primitive agricultural village in which they lived? She herself was pulled unconscious and severely burned from the straw hut in which the rest of the family perished.

"Ask your President Johnson," she said to me, "if our straw huts were made of steel and concrete" (a reference to the President's claim that our targets in North Vietnam are military structures of steel and concrete). "Ask him if our Catholic church that they destroyed was a military target, with its 36 pictures of the Virgin, whom we revere. Tell him that we will continue our life and struggle no matter what future bombings there will be, because we know that without independence and freedom nothing is worthwhile."

I went with her to a nearby "Hate Memorial." it was not dedicated to hatred of those whom the United States labels as aggressors and villains. Instead, on one side of the monument, the inscription said:

In Hatred against the U.S. Pirates
Who Killed our Countrymen
of Phuxa village
Nhat Tan Commune
On August 13, 1966

The other side read:

Firmly Hold the Plow
Firmly Hold the Rifle
Be Determined to Fight and Win
Over the American Aggressors
In order to Avenge our Fellow Countrymen
of Phuxa, Nhat Tan

Of the 237 houses in Phuxa, 40 were destroyed on August 13. Thirty-two persons were killed.

Meanwhile an American mother mourns the death of her son, drafted into the armed forces and shot down on a bombing raid over Vietnam. In the United States we are told that he was defending the Vietnamese people against Chinese aggression, but there are no Chinese soldiers in Vietnam. In fact, the Vietnamese will tell you that the last Chinese soldiers to invade Vietnam were 180,000 U.S.-supported Chiang Kai-Shek troops, in the winter of 1945-46. They helped the Allies suppress the Vietnamese independence which the United States had promised Vietnam when we needed their help during World War II. Earlier, when the Vietnamese first declared their independence, on September 2, 1945, the Allies hastily rearmed 90,000 Japanese soldiers who had been waiting shipment back to Japan. During the next nine years, the United States supplied 80% of the cost of the unsuccessful "French" war to preserve Western colonialism in Indochina. President Eisenhower's refusal, in 1956, to allow democratic elections and reunification of Vietnam, as promised in the Geneva Accords, was not our first flagrant betrayal of Vietnamese independence. Most Americans are ignorant of these facts, or dimly aware of them as unfortunate mistakes committed in a confused and distant past, but there is hardly a Vietnamese family that does not measure America's broken promises in terms of the death of one or more loved ones.

How does one greet a seventeen-year-old boy who limps painfully across the room, looking as if he were fifty (though he will never reach that age) because his face and neck, legs and arms are covered with welts and abscesses from napalm burns? I don't know, but I remember protest meetings in the United States at which Christian clergymen have said: "It may be true that our tax money buys napalm but you can't expect Americans to refuse to pay their income taxes in protest. After all, whatever mistakes the United States may make, this is a democratic country and we must obey its laws."

We weep for your wounds, Thai Binh Dan, and those of your countrymen. But we hope that you don't expect us to be so rash as to revolt against the society that inflicted them. Don't be discouraged. There is a solution and we will tell it to you. You can revolt against your government. Tell your brothers and sisters who are not yet wounded that if they are anxious to avoid your fate, that is what they must do.

We admit that the United States had no business getting involved in Vietnam in the first place, but you must remember that we are a big and powerful country. Now that we are there we can't just withdraw; that is, we can't just stop the murder, stop trying to dictate to your people what kind of economic and political system they can have, stop pretending that our massive terrorization of your people is somehow a way of protecting them against intimidation and terror.

So it's up to you, Thai Binh Dan. You must get your people to come over to our side. You must get them to turn against your government so that it will be forced to surrender. ("Come to the conference table" is the way we put it in the United States; surely you can see how reasonable that sounds.) Meanwhile we shall continue the napalm and the other bombing, which if you stop to think of it, will help you in your struggle against your government.

Be of good cheer, Dan. After the peace that we all desire so earnestly, if your country lines up satisfactorily on our side of the Cold War, our government will probably permit us, after a few years, to bring dozens, possibly even hundreds of your people to the United States.

Here in our warm-hearted, rich and democratic country, they will be given every consolation. Our women will weep over them, our skilled plastic surgeons will remove the worst of the scars, and the most enlightened of our businessmen will write tax-deductible checks to cover their expenses.

What does one say to a seven-year-old lad who (if he manages to survive future attacks) will have to go through life with only one arm, because his right arm was severed near the shoulder in a bombing raid? When I talked with him and a twelve-year-old friend, who had lost a leg in a different attack, I tried to get away from the horrors of war. I asked them about their school and told them about the daily life of my ten- and fourteen-year-olds in the United States.

We had a good conversation. There were the beginnings, at least, of trust and affection. But there was no way we could get away from the war, as one can do in the United States by turning off the news or changing the topic.

School? Seven-year-old Dai had lost his arm when his kindergarten was bombed. Ten of his classmates and the teacher were killed; nine were wounded. Twelve-year-old Chinh had been on his way to his school one morning with a friend when:

> There was the explosion of bombs and I didn't know that my leg was cut but only that I couldn't stand up and that I couldn't walk any longer... My friend Ve put me on his back and got me near the trenches. Then another explosion knocked us into the trenches where there was water and we got all wet. Ve kept pulling me through the water to get away from the bombs. He put me in a dry place and saw that there was lots of blood and was afraid and went to the village to get my father... When my father was carrying me to the first aid station I still could see everything all around and I saw a number of my friends and some of the villagers lying dead on the ground. Then I lost my consciousness and couldn't see anything.

My notes say: "It is amazing how simply and naturally he speaks, without a trace of self-consciousness or self-pity. I wonder if he will be able to preserve such a healthy attitude as he goes through life without a leg."

While we were talking, American planes came suddenly upon us (as they do, day and night, all over Vietnam), roaring over the little complex of primitive shelters and the communal well at which women were washing their supper dishes and the three of us were talking. We took to shelter and continued the conversation. They told me that some of their friends had been killed while herding water buffalo: "The planes swoop down on the fields and machine gun the beasts and the people."

Earlier that day, Miss Tuyen, a twenty-year old peasant woman in the village of Nam Ngan, told me that two of her brothers, one eight and one three, had been killed less than a month earlier in the field where they had been taking care of buffalo. Miss Tuyen had been introduced to me as a "village hero" who had carried twice her weight in ammunition on her shoulder during an attack, transporting crates of shells through the narrow trenches to the anti-aircraft stations. It was only when I tried to turn the conversation to personal subjects, asking about her family, that I learned about the strafing of her brothers. An older brother had been killed at the age of eighteen, at the battle of Dien Bien Phu, the last major battle of the French Resistance War, which led to the Geneva Agreements and (supposedly) recognition of the independence and sovereignty of the unified country of Vietnam.

Perhaps it is worth quoting part of what Miss Tuyen said to me:

> When the planes come bombing and strafing our native land we feel a great indignation. We are making every effort to shoot them down, in order to avenge our young people who have been cut down by the American aggressors... What would young Americans think if they were living peacefully and suddenly another country came and started killing them? For this reason, in spite of the planes all over the skies, we do not fear them... When I was carrying ammunition a bomb exploded near me and covered me with dirt but I struggled free in order to continue fighting. We only have rifles in the ground forces but we are making every effort to bring down the planes. Since August 5, 1964, we have participated in more than a hundred battles (I can't remember the exact number), but we are still firm in the battle.
>
> At night when the planes come, I volunteer to cook rice. I reach every difficult place to serve the soldiers. During the day I go to the fields and gather vegetables for the army. They come, we open fire; they go, we continue picking vegetables... Bombing is continuous but we never feel tired... It is very clear that the young people in my village are ready to sacrifice their lives if necessary to defend our independence. The struggle may last for years, but we realize that we will win.
>
> During the resistance against the French colonialists, when we won our independence, one of my brothers lost his life. He was eighteen at the time. Now the Americans have come, massacring the people in our village. That has fanned our hatred. We know that the American aggressors may commit more crimes against our village, but we have no alternative but to stand firm.

Recently, as I told you, my aunt and my two younger brothers were killed and I can't help feeling a great hatred. I am determined to avenge this blood debt... We know that our battle is very difficult but we can see our victory ahead.

It's hard to find the words to tell you all our experiences but I realize that you can see much for yourself. On your return I hope that you can help the American people to understand the truth and, if you don't mind, I send my regards both to the peace movement in your country and also to your wife and to my brothers and sisters in your family. As for me, I have no alternative but to go on fighting. When one day our country is reunited in freedom, I hope to greet you in our village on your way to Saigon.

The village in which this interview took place was another of those unbelievably primitive agricultural villages, similar to Phuxa, which cover the countryside. There was no way in which it could be considered a military target, except perhaps that its people fire back at attacking American planes. Yet because of the frequency with which bombs are dropped in the vicinity, every primitive straw hut had an individual underground concrete shelter that the family could slip into during night attacks. In addition there was a network of trenches some of them concrete and some brick-lined. These trenches led away from the houses to larger shelters and to anti-aircraft stations. Before such villages have electricity, plumbing or paved roads, they have concrete trenches and bomb shelters to protect them from the advocates of the Great Society. While I was at Nam Ngan, I watched the peasants thresh rice by hand. Although they have no threshing machines, or for that matter sewing machines, washing machines, refrigerators—any of the things most Americans take for granted—they have to have machine guns and rifles to fight off the American attackers.

Now, a few hours after my conversation with Miss Tuyen, I was in another little hamlet, a few miles away, talking with Dai and Chinh and listening to the bombs explode. We estimated by the blast and illumination that they were falling in an area between a mile and perhaps five miles away. I tried to calculate whether some of them might be falling on Nam Ngan village, and wondered whether Miss Tuyen was cooking rice or carrying ammunition. I knew that I would probably never find out, because in a few minutes I would be on the road. It was dark already and nighttime is the only time it is "safe" to travel in North Vietnam. Now the planes were dropping flares, bathing everything in an eerie light, and despite myself I found myself wondering whether this was to make it easier to strafe "anything that moved," as the Vietnamese charge is the common practice.

In the minds of the American gunners, anything that moved would almost certainly be a Red totalitarian or terrorist, or, at the very least, an ignorant and inferior "Gook." I looked at seven-year-old Dai, with his missing arm, and twelve-year-old Chinh, with his missing leg, and thought of Miss Tuyen's three- and eight-year-old brothers who had been shot down a few weeks earlier while tending buffalo. I didn't want to think about what might be happening to any children who had been caught cowering in a field when the flares were dropped. So I turned to Dai and Chinh and tried to explain to them that many American airmen think that they are helping Vietnamese people when they bomb and strafe Vietnamese villages. It wasn't easy.

*

As long as I was in Hanoi, I was able to keep a relatively open mind and raise questions when I was told about the "deliberate bombing" of residential areas, schools and hospitals. Something, perhaps my own type of Americanism rose up inside me and I tried to deny that Americans would knowingly bomb and strafe civilians, at least as part of deliberate governmental policy.

At dusk I sometimes sat on a bench by the lake and enjoyed the beauty of the thunder and lightning in the background—until I became adjusted to the fact that it was not really thunder and lightning but the explosion and illumination of bombs in the outskirts. Occasionally in Hanoi in November, one's eardrums would be threatened by particularly loud explosions, which generally turned out to be Vietnamese anti-aircraft fire from the roofs of nearby buildings. Twice while I was there, after shelter alarms and deafening blasts on all sides, the Vietnamese told me that they had shot down pilotless reconnaissance planes over the inner city. I saw the wreckage of one such plane. I could lie on my bed in the Thong Nhat hotel and watch the flames at the mouths of the guns on the roof of an adjacent building as they fought off occasional intruders. I talked with several people who had fuel tanks or an isolated bomb crash on their houses as an American pilot tried to lighten his load in order to facilitate his getaway. A Polish diplomat told me that from inside the Polish embassy he had caught on tape the explosion of American bombs which fell in the embassy district in June. He said that it caused a sensation in Warsaw when he played the tape on his leave. But the inner city of Hanoi had not suffered any major attack, and, during the time I was in North Vietnam, it was indeed a small island of relative safety.

The Vietnamese, who have suffered from ceaseless escalation, even as President Johnson assured the world that "We seek no wider war," considered the partial sparing of inner Hanoi as a temporary public relations gimmick that would not last much longer. In North Vietnam they say that there are two events which are invariably followed by particularly brutal bombing raids. One is a severe military set-back in the South. ("After they have lost a battle on the ground they seem to need to reassure themselves by dropping tons and tons of bombs on our towns and cities.") The other is a speech by President Johnson assuring the world of his love for little children and his devotion to world peace. (A Vietnamese writer said to me: "We are as offended by Johnson's hypocrisy as by his cruelty." A doctor said: "You have no idea how angry Johnson makes us with his 'carrot' of a million dollars for economic aid. He is as cynical as he is barbarous. Why, do you realize that some days the planes come dropping bombs and killing our children, and then the next day they may drop toys and candy, and leaflets urging us to surrender?")

For my part I shared the Vietnamese expectations of the worst for Hanoi (though I remembered hopefully that even the Nazis did not bomb Paris during World War II, apparently for fear of provoking world-wide indignation). At the same time I could not help being grateful for the delay in bombing the inner city. In a strange way, perhaps the American peace movement, which tends to be rather too quickly discouraged by its inability to reverse twenty years of American foreign policy with a few demonstrations, might take some credit (along with world public opinion) for having saved many Vietnamese lives by forcing the military-industrial complex to accelerate its aggression at a slower rate than it might otherwise have done, thus giving the Vietnamese the opportunity to disperse and decentralize. They had evacuated half or more of the population (including most of the children and older people) and had scattered most of Hanoi's factories and schools throughout rural and jungle areas.

My first trip outside Hanoi was a brief one, to the village of Phuxa, which did not provide conclusive evidence of civilian bombing as governmental policy. Phuxa was clearly not a military target itself and was not near anything that appeared a likely military target. In fact it was surrounded by fields and dikes. Thirty-two civilians had been killed but the damage had been done by three airplanes which dropped a total of five bombs and fourteen rockets. In August, in the United States, I had talked with an ex-Marine, returned from service in Vietnam, who had told me that out of a combination of irritation and boredom he and his buddies had opened fire on civilians in a South Vietnamese village that lay beneath the spot on a hillside where they had been standing guard all day. It is not hard to imagine that from time to time enraged or frightened airmen might drop bombs on "Communist villages" without great qualms of conscience. Clearly such incidents need not reflect government policy. While I was in Phuxa, an alarm was sounded by the ringing of the village bell and all lights were extinguished but the planes passed noisily overhead to drop their bombs on other targets. I was prepared to believe—and still am—that the three offending planes, on August 13, might have been over-anxious to get rid of their load and return to safety, rather than to carry out their original assignment.

Later, however, when I made two extensive trips outside Hanoi, I reluctantly agreed with the Vietnamese that the United States has consciously and deliberately attacked the civilian population in a brutal attempt to destroy civilian morale. The best defense my American pride could muster was to say that the American people would not knowingly tolerate such practices. I urged Vietnamese officials to invite other non-Communist observers, including perhaps a few American newsmen or even someone like Senator Fulbright, to see the damage and report the facts to the American people. I argued that when the American people found out the nature and effects of the bombings, they would put an end to them.

Even apart from the widespread destruction of villages, cities and towns, I see no way to explain away the universal use of fragmentation bombs. Fragmentation bombs are useless against bridges and buildings of any kind but are deadly against people. In fact another name of them is anti-personnel bombs. I saw these bombs everywhere I went in North Vietnam.

There are different types of fragmentation bombs, but they all start with a "mother" bomb. (The term itself tells us something about our culture. Do we know nothing more about motherhood than this? Or is it that we have accepted the fact that mothers produce offspring who are destined to become killers?) The mother bomb explodes in the air over the target area, releasing 300 smaller bombs, typically the size of either a grapefruit or a pineapple. Each of the smaller bombs then ejects a spray of 150 tiny pellets of steel, which are so small that they bounce uselessly off concrete or steel, though they are very effective when they hit a human eye or heart. Vietnamese doctors told me that they have difficulty operating on patients wounded by these bombs, because the steel is so small that it is hard to locate, except through X-rays. (There are more target areas in Vietnam than there are X-ray machines.) According to the Vietnamese, the general pattern of most attacks is to drop heavy explosive bombs and then to follow a few minutes later with fragmentation bombs and strafing, so as to interfere with relief operations and to kill those who are trying to flee the bombed-out area. From personal observation, I learned that the fragmentation bombs are equipped with timing devices so that they do not all eject their murderous barrage right away. When relief workers are trying to rescue the wounded, or later when the planes have departed and the all-clear has been sounded, hundreds of fragmentation bombs may explode, wounding or killing the innocent.

On my return to the United States, I discussed the uses of fragmentation bombs with a representative of the State Department.

The only justification that he could offer was that they cut down the activities of guerrillas. But of course there are no guerrillas in North Vietnam and will be none unless the United States extends its land invasion to the North. And I talked with a mother in Than Hoa province who complained that it is difficult for children and parents to find one another after a raid because of the delayed-action fragmentation bombs.

In practice I know of only two possible explanations for the use of fragmentations bombs: 1) as part of a deliberate attempt to terrorize the civilian population. This explanation is held by everyone I talked with in Vietnam; and 2) as a way of trying to kill any soldiers who might be on their way south. (Perhaps the State Department representative meant "soldiers" when he said "guerrillas.") Technically this would fit in with the American claim that the bombing is aimed at military targets but it would rob such a claim of any moral attractiveness or humanitarian meaning, since fragmentation bombs obviously cannot distinguish between soldiers in transit and children in search of their mothers, or any other category of human beings.

Even if one gives the United States the benefit of the doubt as to intent, the results can only be classified as criminal. Widespread use of fragmentation bombs in the North becomes the equivalent, on a large scale, of the practice in the South of shelling, napalming or setting fire to a village which is suspected of harboring a few guerrillas. There have been some practical restraints on this practice in the South, because of occasional publicity and attendant public reaction, but until now Americans have not been made aware of the nature and implications of their bombing of the North. They have preferred to believe, for the sake of their own illusory peace of mind, that it is possible to send an average of nearly a thousand bombers a day to attack the small country of Vietnam in an essentially sanitary and surgical operation that impedes "aggression" and spares civilians.

The figure of a thousand planes a day is the Vietnamese estimate of the daily average during the period I was in Vietnam (from October 28 through November 15, 1966). The American estimate is somewhat lower but, with typical deception, does not include attacks originating in Thailand, where the United States has built seven large bases with as little publicity as it could get away with. According to Arthur Cook, Bangkok correspondent for the *London Daily Mail*, "more than half of all the air attacks on North Vietnam now originate in Thailand, (*Viet Report*, October 1966)." Even the American figures would imply that Vietnam has a virtually limitless supply of "military targets."

About thirty-five miles south of Hanoi I visited the ruins of what once had been Phu Ly, a city with a population of over ten thousand. It was a gruesome Vietnamese Guernica. Not a building was still standing. Despite the fact that I think that the Air Force and the White House have grossly exaggerated American ability to carry out "pinpoint," "precision" bombing, I do not see how the total destruction of a city of this size can be passed off as an accident—as if a city of more than ten thousand people could be reduced to rubble and ashes by a few bombs that were aimed at a bridge or railroad terminal but missed their mark.

Phu Ly was attacked on six different occasions, five of them between July 14 and November 5, 1966 (when I happened to be in the outskirts). The heaviest attacks were on the mornings of October 1 and 2, when an estimated 250 heavy bombs were dropped on the city. Survivors told me that after the heaviest bombings planes returned at intervals of twenty to thirty minutes to strafe anything that moved.

Before I went to Nam Dinh, North Vietnam's third largest city, I met the mayor, Mrs. Tran Thi Doan, in a rural hideaway some five or six miles outside the city, where it was considered safer to talk. Nam Dinh is a textile city of about 93,000 people, sixty miles southwest of Hanoi and eighteen miles from the seacoast. It is about twenty-five miles from Phu Ly.

In view of the American suspicion that the Vietnamese exaggerate the extent of bombing damage, it is interesting to note that Mayor Doan supplied me with statistics that appear to have underestimated the damage to Nam Dinh. For example, she told me that 881 houses had been destroyed in thirty-three attacks, rendering 12,000 people homeless. She said that thirteen percent of the city had been destroyed. When one walks through block after block that has been completely flattened and in addition surveys dozens and dozens of other buildings that turn out, on examination, to be empty shells, with a section of the roof caved in or a wall shattered, it is hard to estimate percentages. This was particularly true in my case because planes had been in the province off and on all day and my Vietnamese guides, including Mayor Doan, rushed me from location to location in a speeding jeep and kept urging me to hurry when I wandered through the debris. Even so, I had the definite impression that something more than the announced thirteen percent of the city had been destroyed. Later, when we were back in the rural hideaway and bombs could be heard exploding in the background, thereby reminding me of the frequency of attacks, I told my impression that more than thirteen percent had been destroyed and asked if the statistics included damage from raids that had taken place last week. It turned out that the statistics were only up-to-date as of September 20, two weeks earlier, and that since that time there had been seven additional attacks whose grim results had not yet been itemized and added to the totals.

(Since writing the above, I have learned of Harrison Salisbury's visit to Nam Dinh. Interestingly enough, reporting on his visit, which took place on December 25, during the Christmas truce, he repeats the figure of thirteen percent destruction. On the other hand, he speaks of fifty-one attacks, which is an increase of eleven since my visit on November 4 and 5 and eighteen since September 20. He still gives the figure of eighty-nine killed and 405 wounded, which I had been told was the total up to September 20. Salisbury has been criticized for passing Vietnamese statistics as if they were credible, but in the case of Nam Dinh the real statistics are undoubtedly more damaging to American claims than those he used. Certainly he would have been better advised to say in his first dispatch that the statistics came from the Vietnamese and the visual observations were his own. But what did his critics imagine—-that he counted the 881 houses that had been destroyed, most of which had been so totally demolished that no one could possibly have counted them anyway? Obviously an intelligent and honest reporter can only be asked to indicate whether his own observation of the damage makes the official statistics appear credible. The only incredible aspect of these statistics is that with such pulverization of the area, only eighty-nine persons would have been killed. It is a tribute both to Vietnamese honesty and to the success of their evacuation procedures and other safety measures that they announce such a low death rate.)

When I visited Nam Dinh, areas almost totally destroyed included the working class residential areas of Hang Thao Street, where according to official statistics 17,680 persons had lived, and Hoang Van Thu Street, which had housed nearly 8,000. Because of the precautionary policy of evacuating the large cities and other areas of concentrated population, less than 2,600 persons still lived on these two streets when they were subjected to repeated attacks. In passing, let me point out that Mayor Doan's estimate of 12,000 rendered homeless for the entire city apparently could not have been based on the population before evacuation, since more than 25,000 persons lived on Hang Thao and Hoang Van Thu streets in normal times. On the other hand, I cannot state definitely that her figures included only those who remained after evacuation—in this case the 2,600 thought to have lived on these two streets at the time of the attacks—since unfortunately I did not notice the discrepancy until too late to inquire. In any event, the damage was massive—far out of line with any comforting thoughts Americans may have about precision bombing of purely military targets—and the human effects incalculable.

Judging from the neighborhood and from an occasional shell of a building that was not completely demolished, I would call Hang Thao Street a "slum" area. On the other hand, Hoang Van Thu Street appeared to be more "middle class," or at least the buildings adjacent to the gutted area gave this impression. On Hoang Van Thu Street a Catholic church, a Buddhist temple, and the headquarters of the overseas Chinese Businessmen's Association had all been rendered unusable, but not flattened. At least half a mile from either of these streets, I walked in the ruins of the new "social welfare" section, where a hospital, two schools, a kindergarten and some model "workers apartments" had been destroyed.

On the outskirts of the city, I saw three different places where bombs had fallen on dikes and on the brick retaining wall that kept the Black River from flooding the city. I did not see enough or know enough to be able to judge whether or not these attacks on the dikes were deliberate, as charged by the Vietnamese. In any event, here and in many other places the damage to the dikes was indisputable and the Vietnamese have very wisely taken precautions by building auxiliary dikes, through a tremendous expenditure of labor power, and by stockpiling huge mounds of materials ready to plug any gaps. A huge auxiliary dike runs right through the city of Nam Dinh, cutting it in half.

The real impact of the bombing—both human and political— cannot be estimated by a catalogue of the physical damage. To understand this, one must talk as much as possible with the "ordinary people," whom the United States claims to be rescuing from communism. Let me quote excerpts from just two of my conversations with residents of Nam Dinh. The details differ but the response to the bombings is typical of the response of everyone with whom I talked.

Vu Thi Minh spoke to me about the death of her brother, a young poet by the name of Vu Dinh Tanh:

> My brother was a young talented man who was working night and day to sharpen his poems. When the American Norman Morrison burned himself in front of the Pentagon, my brother was inspired by the sacrifice and made a poem which he dedicated to Mrs. Morrison and the children. Tanh was killed at a time when his talents were being developed. The cowardly Americans misused the cloudy skies to intrude in our city and bomb and strafe our people. My brother died on the way to the first aid station. [At this point she handed me a photo of her brother, who was twenty-one when killed. He had an open, sensitive appearing face and wore glasses.]
>
> Since Tanh's death all of his sixteen brothers and sisters are working harder in their posts in order to avenge him. My father is sixty-four and had retired, but he has come back to the city to carry on. My younger brother Kim, seventeen, volunteered to join the army to avenge his brother. Sister Ngoc has graduated from the Polytechnic college but her dream is to serve in the people's army to avenge her brother. For myself and the other teachers, after his death we asked to share his teaching work. In

addition we are ready to take arms against the American planes... We are determined to fight until final victory. Only when the U.S. aggressors go home can we have peace and independence and be finished with all the hardships you have seen in our city.

Mrs. Trung Thi Mai appeared to be in her late twenties or early thirties. She told me that her children had been evacuated to the countryside, because of the expectation of attacks. They lived with their grandmother, while Mrs. Mai and her husband stayed in the city to continue their work at the textile factory. After the children had been gone about a year, the Mais had another child and the other children came to the city to see their new brother.

In view of the American attacks, we prepared for them to be evacuated again. Binh, my oldest son [aged thirteen], brought water to the house from the well and bathed his brother and sister before they were to go to the evacuation place the next morning. As we were going to be separated, we sat up late talking and visiting, 'til 1 A.M.

When we were sleeping I heard a bomb explode and the house fell down on me and the three children. We didn't know what time it was. I had only enough time to call my husband: "Darling, save us," and Binh only enough time to cry out, "Father, save us." My husband heard our voices but it was impossible to dig us out of the debris. I felt my youngest dying be my side and the others too, but it was impossible to do anything. I fainted and then people dug us out and took me and my children to the hospital. I recovered consciousness at the first aid station and saw my father. I asked him where my husband and children were and he said: "The children are all dead and your husband is out in the street helping other people." I lost consciousness again. Then I woke up and saw my three children lying dead by me and I couldn't do anything but cry the whole day.

I didn't expect that the U.S. aggressor was so barbarous. We Vietnamese people do not go to the United States to fight their people, why have they come here to kill my three children? At present when I see other children of the same age as my children I can't help crying. My second son, whose name is Long, when he sees that I am ill, he comes to my bed and consoles me. He says, "Mother you must keep up your health so that you can bring me up. When I am grown up I will avenge the family." The more we grieve at the death of our children, the more we swear not to live under the same skies as the U.S. aggressors.

On another trip through the provinces, I visited the city of Than

Phung Khoc Chinh, Tong Viet Dai and the author.

Several blocks of Than Hoa General Hospital were destroyed.

Hoa, which is about 110 miles south of Hanoi. Here the Vietnamese estimated that by early November about 200 houses, or one dwelling in ten, had been destroyed. The entire city of Than Hoa was wiped out in the French Resistance War of 1945 to 1954 and was painfully rebuilt after the Geneva accords, only to suffer this new destruction.

One must remember, in evaluating the areas of damage, whether in Phu Ly, Nam Dinh or Than Hoa (the three cities that I visited) that the tallest buildings are three stories, and most buildings don't even have a second story. In Than Hoa, block after block of rubble included the ruins of a Franciscan seminary, a Buddhist pagoda and the general hospital. Here again I saw damage to the dikes that protected the city. Outside the city limits, I saw the ruins of the 600-bed Than Hoa tuberculosis sanitorium, which had been attacked on five different occasions. It had the usual identifying huge red crosses and was sitting by itself in an area of rice paddies and irrigation dikes. There was no conceivable military target for miles around. Let me quote from the testimony, undoubtedly biased, of Mrs. Nguyen Thi Tien, a seventy-one-year-old peasant lady from the village of Kieu Dai:

> Last year on the seventh day of the seventh month of the lunar calendar (you'll have to forgive me, I never did learn the new way of figuring the months), when I was doing some housework the American planes came, dropping bombs and cutting off my arm... When my wound was cured and I returned to my village, the villagers helped me in every way. I am very moved by their help. At the same time I feel a great indignation at those who have come and attacked us. The pain in my heart is as big as the pain in my body. More than thirty persons were killed during that attack. Twenty-four were wounded. Probably more than twenty roofs [meaning houses] were knocked down. Before that, in the sixth month of the lunar new year, during the bombing of Than Hoa tuberculosis hospital, two old people were killed and another young person was killed that day. I don't remember the day but I remember it was the sixth month and some other people on the dikes near the hospital were also killed. The crater of the bomb looked like a river. There were a lot of people, about twenty-seven I think, who entered the cave under the dam and they were killed. If we speak of indignation and hatred, we have no words to describe them. The people now working in the fields do not do anything to the Americans, why do they come here to kill us?... The more we hate the Americans the more we unite with each other. We must have unity in order to produce our food and serve our sons in the army. We will keep up this hatred forever. We can never live under the same sky as the American aggressors. I am very old, but I am thinking very much about the children.

Americans often argue that the destruction of villages and the killing of civilians in North Vietnam is an unpleasant but largely unavoidable by-product of the bombing of tactical military targets, such as bridges and railroad depots. Mrs. Tien describes circumstances under which two old people, a young person and about twenty-seven others "who entered the cave under the dam" were killed. It is my belief, based on the testimony of Mrs. Tien and other eyewitnesses and based on my own personal visit to the scene, that these thirty peasants died as a result of a deliberate attack on a tactical *political* target, the Than Hoa tuberculosis sanitorium.

Actually Vietnam has very few cities, and is mostly rural. As I traveled through the countryside I saw many villages that had been attacked, as well as an occasional one that seemed to have been spared completely. At first I thought that I might have been getting an exaggerated sense of the rural destruction because of the fact that I was traveling on main highways, which probably could be thought by the American Air Command to be the main routes for military infiltration from the North to the South. But the frequency of the attacks soon forced us off the main routes, which are only two-lane highways at best. Each time I traveled we detoured through narrow dirt roads and traveled on dikes that might not have been intended as roads at all, except for carts pulled by oxen and on occasion by Vietnamese peasants. After a while I learned that no matter how many miles we left the highway we were never very far from bomb craters and bombed-out villages.

Traveling always by night (and making only occasional brief sorties by daytime) I was unable to get a clear picture of the statistics of the damage, but there was no doubt that it was extensive and ghastly. In Y Ngo, a village of 300 primitive houses, none of which would normally be considered suitable habitation for an American, 100 houses had been destroyed. In Yen Vuc, out of 262 houses, only nine still remained.

When we came to a section that looked like a layman's visualization of the surface of the moon—barren and pockmarked with craters—I could imagine that we were approaching a bridge, but this did not always turn out to be the case. Sometimes it was clear that a whole hamlet had been wiped out in a determined effort to destroy a bridge that was at most twenty to thirty feet long. The stream had been quickly spanned again. More than once we crossed a river an hour or two after its bridge had been knocked out. When a sizable bridge was destroyed, apparently it took a little longer—perhaps half a day—to throw up a crude floating bridge (which would be torn down by day and reassembled at night) or create a ferry (actually a hastily constructed barge powered by a small boat). Unfortunately, though the bridges could be quickly restored, at least to a rough but serviceable state, the houses and the people could not.

Part II

Vietnam Today

9

Even a Brief Visit Tells a Lot About Vietnam—And About the U.S. Media

On a Thursday in late April, 1985, my phone rang, and after the caller identified himself as a member of Vietnam's U.N. Mission, he continued:

> I have the honor to invite you to visit Vietnam for the observances commemorating the tenth anniversary of the end of the U.S.-Vietnam war.

Vietnam was not on my mind, but U.S. policies similar to those that produced the Vietnam War were. I was about to leave for Washington, D.C. for four days of protests, and was planning to commit nonviolent civil disobedience at the South African Embassy on Friday and at the White House on Monday.

"No Vietnam in Central America" is one of the popular slogans at such events, but usually one hears little or nothing about Vietnam itself. It wasn't until after the phone call that I thought of making the connection between Central America and Vietnam from the opposite direction. Just as the U.S. uses terrorist forces to attack Nicaragua from its borders with Honduras and Costa Rica, so it uses terrorist forces to attack Cambodia from its border with Thailand—and for basically the same reasons. Whatever the differences between the Cambodian situation and that in Nicaragua (see Chapter Twenty-two), both countries need to work out their own economic and political models. As long as threats from U.S. proxies force them to divert scarce resources to military efforts, an alternative development path will be blocked.

The Vietnamese diplomat, who was relaying an invitation from the Viet-My Society (My is Vietnamese for the United States), informed me that, "Due to the financial difficulty, the Viet-My Society can only afford you during your stay in Vietnam." I wondered where I would find the plane fare, over two thousand dollars, even if I did decide to cancel two weeks of appointments and was not being held in jail because of the double civil disobedience. The money came from several friends from anti-Vietnam-War days who know the media's unreliability and were anxious for a first-hand report from Vietnam.

"I'll think about it in Washington," I told the caller. "I'll let you know next week." But a hasty call to my travel agent revealed that if I accepted the invitation I would have to forgo the civil disobedience and leave on Monday in order to get to Bangkok in time for the once-a-week flight to Ho Chi Minh City. Despite some ambivalence caused by the urgent situations in Central America, South Africa and the United States, I decided to make the trip. (The urgency in the United States is caused not only by its policies toward Third World peoples within the United States and throughout the world, but because, to cite one example, the number of children who live below the poverty line increased by more than a third between 1979 and 1983, reaching a whopping 22.6 percent of our children, or about fifteen million, the highest since 1967 and still rising. Meanwhile, the government boasts of "economic recovery.")

I mention the last-minute circumstances of the invitation, because the U.S. press consistently emphasized that "only two Americans" accepted the invitation. Or, as the *New York Times* put it,

> Few Americans accepted Hanoi's invitation to attend the celebrations this week as friends of Vietnam.[1]

Most papers listed several prominent anti-war activists who had "turned down" invitations. The clear implication was that Vietnam was isolated from its disillusioned former friends in the anti-war movement. Obviously, then, these people had been dupes of the evil Vietnamese communists rather than opponents of an arrogant and costly war to make Vietnam an economic and political satellite of the United States. This is an idea that conveniently supports any number of similar assumptions today: Those who call for an end to the nuclear buildup are witless dupes of the evil Soviet empire. Those who oppose U.S. aid to the contras in Nicaragua, to the government of El Salvador, to South African attempts to overthrow the government of Angola, and so on around the world, are babes in the woods of realistic international politics. Father knows best.

When I received the invitation, I asked who else from the United States was being invited. Several of those listed by the press were not on the list, including one well known American communist who, I was told in Vietnam, had asked for an invitation and had been turned down. Of the six persons who were invited, along with their spouses, I have spoken with two who wanted to go but could not arrange their schedules on three or four days notice and one whom the Vietnamese could not reach before departure time but wishes that he could have gone. This could also explain the absence of Jane Fonda, who is enmeshed in an extremely busy schedule. However, she has been the target of vicious public attacks because of her visits during wartime and I wouldn't blame her if she decided that whatever benefits might accrue from a hurried visit weren't worth the diversionary attacks that would follow. I decided not to inquire. That leaves two who went, myself and John McAuliff, a Quaker who directs the U.S.-Indochina Reconciliation Project.

The *Times* highlighted its focus on those who have apparently now seen the light with a headline, "Absent Invitees," and a supporting quote: "'Why would you want to come for the anniversary of an occupation?' an elderly shopowner asked a reporter." I had thought that the Vietnamese were celebrating the *end* of an occupation, in fact the end of over a century of occupations. That's what I was celebrating, that and the end of a war that, during the American occupation, had killed 58,721 Americans and nearly 3 million Vietnamese; not to forget the far greater numbers who were wounded or traumatized. The coverage of this question may seem like a small matter, but it is indicative of the animus with which most of the U.S. media approached more significant matters that week.

I am overwhelmingly glad that I went. I learned things about the dynamics of the Vietnamese society that are almost impossible to learn in the United States. As we shall see, for the most part the attending journalists reported an entirely different reality than I experienced. I expected some of this, since I observed the animus of all but a few, during long conversations in the hotel that I shared with a number of them and in the two nearby old French hotels that housed the others. But when I got home and read many of their accounts in newspapers and magazines and in transcripts I secured of the TV shows that originated in Vietnam, I was shocked all over again. Now, it is hard to write about what I saw and experienced without contrasting it with a number of the reports that appeared in this country.

However, in challenging the crude media distortions of a number of events I witnessed, I don't want to suggest that there are not severe limitations to what I was able to learn concerning human and political rights in Vietnam. That is why I will mostly supply information about my personal conversations and experiences rather than to draw sweeping conclusions. Serious questions about civil liberties continue to concern me and I believe should be continually raised and explored in future visits by others who see themselves as citizens of Planet Earth rather than as narrow partisans of the United States and its increasingly prominent slogan: "America Number One." That slogan is dangerously reminiscent of the "Deutschland Uber Alles" slogan of Nazi Germany half a century ago.

Dissatisfied Vietnamese

On the one hand, it is clear that there are a lot of dissatisfied Vietnamese, as the media reports and the U.S. government delights in pointing out. I talked to a number of them during my visit. And the flood of refugees who have taken the desperate course of risking their lives as boat people is a politically sobering phenomenon that reflects negatively on life in post-war Vietnam.

I will return to the boat people later (see Chapter Nineteen), but for now it may help put them into preliminary perspective to remember that during and immediately after the American revolution, a higher percentage of the colonists fled to Canada than the percentage of the Vietnamese population who fled as boat people or through avenues. It may also help to note the horrendous economic conditions that drove most of the Vietnamese boat people to leave. It is fashionable to blame these conditions on the communists—and, indeed, they are not blameless. But we can't overlook the greater role of the United States in first destroying much of the country and its economy and then imposing a murderous economic boycott. Moreover, even in Third World countries that the U.S. deems worthy of its approval, trade and investments, there is a veritable flood of impoverished people who are trying desperately to get to the United States. Under the influence of American films, the Voice of America and other questionable sources, they want in. The more realistic ones believe that even if our streets are not quite paved with gold, those who make it past the border guards will at least be able to eat regularly and eventually enjoy some of the crumbs that spill ("trickle down") from the tables of our fabulous affluence. Finally, we should consider something that ABC correspondent James Walker pointed out on April 25, 1985, in a program that featured Alexander Haig and Nguyen Cao Ky as its "experts" on Vietnam. Typically, the program failed to ask any embarrassing questions of either Haig or Ky, even though Ky had announced, when he was Prime Minister of South Vietnam, that his personal hero was Adolf Hitler. But there was one realistic moment when Walker reported that

> There are now in this region [from Malaysia to Hong Kong] roughly 100,000 Vietnamese still waiting to be resettled... [The] most desperate of Vietnam's refugees...*have been here for as many as six years [and]...have nowhere to go because no country will take them* [emphasis added]... The problem is that...the

people who escape are largely the uneducated, the unskilled and therefore, the unwanted... The hope is that Washington will relax its strict entrance requirement and allow the Vietnamese refugees at this camp and at other camps throughout Southeast Asia to come to the United States.

Le Duc Tho[2] and other officials with whom I talked in Vietnam insist that they want all of their dissatisfied people to leave under the Orderly Departure Program of the U. N. Commission on Refugees, but that the United States refuses to do its part by granting them immigration visas.

None of these factors should be used to minimize the human tragedy involved or to justify the failings of the Vietnamese government in their dealings with these people, failings that were particularly shocking in the early days of the exodus. The Vietnamese put a lot of the blame for this on low-level officials in a reunified but not yet politically or morally integrated South Vietnam. Le Duc Tho told me that as former officers of the South's Army of the Republic of Vietnam (ARVN) were released from re-education camps, some of them gravitated back into positions of responsibility, where they showed that they had not really been won over to the mores and ethics of the new society. I couldn't check this carefully in my short visit, but I talked with one man who had used this kind of connection to leave in a boat. He and his companions were caught before they got very far, held in jail overnight and then released without penalty. He is now somewhat more ambivalent about the new regime and way of life and tempers his criticisms by saying that "There are good things and bad things here, just like anywhere else."

Tho says that by now somewhere between thirty and forty thousand former ARVN officers have been released from re-education camps. These are former collaborators with the U.S. The U.S. paid the entire ARVN payroll, supplied all its weapons and trained the troops. Similarly, a federally funded team from Michigan State University trained the secret police, a scandal that rocked American university campuses in the late Sixties. Both sets of Vietnamese collaborators were abandoned when the U.S. left precipitately in April 1975. In later years Vietnam offered to release all of them from the re-education camps in which they were confined if the U.S. would take them, but the U.S. refused. As they have been released, they have contributed heavily to the ranks of boat people, much as Tories comprised the bulk of American colonists who fled to Canada.

10

Everybody Loves a Parade—Except the American Media

However one interprets the phenomenon of the boat people, there was no mistaking the joy and pride that were demonstrated in Ho Chi Minh City by hundreds of thousands of people who marched in or watched the parade on April 30, 1985 or who participated in the other festivities that week in celebration of ten years of independence and freedom. I can't think of an American celebration since those at the end of World War II in which I have witnessed so many people sharing so much euphoria. The remarkable thing is that this was ten years after the end of their war and in the midst of straitened circumstances and intense international pressures. I detected no acknowledgement of this exuberance in the American reports of the occasion. Quite to the contrary, the *New York Times* reported that "There were no cheers or applause except from the invited guests."[1] This remarkable statement followed its ominous announcement of three days earlier that

> There is little sense of festivity here this weekend, outside the areas set aside for the celebrations. Residents say districts have been assigned quotas to provide the crowds at Tuesday's parade.[2]

Americans who saw the event on television tell me that the emphasis was on the military side of the parade—and this was evident in the transcripts I read. As I told my Vietnamese hosts, displays of military weaponry always sadden me wherever they take place and whatever the circumstances. But I carefullly clocked this part of the festivities and was relieved when they took only fifteen minutes and were followed by a full two hours of singing, dancing civilians with

90

love and joy clearly visible on their faces and in their voices and movements.

If the parade began with marching soldiers, military weaponry and aircraft (all of twelve military transport planes, 12 jets and 4 helicopters), it ended with a small cart drawn by a donkey, with three little children inside. Immediately preceding this touching and symbolic finale, three teenagers (two boys and a girl) rode up the street on prancing horses that they could barely control, probably because they had been held up so often by the stops of preceding contingents to do a little joyful number in front of the reviewing stands. When I asked several U.S. newspeople what they thought the intended significance was of closing the parade with these two groups of children, most of them hadn't even noticed and none showed any interest in thinking about what they symbolized. That the future belongs to the children, perhaps? Or will be better for future generations than it was for the adults? Whatever the Vietnamese intended, as a person exposed from an early age to the Christian scriptures, I couldn't help thinking of Jesus's love for little children ("of such is the Kingdom of Heaven") and his choice of a donkey to carry him on his triumphal entry into Jerusalem.

In this mood, I linked these two final displays of the spirit of Ho Chi Minh City that day with the emphasis on the ten-year-olds— children who had been born in the first year after the end of the war. "A new generation of peace," the war-weary adults kept explaining, with what seemed to be mingled hope and determination. They marched as a unit in the parade, and more than a hundred of them [See Photo] opened the gala performance at the National Theatre the evening before. As the curtain rose on that event, no adult took the podium. Instead, a ten-year-old girl came forward and made a welcoming speech. Then a boy took the podium to conduct two songs, to the accompaniment of a small orchestra. Each time a girl from their number came to the mike and sang a solo.

The ten-year-olds were also featured at a concert I attended a few nights earlier at a newly opened Cultural Center, packed with happy Vietnamese. On neither of these occasions did I see any American photographers or television cameras to send the images of the children back to the American public. Is it farfetched to think that combining such images with the famous wartime photograph of a young girl (Phan Thi Kim Phuc, aged nine), naked, covered with napalm burns and screaming in anguish as she ran down the road away from the blast, would have been an appropriate part of the media's coverage of Vietnam ten years after the end of the war?

This is my initial report on the parade and two of the events that preceded it. But when I got back to the United States, I read the transcript of the coverage on ABC's *Night Line* that day. I found the following comments by Richard Threlkeld:

Well, we're here at the reviewing stand, Ted... And what we've been seeing, as you inferred, is the display, a rather awesome display, of the military power of the fourth largest army in the world... We've been looking at most of the equipment, and as you've seen it's all Russian.

Undoubtedly a lot of it was Russian. I don't know enough about such equipment to tell. To me it's all offensive, wherever it comes from. But the American reporters I spoke with that day commented about the prominence in the parade of American military equipment (either captured during the war or abandoned when the Americans left). Threlkeld, however, had something else on his mind. He was creating a mood. And Koppel helped him:

KOPPELL: As we both know, there are very few spontaneous demonstrations in socialist countries, and I'm just wondering...is some of this being done just for our benefit? ...
THRELKELD: Sure it's being done for our benefit. And it's interesting to me to watch this parade because I think you're going to see the same flavor, the same sort of socialist totalitarian flavor tomorrow, May 1st, in Moscow in Red Square. It's that kind of feeling.

But wait, there *was* a reference to Phan Thi Kim Phuc on American television. Bob Simon of CBS interviewed her briefly the week before these events, an indiscretion that led the *New York Times* television critic to quote a few words from the interview and complain about them:

"I still suffer from the burns," she told Mr. Simon. "I am sad. I don't have strength to study like the others."
And indeed, Miss Phan is a victim, deserving of help and pity. At the same time, it's ingenuous not to recognize that she's also a propaganda symbol... To survive is to forgive in the world of Kim Phuc. What she really wants to do is to study one day in the United States.

Personally, I am attracted to the idea that "to survive is to forgive." I was encouraged to find this a common sentiment in Vietnam today. And I find it depressing to note its absence from both the words and the policies of our own government. I was sorry to see the television critic of the *New York Times* take a stand against allowing someone we have injured to tell us, on TV, that she forgives us and would like to come to our country to study. Perhaps he has watched so much American TV that he doesn't believe anyone could speak the truth on television.

This enlightened commentary appeared in an article entitled "Sorting Out Coverage of Hanoi's Celebration," by John Corry.[3] Corry began his "sorting out" by quoting Henry Kissinger's criticism of the "absolutely one-sided account of the correspondents" and his complaint that there was "something demeaning about having the three networks cover a victory parade over the United States." "In fact," Corry says, "Mr. Kissinger was onto something..." And straining to prove his own contention that the "coverage has served Vietnamese interests," he writes, "Correspondents...do not mention that they must hire transportation from the Vietnamese Government."

Did he think they should have complained that they were not provided free transportation? Or did he want them to damn the Vietnamese for having no democratically owned and operated rental agencies like Hertz and Avis, our own suppliers of cars on the democratic principle of making them available to anyone with enough money to pay for them? Perhaps they should have told the Vietnamese that they were flying in their own limousines on a U.S. Army transport plane, and stayed home if the Vietnamese had refused to permit it. That way Henry Kissinger could have been pleased that there were no captive American reporters or TV crews covering the parade (or any of the other sights they found so admirable) and subjecting the American people to Vietnamese propaganda.

Having walked to the parade, I freely wrote the following in my notes:

> Everyone is so joyous and relaxed that every time there is a little space between marching contingents, it is filled with people who advance onto the street to look down and see who or what is coming next. The police are either powerless to prevent it or are caught up in the general euphoria and don't care. They seem to know that the crowd will move back, if necessary with a little prodding with open palms [no clubs], when more space is needed. Just now a float had to angle across from the right side of the street to the left in order to find an opening through the slowly retreating crowd.

Usually the gap in the parade was created when a group stopped in front of the reviewing stand to do a little dance or choreograph some other artistic, gymnastic or musical feat. In one of them, a group of fifty or more women wove in and out in varied patterns while linked by long colorful paper streamers. This and other maneuvers, by both women and men, children and adults, reminded me of some of the impressive designs and patterns acted out by American women in recent years, at demonstrations at the Pentagon and elsewhere. At such times, the entire street was filled with people all the way from the reviewing stand to the old Presidential Palace (now the Reunification Palace), a distance of perhaps a quarter of a mile. But when the performers finished their little act, the streets were cleared just enough to permit them to pass, mostly by a voluntary moving back and partly by a certain amount of pushing by the police.

When these performances were taking place, I looked carefully

*Crowds lining the streets with only
one policeman visible and no barricades.*

Ten-year-olds marching in the April 30th parade.

into the faces of the performers and of the quickly gathering crowd as it moved onto the street and surrounded them. There could be no doubting the genuineness of the smiles and other unselfconscious expressions of joy. And I was impressed at how few police and soldiers there were to restrain the crowd and how gentle they were with the people. There were absolutely no barricades. [See Photo] If an American crowd pushed out into the street on a similar occasion and was in apparent danger of interfering with the orderly procession, I would be surprised if the police (or Secret Service: eight of the thirteen top governmental leaders were in the main reviewing stand) did not take stronger, more violent steps against them than any I saw from my unexcelled vantage point.

After a while I tired of sitting in the stand, surrounded by dignitaries and separated from the madding crowd. So I excused myself, descended to street level and, unaccompanied, pushed myself through the throngs to a spot some distance down the street in the opposite direction from the Presidential Palace. Away from American reporters, Vietnamese officials and visiting dignitaries, the scene was very similar. There was no question about the exuberance of the marchers and the crowds, or the camaraderie between the police and the people as they shared the enthusiasm of the occasion.

Newsweek "Strikes Out" with a Bamboo Cane

In contrast to what I saw, *Newsweek* reports that

> As the crowd watching the parade spilled into the street, police struck out with bamboo canes.

Not once did I see any police with a bamboo cane, although I would not have been surprised (or shocked) if some had carried them. Having seen Japanese police use such canes viciously, and having experienced the crunch of police clubs in nonviolent demonstrations in the United States, I scrupulously examined the surging crowd and the police response during the Vietnam parade and on other occasions when crowd control was necessary. At the parade, most of those who handled the crowd were not armed, but there were others in nearby areas, well back from the street and crowds, who were wearing small holsters from which the tips of gun handles could be observed. And on my way to and from the parade, I saw soldiers on duty, with shouldered guns. Was it because bamboo canes are so "Oriental," so good for dressing up a story with "local color," that the account reads "struck out with bamboo canes"? "Forced back by armed police" would have given a false picture of the relationship between the crowd and the police, but at least it would have been a little more accurate as to the only weapons some police and soldiers were carrying. I wonder who supplied this deceptive note, the reporter on the spot or an imaginative rewrite man in New York.

"Contact With Foreigners Is Forbidden"

Obviously, if there is a lot one can not ascertain in a brief visit, experiences such as these indicate that there is a lot that one *can* learn by being on the spot. This is especially true if one makes a point of being out and around for eighteen to twenty hours a day for seven days. By spending a relatively sleepless week, I was able to spend a good two-thirds of my time unchaperoned, either meeting old friends from earlier visits or striking up conversations and making new acquaintances. I did this on street corners, in public parks, in restaurants, bars, sidewalk cafes and "free market" stalls (misleadingly called the Black Market in most American accounts), a department store, smaller commercial shops, two bookstores, a museum, at two concerts and two fairs dedicated to showing the country's accomplishments during ten years of liberation. Also, I made two unaccompanied visits to Buddhist pagodas (in addition to a visit to another pagoda in the company of two Vietnamese friends), two visits, without a guide, to Catholic churches, and one unannounced, unaccompanied drop-in session of forty-five minutes with a priest. I looked up the priest because he has been reported in the American press as a former supporter of the regime who is now disillusioned.

When I did have a translator, mostly in my meetings with officials, I could usually tell from the context of the responses I received that he or she had unhesitatingly communicated my most "embarrassing" questions, ones that would have been considered offensive by a rigid, repressive official. Even so, I felt it wise to go out as much as possible alone, to give people the freedom to approach me on their own and to speak outside the presence of anyone who might appear to be connected with the government. Besides, a solitary person is less intimidating, more approachable. Obviously, the language barrier restricted my contacts and conversations. But I was rarely abroad for many minutes without someone approaching me and starting a conversation. Sometimes the extent of our dialogue was limited by elementary English, but overall I managed to meet quite a few people, singly or in groups of two or three, with whom I could converse at length, either in English or in French (the languages of the two most recent occupying powers). Usually the conversations took place in the public places I have mentioned and in full view of other Vietnamese (although on three occasions I was invited inside by either two or three Vietnamese. Often we talked within the purview of uniformed police or of soldiers who were passing on the street or guarding a public establishment.

At the parade, my position in one of the reviewing stands was directly opposite the American press, who were on the street, and I saw them standing shoulder to shoulder with the crowd. From time to time, I saw reporters engaging in conversation with one or more of the bystanders, sometimes with a policman nearby and sometimes not. Some of the conversations went on a long time.

So what shall I say of an account in the *New York Times* in the reportage from the April 30th parade?

> There were no cheers or applause from the crowds. A man in the crowd who talked with a Western Reporter was hauled off by the police. Contact with foreigners is against the law.[4]

Did it happen? I don't know. If it didn't happen, did the reporter, Barbara Crosette, who was an admitted newcomer to Southeast Asia and on her first visit to Vietnam[5] conclude inaccurately but honestly that it did happen? This would have been easy to do, since she had been told, before arriving and by other American press people in conversations I was part of, that contact with foreigners is against the law and that this kind of interference does occur.[6]

Given a predisposition to expect it, it might not have been hard to think it happened, during one of the frequent occasions when the police partially cleared the streets by pushing back the eager, buoyant crowd. Was it at one of those times that she was uncermoniously separated from the man who was talking to her?[7]

On the other hand, I talked with Crosette and at least a dozen of the other American reporters, shortly after the parade and again at breakfast the next morning. No one, including Barbara, mentioned an arrest. Given the nature of our dialogues (often friendly arguments in which I told them of my own free access to "ordinary Vietnamese" and asked unsuccessfully for specific instances in which their own access had been interfered with), I would be surprised if they had not told me, gleefully, if an arrest had taken place. Was this, perhaps, another insert by a New York editor?

Whatever did or did not happen on that occasion, the *Times* managed to say in an editorial about the sad state of affairs in Vietnam, that on a few occasions some Vietnamese "risked their lives talking with her [Barbara Crosette]." This kind of statement is both sensationalistic and false. Similar statements in the *Times* in the late Fifties and early Sixties helped put the lives of a lot of Americans and Vietnamese at risk in the U.S. invasion of Vietnam. Today, such irresponsible comments in America's staid "newspaper of record" help inflame the cold war, with all the dangers that represents to the lives of Americans and others.

Perhaps I am being unduly kind to Crosette when I mention the circumstances under which she could have made an honest mistake about the arrest. Or when I suggest the possibility that her report was doctored for maximum effect. I include these possibilities because they were my first thoughts when I read the story. But several days later, back in the United States, I read another of her stories, one that permits no similar explanation. In it she wrote of a crackdown on religion by the Vietnamese government and reported that the identification of churches and pagodas on the new maps of Ho Chi Minh City has mysteriously faded out to a faint grey, so that it is virtually impossible to read them.

The reason I can think of no similar excuse for this story is that one day when I told Barbara that I was about to set out for the An Quang pagoda, she got out her map and we looked at it together. We had no trouble finding a number of pagodas, including the one I was going to visit. They were all identified in clear black type. She lent the map to me, so that I would have it on my trip. I was going to travel in a pedicab, the form of travel used by most Vietnamese (and one which adventuresome American press people could have used inside the city without having to "hire transportation from the Vietnamese government" (John Corry). Barbara's very readable map provided a check on where the driver was taking me, a precaution based on my knowledge of what sometimes happens to foreign visitors in New York, when an opportunistic taxi driver sees a chance to take advantage of their lack of familiarity with the terrain.

Imagine my surprise when, on my return to the United States, I discovered her story about the "mysterious," obviously intentional, "fading" of any markings that would have made it possible to make the kind of independent visit that I did make.

"They Are Evil, Truly Evil"

CHAPTER ELEVEN

Introducing Ngo Ba Thanh

As soon as we normalize relations with the United States, we want to send many young people to your country for professional education. It is one of our needs and we prefer the American approach to higher education rather than the Soviet model.

I'm not talking about U.S. imperialism. I'm talking about the America that produced so many advances in science, medicine and technology—and gave birth to the peace movement. We share that America's thirst for knowledge and peace.

We know about McCarthyism, the rise of the New Right and the current U.S. interventions in Central America, but in the long run we believe in the American people.

Why can't our two peoples put the war behind us and be friends?

The speaker was Ngo Ba Thanh, a former member of the Urban Resistance Movement in Saigon. She was in prison when I visited that city in 1966, but I met twice with her husband, behind locked doors and with the blinds closed, wondering when Nguyen Cao Ky's police would break in and take him (us?) away. I first met Thanh herself in September 1975, on the first celebration of Vietnam's Independence Day after reunification—my last visit to Vietnam before 1985. In 1975, I had been told in the United States that she had disappeared—liquidated or in re-education camp along with other members of the non-communist resistance in the South. So I was relieved to find her alive, free and

99

Ngo Ba Thanh with the author.

Nguyen Ngoc Dung with the author.

serving in the National Assembly.

A feisty, independent woman, Thanh wrote a book in the early Sixties on the history of non-communist opposition movements. It was banned by the U.S.-sponsored regime. She had graduated from New York's Columbia University Law School in 1958, so her imprisonment in the early Sixties attracted the attention of American friends in the anti-war movement and, through them, of some American congressmen. She believes that this saved her life, but it did not save her from spending six years in prison, with an interlude on the outside that was ended when she announced that she was going to run for office on a program of negotiations to end the war and reunify the country.

In 1975, I told her of the American reports of her demise under the new regime but, perhaps foolishly, was not satisfied to leave the question there. Not after she spoke with such scorn of "these American fabrications" and talked so matter-of-factly about her participation in an "alliance of all resistance forces," as if no other course was conceivable. I felt it necessary to remind her that the American propaganda, fabricated as it surely was, had been at least partly believable because of the countless non-communist anti-Nazi resistance leaders who had been liquidated in Czechoslovakia, Hungary, Poland, etc., after the Soviet Union and its local supporters had taken over at the end of World War II. Then, my heart pounding at the indiscretion, I told her that while her American friends would be glad to know that she was functioning in a key position, they would wonder if she was not a "dupe" who would be used for a while during the difficult transitional period, and then stripped of office—or meet a worse fate—when her usefulness had passed.

Her eyes flashed and she replied:

I have run into these hypothetical formulations before, fears from another epoch and far-away countries. I was schooled in them during my years in the United States and I certainly heard them enough in Saigon. But I am living in Saigon after liberation and I have never had so much freedom. I have never had so much opportunity to help my people by being part of building a new society.

By now she has been re-elected twice to the National Assembly, serves on its Legal Rights Commission and is a lawyer for the United Buddhist Movement.

Recently Thanh was invited by the National Lawyers Guild to come to this country to discuss the worrisome matter of Vietnamese re-education camps (see Chapters Seventeen and Eighteen). The camps are a concern not only of the Reagan administration (hypocritically, given its attitude toward human rights in El Salvador, South Africa, South Korea, and other client states) but also of Amnesty International and of many veterans of the anti-war movement, including myself.

Her visit could have been instructive for us and Americans could have expressed to her their concerns for those still being held in the camps. But the Reagan administration denied her a visa. Once again it decided that in order to save our freedom it had to deny us the freedom to meet with one of our dangerous "enemies."

I hadn't seen a report of this denial anywhere in the American press. But when she told me about it, I remembered that one of the first things I learned when I visited Nicaragua—in October 1984—was a similar defense of our freedom that I hadn't known about until I got there. The United States denied entry to a Nicaraguan commission appointed in 1983 to study U.S. electoral procedures, with the aim of making their own elections as democratic as possible. Similar commissions were admitted without difficulty in Europe and a number of Latin American countries.

Introducing Do Xuan Oanh

We are nationalists who fought for independence and freedom. The best way to be independent is to have good relations with all countries, not just one bloc. But the United States refuses to enter into trade relations and other exchanges with us. Instead it works internationally to deny us Western development funds and forces us to go to the Soviet Union to survive. The Russians help us and we are grateful, but it is not enough. We have a saying that "The Russians are Americans without dollars." To this day, we have refused to allow them to turn Cam Ranh Bay into a naval base. They have to get permission every time a Soviet ship enters. But we are not a superpower and our needs are great, so how far can we go?

The words are by Do Xuan Oanh, a friend of the late Ho Chi Minh. He is a poet and the composer of their national anthem. I first met Oanh in Hanoi in 1966, and between then and September 1975 saw him quite a few times, in Europe and in Vietnam. A close friend, this is the first time I have seen him in ten years. He is identified in an article in the April, 1985 *Atlantic* as "one of Hanoi's leading authorities on America." William Broyles, Jr., author of the article, quotes him there as follows:

The Communist Party inspired the people to fight out of patriotism. Then when we had their allegiance, we could persuade them of our ideology.

I took the article with me and showed it to Oanh. "That's stupid," he says, "I would never say such a thing." He tells me he resents the implication of scheming to take advantage of the people's patriotism for the Party's hidden agendas.

As he says this, I re-read the two sentences attributed to him and wonder why he is so upset. It doesn't seem so unlikely to me that in some contexts he would have said them or something close to them. They don't necesssarily imply dishonesty or manipulation. And I think of how in the best days of the anti-war movement we focussed not on the ideologies and ultimate politics of the movement's organizers, varied as they were anyway, but on first things first. We concentrated on the brutality of the napalm and bombings; the burning and bulldozing of native villages and herding of the inhabitants into concentration camps that were called "Strategic Hamlets" and "Freedom Villages"; the tragic toll of G.I. deaths, 200 a week at the war's height; the corruption and brutality of the Saigon regime; the lies of the U.S. government. These were the things that united us and could "persuade" growing sections of the American public of the arrogance, folly and human costs of invading an undeveloped country half way around the globe from us, in pursuit of the elusive American Century.[1] The movement went down hill when a growing number of its organizers began to push ideology and dogma more than elementary humanism. It was one thing to analyze and discuss the causes, another thing to demand ideological conformity as a test of anti-war "seriousness."

Then I read on and saw the uses Broyles had made of Oanh's supposed words, whether the original quotation was roughly accurate or not. He had written, as if it were the meaning behind Oanh's statement:

> Now the only incentive is the Party's own authority: you will follow this ideology not because it is the only way to liberate the country but because we say so.

No wonder Oanh felt that "stupid" ideas had been dishonestly attributed to him.

A further look at Broyles' article reveals some important facts both about Vietnam and about the limitations of mass media journalism in the United States. At one point, for example, he writes

> I talked to Viet Cong veterans several times about American veterans. I tried to explain post-traumatic stress syndrome—the flashbacks, the blackouts, the bitterness, the paralysis of will, that still seem to afflict many Americans. It was incomprehensible to them. "We had to rebuild our country. We had too much to do to think that adjusting to peace was a problem," Tran Hien, a former Viet Cong company commander, told me. "Life goes on." Simple ideas...sustained men like Hien then and sustain them now. Truly nothing, in their minds, is more

important than independence and freedom.

This is honest reporting and has implications that run directly counter to the general line promoted by the mass media and the government. There are other examples in the article, along with some obvious soul-searching by Broyles as a Vietnam veteran. It is because of nuggets like this that crop up from time to time in the media, like grass growing through the cracks in cement, that the Right Wing attacks the media for its "liberalism." But ambitious reporters and editors know what the line is—or soon find out—so such examples are rare, not prominently displayed and not followed up.

As a former editor-in-chief of *Newsweek*, Broyles is familiar with the combinations of fact and fiction, pride and prejudice (American) that are required in such publications. So he keeps returning to the virtually compulsory throwaway lines that dominate most American reports from Vietnam. There are a lot of sentences like the ones that offended Oanh. Here is an offensive story that tells us less about Vietnam than about some of its critics:

> A European diplomat paused, looked out the window, and said in a flat voice: "All this is just bureaucracy. What matters is that they are evil, truly evil." He said this softly but with such passion that the whole table became quiet.

Perhaps I am unfair to Broyles, but as I read this in the context of the evil things about Vietnam that he uses as a lead-in to the story, he agrees with the diplomat—and misses the irony of the very next sentence, with which he concludes the episode:

> When the conversation picked up again, it centered on how to smuggle antiques out in diplomatic pouches.

In my mind this tells us not who is truly evil, but who has been falsely conditioned by the evil heritage of white Western arrogance and plunder. Later, as if it has nothing to do with this continuing tradition, Broyles writes that

> Vietnam is a terribly poor country [with] a per capita income lower than India's. Its people suffer from malnutrition and curable diseases "out of a nineteenth-century textbook," as one Western doctor described them to me.

12

Introducing Nguyen Ngoc Dung, General Nguyen, Huu Hang, and China's Vietnam Policy

The enthusiasm, patriotism and courage with which we fought to liberate our country are not enough for us to make the economic jumps required after forty years of warfare. Besides the devastation, we weren't able to keep up with the advances in agriculture and industrial development of other Third World countries. How could we? In the South we became a consumer society, corrupted and propped up by American money. We even imported rice, from the Philippines. At least we are self-sufficient now in rice—since 1983—but we have a long way to go in meeting our other needs. Our problems are very complex and we keep making a lot of mistakes, but at last we are beginning to make some progress in overcoming them.

Nguyen Ngoc Dung was telling me of the psychological as well as economic and cultural difficulties under which Vietnam has been laboring. Dung is a national executive of the Women's Union and Deputy Secretary General of the Fatherland Front. The Fatherland Front is a coalition headed by elected representatives of all mass organizations—women, youth, Buddhists, trade union, peasants, etc. (see Chapter Seventeen). It educates and agitates in support of their rights. For me, its sexist name serves as a reminder that the work of the Women's Union (and supportive men) is still incomplete.

"We were utopic [utopian]," she says:

Even the Central Committee was utopic. We thought that with the end of the war, we would have a beautiful society, just like that. But our economic understanding was behind our political understanding. Our society was geared for war, not peace. Many people became disillusioned when we couldn't immediately have the full rewards of peace that we had dreamed of all those years.

Suddenly the U.S. money was withdrawn from the South, removing the resources millions had been dependent on, and the economic aid promised in Article 21 of the Paris Peace accords was denied. To make matters worse, China cut off the aid it had been providing the North. Later it began attacking us militarily, first on the Cambodian border, through its ally Pol Pot, then with its own troops, from the North.

Later, Dung returned to the psychological toll that went with these unexpected difficulties. But before going further into that subject, I want to pick up on her reference to China's withdrawal of material aid.

In my conversations in the United States, whenever Americans had spoken of Vietnam's economic problems the majority had blamed them exclusively on the inefficiencies of communism and the costs of Vietnam's "expansionist" invasion and occupation of Cambodia. A few had spoken, as Dung did, of the continuing effects of wartime devastation, the difficulties created by U.S. post-war policies, and the costly Cambodian and Chinese attacks on Vietnam. It wasn't until I got to Vietnam that I heard anyone include as a major factor the economic shock of losing millions of dollars worth of Chinese aid to the North shortly after millions of U.S. dollars were suddenly withdrawn from the South. I offer this as a humble example of the importance of people-to-people cultural exchanges. Simple truths that should be obvious often elude us until we are on the spot hearing and seeing through the ears and eyes of the inhabitants. I had known, intellectually, about the Chinese aid cutoff before I went to Vietnam, but it wasn't until I escaped the U.S. environment and was talking with Dung and others that its significance came home to me.

When Dung spoke of the aid cutoff, I recalled two earlier periods when China had used its power to grant or withhold aid as a means of advancing its own interests. The first was when Vietnam entered into peace negotiations with the United States, in 1968. China responded by cutting its aid by 20% the first year and 50% the next year. The figures are Vietnam's, but China's opposition to negotiations was well known at the time.

American Maoists interpreted China's opposition to negotiations as an example of its revolutionary fervor: China would have no truck with Vietnam's negotiating with the American Paper Tiger because it wanted the anti-imperialist war to be fought on to a victorious conclusion.

Most of us who were not Maoists accepted this explanation, but disapproved of China's seeming ultra-leftism. We condemned it as a policy of continuing the war to the last Vietnamese. We took a position of welcoming the peace negotiations but placed our reliance on increasing the domestic pressures by demonstrating and organizing to "Bring the Boys Home." In a way our position was the nonviolent equivalent of the Vietnamese position, which was "Danh va dam, dam va danh" or "fighting and talking; talking and fighting."

We were right about Chinese policy, but not because it was ultra-leftist, at least not in its foreign policy. The "interests" of the superpowers and would-be superpowers of any camp rarely coincide for long with the aspirations of Third World countries, and China, under a series of regimes, was no exception. It was perfectly willing to see Vietnam—and of course the United States—drained and weakened by continued warfare, but not in the interests of achieving a united and revolutionary Vietnam. For its own reasons, it wanted the war to end, when it ended, with a divided Vietnam. We should have known this—even the Maoists—because it was not a new policy, but a continuation of the policy it had pursued in Geneva, in 1954. Only the combined military and political strength of the Vietnamese nationalists, empha-sized by their spectacular victory over the French at Dien Bien Phu as the peace talks began, had been able to force through a compromise, a temporary division that was supposed to have ended when national elections took place, two years later.

If China's underlying objectives were not clear to many of us in 1968, they became clear in 1971 and 1972, when the negotiations in Paris reached a critical stage and Henry Kissinger began meeting alternately with the Chinese, the Russians and, of course, Le Duc Tho, the chief Vietnamese negotiator. During that period, China simulta-neously increased its Vietnam aid to an unprecedented level and used its talks with the U.S. as a means of bringing "unrelenting pressure" on Vietnam to accept U.S. peace proposals. These proposals would have surrendered the principle of a united Vietnam.

During my 1985 visit, Le Mai, the Vietnamese Assistant Foreign Minister, told me that China had used the increased aid as a carrot and the negotiations with the United States as a stick. When he said this, I realized that, conversely, the increased aid to Vietnam confronted the United States with a Chinese stick, while the promise to pressure Vietnam to accept a peace plan favorable to the United States offered Kissinger and Nixon a juicy carrot. In effect, it was not only Kissinger who was attempting to "create incentives or pressures in one part of the world to influence events in another." (See Chapter Three.)

China's plan worked well as far as the U.S. was concerned. On October 25, 1971, the Peoples Republic of China, with U.S. support, replaced Nationalist China (Taiwan) in the United Nations, with a permanent seat (with veto power) on the Security Council. And in February, 1972 at the conclusion of Nixon's visit to Beijing, the

Shanghai Communique, signed by China and the United States, stated

> The United States confirms its ultimate objective of with-
> drawing all U.S. forces and military installations from Taiwan.
> In the meantime, it will progressively reduce its forces and
> military installations on Taiwan as the tension in this area
> diminishes.

The Taiwan portion of the agreement is interesting because
China's argument with Vietnam in favor of accepting a divided country
was put in terms of the limits of the "brooms" with which China and
Vietnam were seeking to sweep their respective countries clean of
hostile forces. They insisted that Vietnam's broom was "not long
enough to reach Saigon," just as theirs was "not long enough to reach
Taiwan."

But Chinese pressures on Vietnam were no more successful than
the Soviet pressures during the same period. In the end it was Nixon
and Kissinger who were forced to yield on the terms of the January, 1973
Peace Agreement between Vietnam and the United States. On the one
hand, the terms provided procedures for eventual reunification of
North and South Vietnam. On the other hand, they required the final
withdrawal of U.S. troops but permitted the North Vietnamese army to
stay put in territories that it controlled in South Vietnam. When South
Vietnam violated the accords by attacking the areas under North
Vietnamese control, the communists were in a position to counter-
attack successfully and eventually to win the war.

With the 1973 signing of these accords, China showed its dis-
pleasure by making major cutbacks in aid, withholding some items
already promised and leaving some construction projects unfinished.
The final, total cutoff of aid came in 1977.

General Hang

A few days before Dung told me of the hardships this created for
Vietnam, and before Le Mai analyzed the reasons for the ups and downs
in Chinese assistance, I had spoken with an ex-Saigon General,
Nguyen Huu Hang. Hang served as top assistant to Big Minh, the
U.S.-backed Head of State in South Vietnam in the last desperate days,
after Nguyen Van Thieu had fled. He told me another result of the
Chinese aid cutback, one that in the end was the opposite of what China
had intended. After the signing of the peace agreement, Hang said that
Saigon and the United States underestimated the strength of the North
Vietnamese Army and attacked it inside territories it controlled. These
attacks initiated the series of events which eventually led to the fall of

Saigon and reunification of the country.

Along with this overestimation of the effects of the Chinese action, the U.S. also overestimated the effects of its own simultaneous expansion of its military aid to Saigon. Ngo Vinh Long, a Vietnamese scholar at Harvard, describes this:

> Too much, and not too little, aid from the United States to the Thieu regime, especially after the signing of the Paris Agreement, brought about the fall of Saigon. Propaganda to the contrary, in the two years after the signing of the Paris Agreement, Congress actually voted more economic and military aid to Saigon than ever before. Immediately before and after the signing...the Nixon administration sent nearly $1 billion worth of military aid to Saigon. The United States supplied the Thieu regime with so many arms that, as Maj. Gen. Peter Olenchuk testified before the Senate Armed Services committee on May 8, 1973, "We shortchanged ourselves within our overall inventories. We also shortchanged the reserve units in terms of prime assets... We also diverted equipment...[from] Europe"
>
> In fiscal year 1974, Congress gave Saigon $1 billion more in military aid. Saigon expended as much ammunition as it could—$700 million. This left a stockpile of at least $300 million, a violation of the Paris Agreement, which had stipulated that equipment only be replaced on a one-to-one basis.
>
> For fiscal year 1975, Congress again authorized $1 billion in military aid, but appropriated $700 million—about what was actually spent in 1974.
>
> The military aid granted Thieu encouraged him to sabotage the Paris Agreement by attacking areas controlled by the Provisional Revolutionary Government [PRG]. A study by the U.S. Defense Attache's office in Saigon revealed that "the countryside ration of the number of rounds fired by South Vietnamese forces [since the signing of the Paris Agreement] to that fired by the Communist forces was about 16 to 1.[1]

Something more important than arms, then, was responsible for the final victory of the liberation forces.

General Hang also told a story of a last minute attempt by China to collaborate with the United States in an effort to prevent this. As the South's defenses crumbled and the North Vietnamese were sweeping toward Saigon, General Winants, the top U.S. military "adviser"in Vietnam at the time, met secretly with Minh and Hang and told them that Washington would speed increased military aid (as if that were the problem) if they would refuse to surrender. He assured them that the plan to drive the NVA back and keep the war going had been cleared with China, through its ambassador in Washington.

More guns and ammunition wouldn't have saved the Saigon regime, but the U.S. government kept clinging to the illusion that firepower would be more powerful than justice and independence, even after those were two ideas whose time had come for the vast majority of the Vietnamese people. The U.S. had finally withdrawn its own increasingly restless and resistant troops, thereby "changing the color of the corpses" (on its side) and gaining a partial political respite at home. But, like China, it was eager to continue the war to the last Vietnamese.

Being conscious of the current bitterness between China and Vietnam, I pressed Hang on China's participation in this effort, leaning over backwards to see if I could sniff out any indications that this was a convenient ex post facto addition to the account. Hang's response was to say that since the U.S. government rarely told the truth, he didn't know for sure whether China had really agreed to collaborate with the U.S. in this attempt to prolong the war, or not. "All I know," he said, "is what General Winants told us."

I didn't know it at the time, but the very day that General Hang told me of this secret meeting, Alexander Haig was providing corroboration of even earlier collusion between China and the United States against Vietnam. On ABC's *Nightline*, he was telling Ted Koppel and his other honored guest, Nguyen Cao Ky, that

> In my first discussions with Zhou Enlai prior to President Nixon's visit in 1972, it was clear that...he didn't want us to lose in Southeast Asia, and he didn't want the United States to withdraw.[2]

A Heritage of Spiritual Decadence and Chemical Poisons

"The transition from the jungle to the workplace was hard," Dung continued.

> Our poverty was abysmal, our problems immense and our people exhausted. Many lost hope. And it wasn't just the combatants in the South; it was also the war fighters in the North. Even my husband, who was a colonel in the army and saw so many fall, became discouraged. To this day, we have arguments right within the family. I say that our progress is disappointing but has to be measured against the problems we inherited and the pressures we have faced from China and the United States. He says that that's not good enough. The war ended and our problems began. And we have not solved them. The way things are today, he says, is not fair to those who died.

When Dung spoke of "the problems we inherited," I thought of my visit to Saigon in September, 1975, four months after the U.S.-backed regime had surrendered. Here are the first few paragraphs of the report I made on my return to the United States. They begin with a quotation from Nguyen Minh Vy, a member of Vietnam's National Assembly who had served on the Vietnamese negotiating team in Paris.

> The heritage the Americans left in Saigon is far worse than the heritage the French colonialists left in Hanoi. The Americans created a numerically significant section of the population who value money more than human relationships. For them everything can be bought and sold. Everything has a price and nothing else matters. It will take a long time to cleanse the

society of the spiritual decadence left by the Americans.

This was a theme I heard often during our ten days in Vietnam, not only in Hanoi and the provinces but in Saigon itself. Ngo Ba Thanh...spoke of a "society of prostitutes and bankers, backed by the United States." Nguyen Van Hieu, the acting mayor of Saigon, told me of that city's need to re-educate and reform an estimated 200,000 prostitutes, 300,000 full-time thieves and over 150,000 drug addicts—a smaller number of addicts than I had expected, living as I do in New York City.

A 1974 study by the University of Michigan had estimated a higher number of prostitutes (half a million) and drug addicts (also half a million). In addition, it estimated that for the whole of occupied South Vietnam there were three million afflicted with venereal disease, a million suffering from tuberculosis and an average of 430,000 children dying every year from malnutrition, disease and American bombings.

Some of Hieu's statistics did not surprise me, grim as they were: an estimated two million unemployed in Saigaon and another million in the provinces; a half million disabled veterans in Saigon itself. Earlier, in Than Hoa, doctors at the hospital had said, "We have five factories that make nothing but artificial legs and arms, and they cannot make enough to supply our needs."

But I was shocked to hear that 85 percent of the population in U.S.-Saigon areas were illiterate, although illiteracy had been wiped out in the North by the regime from which the United States was determined to protect the South.

We saw a number of children in Saigon who were suffering grotesque birth defects, a heart-rending reminder of Vietnamese claims that American chemical warfare had caused a multiplication of such births.

Other children were either white enough or black enough to remind me that in addition to 370,000 orphans produced in the South by American firepower, half a million Amerasian children had been produced by the sex drives of alienated and insecure American intruders. "Eat, drink and make love, because tomorrow we may die."

[In line with my consistent experience of observing that the Vietnamese are remarkably cautious about overstating statistics, (see Chapter Eight), a U.N. investigation in 1977 estimated that in reality there were 800-900,000 orphans in the South.[1] We have already seen that Hieu's 1975 statistics on prostitutes and drug addicts were lower than those of the University of Michigan study a year earlier.]

The statistics on the number of children by American G.I.s comes from an exhibition of U.S. War Crimes, in downtown

Saigon. A whole section was devoted to "Examples of American Sexual Depravity." Besides crude sex comics and copies of *Playboy*, both of which one might expect to see in an American exhibit devoted to sexual decadence, there was a surprise— blown up reproductions of advertisements from the *New Yorker* and other posh American magazines. They featured the chic bodies and elegant adornments and trappings of the "Beautiful People" who make themselves sexually attractive by using the right perfume, wearing the right jewelry, driving the right cars, etc. Interspersed among these displays were American bombs and instruments of torture. Havelock Ellis and the Marquis de Sade would have admired the Vietnamese insight. All in all it was a very sophisticated exhibit, albeit different from the kind of sophistication it deprecated.

"Bombs kill the body," my Vietnamese friend explained, "but the other things lessen the spirit. They weaken the will to struggle for a just society."

Chemical Warfare

During my 1985 visit, I talked with Dr. Nguyen Thi Ngoc Phuong, who works with victims of Agent Orange. She said that defective births and aborted fetuses continue at an alarming rate, ten years after the end of the war. Here is a Vietnamese description of the nature, purposes and consequences of U.S. chemical warfare:

Among the defoliants used were 2,4-D and 2,4-T...which were first produced in 1941 at the Biological Weapons Research Center at Fort Dietrick, Maryland. Their aim was to destroy both food crops and all other vegetation so as to entice them [the rural population] into strategic hamlets set up by the U.S. and the Saigon administration, with the food available there... Their ultimate goal was to deny the patriotic forces the natural and human cover essential to their guerrilla activities. Toxic chemical spraying was followed by the spreading of toxic gases, including CS...which was blown by Mity Mites into underground shelters, caves and tunnels to kill members of the resistance and their supporters... In 1966, when defoliation operations were being stepped up, a sharp increase in birth defects at the Pediatric Hospital in Saigon was noted. In 1969, the Saigon press shocked the public with reports of many molar pregnancies and malformed babies born to healthy peasants in defoliated areas... Scientists [many of whom were Americans] accused the White House and the Pentagon of both genocide and biocide against Vietnam.

In South Vietnam alone, [the U.S.] spread more than 100,000 tons over [about 43 percent of the cultivated area and about 44 percent of the total area]. These products destroyed 70 percent of the coconut groves, 60 percent of the rubber plantations, 110,000 hectares of coastal filao forest, 150,000 hectares of mangroves, and crops enough to feed millions of people... In his report of August, 1970 to the U.S. Senate, Senator Gaylord A. Nelson admitted [I would say "protested"— D.D.] that "The U.S. has dumped [on Southern Vietnam] a quantity of toxic chemicals amounting to six pounds per head of population, including men, women and children."[2]

I was unable to accept Dr. Phuong's invitation to visit her clinic, but Robert Shaplen wrote in the *New Yorker* of a visit he had made:

> I was fortunate, or perhaps unfortunate, enough to go to Tu Du Hospital, where Dr. Nguyen Thi Ngoc Phuong, one of Vietnam's foremost gynecologists, gave me an hour's tour and a talk on what she maintained were the effects of the toxic sprays, including Agent Orange, on women who become pregnant. Dr. Phuong, an energetic and impassioned woman who has devoted much of the past ten years to this subject, methodically puts her foreign visitors through a wringer. Both Tim Page and I, who went there separately, left wet-eyed after we saw her "exhibits"... The exhibits consisted mainly of deformed fetuses, including some without brains (examples of anencephaly) and some with enlarged heads (or hydrocephaly) and of samples of hydratidiform moles, which are abnormal tissue formations that appear in the placenta in place of normal fetal forms. Dr. Phuong, who told me that she has lectured at a number of international forums but *has been unable to obtain a visa for the United States* [emphasis added], also led me through the hospital rooms, including a ward for young girls, all of whom had hydratidiform moles. Some were sharing beds, because the hospital was overcrowded. The rate of choriocarcinoma cases, in which the mole becomes a malignant tumor, Dr. Phuong said, is still increasing in Vietnam, ten years after the war and...the incidence of such cases and of other defects has been highest in...provinces...where the Vietcong were most active, and which therefore were most heavily sprayed with toxic substances. For example, one set of figures showed a 7.4 per cent incidence of birth defects among pregnant women in a heavily sprayed village, as against less then one per cent in a village in another province that wasn't sprayed at all. The choriocarcinoma patients we saw, most of whom were in their twenties, were receiving chemotherapy treatments after hysterectomies. "Ninety per cent of them will recover," Dr. Phuong said, "but, of course, they will never be able to have children." She gave me a hard stare and added, "That means a lot to women in Vietnam."[3]

Another American, Frank Wilkinson, visited hospitals in Ho Chi Minh City and Hanoi in May 1984, as part of a delegation arranged by the U.S. Committee for Scientific Cooperation with Vietnam. He reports the following:

> We witnessed...the birth defects of children born in the sprayed areas of Vietnam... We were shown bottles, hundreds and hundreds of bottles, containing deformed fetuses, babies without heads or with heads that were like sponges, arms coming out of chests, legs coming out of stomachs, the most horrible examples of deformity in terms of the fetuses.
>
> Their research indicated that in the case of the mothers and/or fathers from the sprayed areas...birth defects are six times greater in comparison with...mothers or fathers from areas that were not sprayed by the U.S. forces.[4]

Although my own conversations with Dr. Phuong took place away from the hospital and her exhibits, her descriptions were graphic. As I listened to her, I was torn between two emotions. One was horror at her clinical descriptions of the human price thousands and thousands of Vietnamese are still paying for U.S. war crimes. The other was a surge of hope for the human race, based on her unselfconscious identification with these victims. As she spoke, it was clear that she had been moved by their sufferings to commit herself both to helping them as individuals and to doing everything she could to prevent any future recurrences of such warfare anywhere in the world.

If Dr. Phuong were an isolated embodiment of this spirit, it would have been inspiring but wouldn't have told me much about the society and its people. But she was not alone. During my visit I of course met people who did not reveal such admirable qualities. One or two of them were relatively uncritical advocates of the Vietnamese status quo, at least when talking to me, a foreign visitor. A few were as undiscriminatingly hostile in their opposition and, conversely, uncritically romantic about the anti-communist "freedom and prosperity" in the United States. But over and over again I met people, both in and out of the government, whose clarity of spirit and unselfconscious sense of sister/brotherhood, each in her or his own way, at least approached those of Dr. Phuong. I think it is part of any honest "objective" report to cite these people as a contrast to the images of Vietnamese communists and their terrorized victims that are rampant in the United States.

In Vietnam today, there are problems and there is hope. There is hope and there are problems beyond our ability to comprehend or express them.

Post-War Let-Down in the U.S.

In 1975, Nguyen Minh Vy had spoken to me of the "lessening of the spirit" produced in sections of the South Vietnamese population by Americans who valued money more than human relationships and taught that everything worthwhile, including love, could be bought and sold. In 1985, Nguyen Ngoc Dung spoke of another "lessening of the spirit" in another section of the Vietnamese population. With sadness, she spoke of the struggle against post-war weariness and disillusionment, a weakening of the spirit that had sustained Vietnam through forty years of brutal warfare for independence and freedom.

As she was speaking, I thought of what had happened to some participants in the U.S. civil rights and anti-war movements after a much shorter and far less demanding period of emergency actions and lives. I want to discuss this briefly now, before continuing with a report on my 1985 visit.

Here too, there was a dimming of "utopic" dreams that had been symbolized by slogans such as "Freedom Now" and "Participatory Democracy"; dreams of a society based on cooperation and love rather than on competition, profits, and power over the lives of others:

> Money is violence. Money is not so dramatic a killer as napalm, but Amerika kills far more people with her dollar than with her bombs. Instead of U.S. Latin American export-import statistics, read "infant deaths, human beings exploited and sacrificed, dignity denied."
>
> —Jerry Rubin, *Do It*, 1970

And Jerry in 1981: "Leverage in financial terms is when a small amount of money controls a larger amount. Leverage is therefore power. I'm into leverage."(*Boston Globe*, Oct. 23, 1981)

I think that the media exaggerate the numbers of Sixties' activists who have lost their social consciences, even as they exaggerate the disillusionment and failings of contemporary Vietnam. And distorted claims about both realities are made by ambitious politicians who take their cues from those who can put up the vast sums required for election in a society that thinks it's possible to have political democracy without economic democracy.

One of the reasons for these exaggerations is that those who are anxious to cling to their undemocratic positions of wealth and power face a problem against which they must defend themselves. The country's most famous rhetoric tells us that "all men are created equal." Its established practice violates that insight.

Clearly the American people are not equal in opportunity, power or rewards, not even in access to the minimal necessities of life and dignity. Today, the inequalities are made obvious by the conspicuous extravagances of the rich and the increasingly visible plights of the jobless, the homeless, the inhabitants of our ghettoes, the aged, and others who cannot even afford basic medical care. According to the U.S. Census Bureau, 34,400,000 people lived below the poverty level in 1982, with the poverty rate for blacks three times as high as for whites—and the statistics have worsened considerably since then. It is increasingly difficult to believe that the rich help the poor by their hard work, skillful management, and wise investments—and that the poor are burdened down by their own short-sighted failures to apply themselves intelligently to bettering their lives. It's more believable that inexcusable inequalities and injustices are built into our system of selfish competition for unequal rewards. Even if the competition weren't weighted in favor of the already well-heeled, why should our economic system be based on a competitive scramble to rise above our fellow humans rather than on mutual aid and cooperation so that we can all advance together?

Working out an alternative system is not easy, and we will have to learn details and methods by trial and error.[1] But, meanwhile, because we fail as a society to explore the possibilities of cooperation and sharing, and because the results of clinging to competition and private profit are so catastrophic, a seething volcano of misery, frustration and potential revolt stirs uneasily beneath the surface of our society.

The Sixties graphically illustrated that the potential for an explosion extends beyond the prime victims to those members of *all* classes who are affronted by injustice and hypocrisy. Whatever their personal situations of privilege or oppression, all human beings experience from time to time strange, potentially energizing stirrings of human solidarity and love—intuitions that we are all members of the same human family, that "All the peoples on the earth are equal [not just *at* but] *from* birth, all the peoples have a right to live, to be happy and free." (From Vietnam's 1945 Declaration of Independence)

Stirring the soup of discontent more deeply, the imperatives that dominate our domestic relationships dominate our foreign policy as well. The American people may respond generously to earthquake, flood, and famine, thereby providing a visible sign of the impulses to love and solidarity. Within the context of the biased and one-sided information that is readily available, they may be genuinely concerned for the victims of human rights violations in far-away places. But U.S. foreign policy, for all its pious rhetoric, violates these familial instincts. Its aim is *not* to promote equality, happiness and freedom for "all the peoples on the earth." Its goal is "freedom" to secure and preserve corporate access to cheap foreign labor, cheap raw materials, profitable markets, and investments in runaway enterprises that are freed from domestic ecological restrictions, minimum wage laws, freedom of speech and assembly, etc. As these "freedoms" are challenged in more and more countries, a second imperative arises: to prevent Third World breakaways from the private-profit system of institutionalized domestic and international inequality. If a country such as Vietnam or Nicaragua succeeds in breaking away, it must be prevented from successfully developing an alternative model that could inspire other peoples ("dominos") to try to do likewise, in other Third World countries *and in the United States.*

Hence the reliance on covert action all over the world—to install or sustain terrorist governments that can suppress popular movements (or replace governments) that aim to develop their own independent models. Hence the Rapid Deployment Force, the financial pressures, the trade embargoes, and the maintenance of the ultimate threat, The Bomb.

From time to time the veil of governmental secrecy and subterfuge is lifted for a moment and people see these realities. For some it is easier to see them today in the poverty and crime of our cities, the communities abandoned by runaway industry, the mortgage-sales of family farms and their replacement by agribusinesses that deplete the soil and pollute the fruit of the earth (our daily food) with cancer-producing chemicals. For others it is easier to see the ugly reality in our support for Central American death squads or South African racism. Everyone is nervous about the threat of nuclear suicide. Wherever one notices it first, or is most offended, it's all the same seamless web of violence and deceit, arrogance and danger.

In the Sixties, more people than usual saw the reality behind the facade of democracy, thanks among other influences to the black civil rights explosion and then to the focus on the Vietnam War, with its genocidal bombings and heartless sacrifice of American soldiers. More people than usual felt hope that together we could change the way things are to bring us closer to the country's professed ideals. Ever since, it has been important for those who wield the power and receive the unequal rewards to "prove" that these people were wrong, that the system didn't change, couldn't change, didn't need to be changed; that instead the activists of the Sixties have changed, as Jerry Rubin and the other Yuppies have changed. It is important for them to show, from the failures of the Sixties in the United States and from the failures of the communists in post-war Vietnam (and of course there are real failures in both cases), that efforts to create a society based on anything even remotely aspiring to equality and love are exercises in futility. "You can't fight City Hall (or Washington)," so don't waste your time trying. Anyway, they say—and "Vietnam proves it"—the only alternative to what we have and to the even worse conditions in our Third World client states is totalitarian misery and disillusionment.

Every war (and every anti-war movement) involves tremendous outpourings of energy, accompanied by unrealistic visions of the gains that will accompany victory: World War One—"This is a war to end war"; World War Two—"After we get rid of fascism in Europe, we will come back home and keep right on fighting for racial equality, social justice and real democracy in the United States." Historically, wartime idealism is followed by a period of reduced energies available for public pursuits and campaigns for justice. For some it is a period of catching up with education, career and family; for others, these basic needs combine with "struggle weariness" and the inevitable human failings of the movements they have worked with, to produce a sense of hopelessness and in some cases disillusionment. Sometimes it takes the form of political apathy and sometimes it causes surrender to the cynicism of trying to get "ahead" in the world without regard to what happens to one's fellow human beings.

To me, this surrender is the real "narcissism," not the search for spiritual roots or explorations of the many facets of a holistic way of life. For the personal really is the political; and there is no gap between inner peace and outer peace. There is no contradiction among global concerns, national concerns, regional concerns, community concerns and personal concerns. What a strange notion it is that there is an antipathy between struggling for a just and loving society and attempting to achieve a non-polluting agriculture and industry, a life-enhancing diet, a satisfying work and workplace, control of one's own body and life, a healthy, non-exploitative sexuality and a similarly non-exploitative, harmonious relationship with the natural universe.

The irony is that some of those who reject one aspect or another of the politics of City Hall, Washington and Moscow fall into the trap of accepting some of these artificial dichotomies. But in the long run, we can't breathe in without breathing out; we can't change our world without simultaneously changing ourselves; and more and more people are seeing that there can be no such separations. It's a time of exploration and experimentation to bring inner and outer realms together in a sound, common-sense way, with many variations according to time and place and individual characteristics. But those who benefit from the one-sided separations are doing their best to preserve them in a new version of "divide and rule."

In this country, the Montgomery, Alabama bus boycott, which came ten years after the end of World War II, signalled the advent of a new period. That period climaxed in the Sixties and early Seventies. Now, the recent rash of public activities challenging U.S. policies in Central America and South Africa may be giving advance notice of the coming birth of a new period of heightened activity. If so, given the insights gained from the anti-nuclear, environmental, feminist, gay and lesbian, human-potential and liberation theology movements (flawed and subject to human error as all of them are), one can expect that "the enthusiasm, patriotism and courage" of the Sixties will return not just with new vigor but with expanded and enriched perspectives and greater maturity.

All during the Vietnam war, the Vietnamese freedom fighters kept telling Americans who were in touch with them that "It's a protracted struggle." And now Dung was saying the same thing to me: "We always said that it's a protracted struggle, but sometimes we didn't understand how protracted it is, even after getting rid of our foreign oppressors."

At the same time, for all the down-to-earth realism of Dung and others, it is clear that they feel that Vietnam, too, has turned an important corner after the days of bewilderment and mistakes that followed hard on the success of their forty-year preoccupation with gaining their independence and national freedom. Dung says:

> Now we have accelerated programs in economic education, in electoral methods, in the technological society—and in making people aware of their human rights. But the biggest progress is that we have faced up to our backwardness and our mistakes. We don't hide our mistakes, so now we are going forward.

Introducing My Friend Phan

Not all the American activists of the Sixties are active now in movements for social justice. Some defections persist, especially among those whose involvement in the noble causes of the period included an impulsive plunge into heady new freedoms that overwhelmed their common sense and threw them off balance. For some it was the pursuit of the "instant gratifications" of drugs and sex without sufficient regard to the consequences for oneself and others; for others, indulging in "utopic" dreams of an imminent apocalypse:

> The next six weeks will determine the future of Western Civilization.—Rennie Davis, recruiting people for the May Day 1971 anti-war protest in Washington, D.C.

This apocalyptic spirit is hard to avoid when the stakes are high. In January 1986, I came across a news item from July, 1984, that quoted anti-nuclear activist Helen Caldicott as stating that "We have four months to save our planet." More often than not such an approach brings short-run gains and long-range losses.

There are parallels in Vietnam, both the Vietnam of the serious freedom fighters and the Vietnam of those who succumbed to the instant gratifications and corruptions prevalent in areas dominated by American money, drugs, loneliness, fear and ambivalence about the war. My friend Phan, an active freedom fighter during the years of the American emergency, is a case in point.

Early one morning a letter from Phan was waiting for me at my hotel desk. The evening before we had spent three hours together, dining and talking in a restaurant on the city's most famous street. (The street provides a capsule history of Saigon's most recent tortured history. It was called Rue Catinat during the French occupation, after a French naval vessel that had shelled the Vietnamese port of Tourane in 1856. When the Americans took over from the French, they renamed the street Tu Do (Freedom) Street; now it is called Dong Xoi (Uprising) Street, in honor of the Saigon residents who rose up in 1975 against the U.S.-imposed regime.)

Here are a few key lines from Phan's letter:

> Dear Dave—I and my wife are very delighted to see you in person, in good health and still active in the peace movement... Could you help us to write for [obviously he means "by writing to"] Prime Minister Dong or Foreign Minister Thach on my case, the permission to go on humanitarian reasons of family reunification in Canada.

My friend wants to go to Canada, where his mother and most of his ten siblings live. When I was in Saigon in 1966, he was in prison but I met his then girlfriend, now wife, in one of several meetings I had with underground student leaders. Phan reminds me that I carried a secret letter and some underground literature from some of them to someone else. I had forgotten all about this and him until he looked me up on this trip.

What I had done was very little, but it meant a lot to Thai and his wife, because they had remembered it all those years. He told me that they had followed my "activities" ever since and had my picture on their living room wall. I knew, of course, that this was not so much a personal tribute as one of many indications of the spiritual importance of the American anti-war movement to the beleaguered Vietnamese. The day after Phan told me this, Pham Van Dong, the prime minister, told me with tears in his eyes how important the support of the American anti-war movement had been during their most difficult days and asked me to convey this sentiment to my American comrades when I returned home. The heroism of the Vietnamese freedom fighters energized many Americans to make new commitments to justice and freedom, both in our own country and in countries ravaged by American imperialism. These commitments and the activities they led to, minimal though they were, also communicated an important sense of human solidarity and hope to the Vietnamese. Beyond hope, their actions for us and our actions for them were living examples, from half way around the globe, of a spirit that today is beginning to unite millions who, according to our government, are supposed to be enemies.

Phan kept enthusing from time to time about my good health, and this puzzled me until finally I asked him why he kept mentioning it.

"Because you are seventy years old, and we were afraid that you would be bent over and feeble, probably not able to walk without a cane, let alone travel to Vietnam." This still puzzled me until I thought of the life expectancy in most Third World countries. Jerry Rubin was right that both U.S. bombs and the U.S. dollar have killed a lot of Vietnamese. And the dollar has played the more lethal role in the last ten years. Life expectancy in Vietnam is lower, and the health of many of its people poorer, because of the economic war carried out by the United States. The current embargo on trade with Nicaragua has a precedent in United States efforts to deny necessary, life-sustaining food and medicine to Vietnam during ten years of "peace." The Prussian General von Clauswitz said that "War is the continuation of the politics of diplomacy by other means." And for the United States, ten years of "peace" with Vietnam have been the continuation of the politics of war by other means.

Phan said that he had been struggling for six months with the question of whether or not to leave Vietnam. His mother, brothers and sisters have all left, most of them during the American occupation and the rest more recently. Obviously he comes from a privileged family and life has not been easy for him in post-war Vietnam. But he has political disagreements with the regime as well, centering on what he considers the arbitrariness of some of their attempts to regulate the economy.

"Does this mean that it is a totalitarian society?" I asked. "Or is in danger of becoming one?"

"Oh no," he replied. "It definitely is not totalitarian. After all the Vietnamese people have been through in the search for freedom, they would not stand for it."

"Is it pro-Russian?"

Again the answer was an emphatic "No."

Phan ran through the familiar litany of the difficulties Vietnam has faced and the necessity of turning to the Soviet Union for aid. By now I had heard it so often that my notes merely summarize it in my own words: Struggle, sacrifice and pressures followed by victory and more pressures, from the United States, China and a corrupted Saigon population; problems of devastation, boycott and embargo complicated by a non-productive consumer society. And then he ended with the usual words about the Russians

> The Russians came to our aid and we are glad for that, even though they don't mingle well and aren't well liked personally. But we are not the least bit pro-Russian. That will never happen. Their ways are different than ours, and we are too proud a people to permit it.

Phan says that the government's aim has been to produce greater equality during a period of inevitable austerity, but that some of the measures have been ill thought out and in particular have unnecessarily reduced the freedom and prerogatives of the patriotic professional class, of which he is a member. He is an architect who feels that his creativity and inventiveness have not been given free rein but have been inhibited by bureaucratic supervision. One of the measures that inhibits him now is an attempt to restrict the "brain drain" by making it hard for professionals to get permission to leave, under the current Orderly Departure Program. As always when I hear of such restrictions, I wonder how valuable the brains of people are if their hearts and egos are alienated.

It is hard to say how much Phan's dissatisfaction is related to his own lowered status, although clearly that is not its only source. On the other hand, he answers a question about his family by saying that his two teen-aged children are extremely happy with the state of affairs and find healthy fulfillments in their daily life. They don't want to leave. He feels good about his kids and doesn't resent their devotion to the regime, but he has decided to try to leave and to take them with him.

After a while, Phan volunteered what he thought was the real reason for finally coming to this decision.

> You know, I've thought and thought about it and I have finally decided that I want to leave because I want to see the world. I think that's the real reason, although also I want to write a book giving an objective account of what has happened here during the last twenty years. What I write will be different than the official versions and different than the accusations of stupid people like Tang [see next chapter]. To write as I want to write, I need to get away to a quiet place, somewhere where I can gain a fresh perspective away from the turmoil and pressures of my life here.

Phan talked at greatest length about his desire to see the world. That seemed to be his overriding passion. "You know," he said,

> I was in prison during most of the years when young people travel and see the world. When I wasn't in prison I was involved in active political struggle. Now I have a passion to make up for all those years. I want to travel. I want to see other countries. Perhaps I will come back and take up the struggle again after a time away.

I couldn't help thinking that ordinarily "most young people," in Vietnam or anywhere else, aren't free to "travel and see the world." During the period he was referring to, a few young Vietnamese of privileged families could do it, but not many others. Phan had set aside his class privileges, stayed in Vietnam, and risked his life for the welfare of all his people. Now, in a sense, he longed for one of the class privileges he had denied himself, something that should not have been a class privilege in the first place. And apparently he has the private funds to think of doing so.

I also thought that there must have been moments in the Sixties when Phan felt some ambivalence about the decision he made. Clearly he feels a lot of ambivalence now, as he decides to indulge his private desires, if the government will allow it, and then "perhaps...come back and take up the struggle again." I thought of some of our movement dropouts in the United States who go through much the same struggle, as in one way or another, at one time or another, everyone does. When does the personal take priority? When the communal? Who of us is qualified to judge for another person? Who can weigh the seasons of another person's discontents and her or his balancing of personal and political imperatives?

Guilt-tripping and psychological coercion rarely contribute either to personal growth or to the development of a sound long-term movement for peace and social justice. There are many situations in which I remember the wisdom of Quaker William Penn's advice to an ambivalent soldier: "Wear the sword as long as you can." So I told Phan that I would do whatever I could to help him leave. And the next day his letter spelled out what he wanted me to do, although it had been pretty well agreed on the night before.

A Vietcong Memoir: A Case History

When Phan said that the book he wanted to write would be different than the "accusations of stupid people like Tang," I knew very little about Tang. I knew that his full name was Truong Nhu Tang; that during the latter days of the war he had been Minister of Justice in the Provisional Revolutionary Government of South Vietnam in exile (the PRG); that he is living in Paris; and that he has written a book, *A Vietcong Memoir*.[1] That was about all. But I have done some follow-up work and want to discuss his case.

In Vietnam, the first persons I asked about Tang were Dr. Duong Quynh Hoa and her husband, Huyn Van Nghi, with whom I had breakfast the morning after my meeting with Phan. At the time I had no way of knowing that the front jacket of Tang's book features a photo of the two of them in the jungle with Tang; or that they appear in the book, in the text and in two other photos showing them with Tang. Dr Hoa is a pediatrician who, from 1969 to 1975, was Minister of Health in the PRG. After the fall of Saigon, she served as Deputy Minister of Health of the unified government, but later resigned to return to full-time work in the private pediatric clinic she now operates. Nghi was a leader of South Vietnam's Alliance of National Democractic and Peace Forces.

Tang praises both Hoa and Nghi and says that Dr. Hoa left her government post because, like him, she was disgusted at being "involved in a farce" in which the North held all the power and used it tyrannically. Who knows what combination of reasons may have led to Hoa's resignation? But when I asked her in an earlier meeting why she had resigned, she replied that she was a doctor and wanted to work as one, in regular, personal contact with patients. Her obvious devotion to the children and their worried parents who come to her clinic reminded me of Dr. Phuong's empathy with her patients. Hoa said that the government had pressed her to stay but she loved her doctor's role too much to settle in as a bureaucrat. It makes sense and reflects an ancient dilemma, one that suggests that a sound society would provide for the rotation of administrative and direct-contact roles—for the sake of the bureaucrats, the professionals, and those with whom they work.

In both of our meetings, Hoa and Nghi freely expressed their own criticisms of the government's bureaucratic bungling and hangups. But when I asked about Tang, they spoke of him with a scorn as great as Phan's. They said that he was an ambitious opportunist who would have stayed in Vietnam if he had been given a sufficiently prestigious position with bountiful perquisites. According to them, his arrogance and incompetence violated the standards aimed at by the government and made it impossible for him to get the type of high political post he coveted. Rebuffed, they said, he "took his opportunism" to Vietnam's disgruntled former rulers (France and the United States), where he could be "hailed and rewarded for inventing tales against his native country." They made him sound a lot like a Vietnamese egotistical Eden Pastora.

Before I left Vietnam, several others who knew Tang said much the same. This opinion was so widely held by people of varied views on other subjects that I concluded that there must be some truth in it. However, Tang had left by embarking on a perilous voyage as a boat person, so I thought that I should take this into account as well. It hardly seemed to be a step that would be taken by a self-serving careerist, unless, perhaps, he did not realize just how perilous a voyage he was undertaking. Or maybe, like some other ambitious self-seekers, he was willing to undertake great risks of a temporary nature in order to achieve his egoistic, basically anti-social ends.

Thinking of Jerry Rubin and some others I have known, I considered the possibility that Tang was torn between a driving personal ambition and a genuine concern for those who suffer repression, injustice and even death under the status quo. If so, certain periods of heady revolt (the Sixties, for example, in both Saigon and the United States) could bring out the more positive side; less glamorous, more difficult periods in which the enthusiasm and visible dynamics have abated could bring out the private ambitions and opportunism. After all, Jerry risked his life and freedom in the struggle to end the war. It may have brought him fame and the adulation of numerous groupies—and he may have played to these "rewards" throughout the Sixties—but every time he faced police clubs and vigilante anger, he laid everything on the line. And when, together, we faced ten years in jail, in 1969-70, as members of the Chicago Seven (originally Eight),

Jerry never compromised his strong anti-war and pro-youth-liberation positions in order to save his skin. He was one of the first to argue in favor of putting forward our full position, in and out of the courtroom, as a media-assisted consciousness-raising device, even though it might increase our chances of conviction and a long sentence.

I decided to reserve judgment on Tang until I could return to the United States and read his book. Now I have read *A Vietcong Memoir*. A close reading of the text does not justify the loving praise showered on him by non-revolutionary Americans who hail him as a true revolutionary who is protesting the betrayal of his revolutionary ideals. This myth is on a par with the claim that Arturo Cruz, Adolpho Calero and Alfonso Robelo, leaders of the Nicaraguan Contras, wanted a genuine revolution in Nicaragua and are now trying to save the revolution from its Sandinista betrayers.

A more possible interpretation is that Tang does have a lot in common with both Jerry Rubin and Eden Pastora—and in a different way with Cruz and Robelo (but not with Calero, who worked with the C.I.A. as far back as 1960). This interpretation would suggest he was initially a relatively honest person who combined an honorable intent with a competing private ambition that now dominates his politics. According to this view, he could stomach just so much of the tyranny of the Saigon regimes but was not prepared to accept more than cosmetic changes in the society that produced it. Significantly, a close reading of the text reveals that he never did favor independence for a reunified Vietnam, and that he opposes all forms of socialism, not just its totalitarian varieties.

But there is a second level of questions that arises when one looks beyond the immediate text to two important historical considerations. The first involves a look at what was happening in South Vietnam when Tang suffered the first of two painful arrests. The second is the known history of one of the co-authors of Tang's first-person life story, Doan Van Toai (see Chapter Sixteen, Postscript). As we shall see, these suggest the possibility of a far less honorable role.

At the first level, the book tells us some important things about the range of people who became involved in the anti-Diem, anti-Thieu, anti-U.S. movement and later became critics of the regime that is now in power in Vietnam. It is instructive not only in respect to Vietnam but also in respect to other countries, (Nicaragua and Cuba, for example) in which cruel and corrupt, U.S.-sponsored, dictators eventually provoked opposition from people whose personal and political objectives were limited at best, objectionable at worst. At this level, Tang brings out not only the self-seeking objectives of persons like himself but also some of the failings of those who are dedicated to achieving more fundamental changes in the society. He reminds us of the serious and difficult problems faced by any movement seeking to achieve a transition from a basically selfish, competitive society to a more public-spirited and cooperative one.

Most of *A Vietcong Memoir* is an account of Tang's gradual disillusionment with the cruelty and hypocrisy of the society in which he was a wealthy, privileged and prominent member, and of his subsequent participation in the struggle to rid Vietnam of the American invaders and their South Vietnamese henchmen. If he is playing up to the Americans, he doesn't do it by retroactively muting his criticisms of U. S. policy and of the U. S.-supported regimes. This has to be made clear, to maintain a proper perspective on Tang. But a long chapter praising the efforts of one of his friends and allies, Albert Phan Ngoc Thao, also has to be taken into account for telling us as much about Tang as about Thao.

Tang praises Albert Thao as a heroic figure who cleverly advanced the progressive cause by serving in higher and higher positions in the repressive Diem government. He explains that Albert vigorously carried out the regime's oppressive policies in order to intensify popular opposition and enhance prospects for the regime's overthrow.

In one example, Tang says that Albert Thao managed to get himself put "in charge" of the brutal program of forcing the rural population out of their native villages and into newly constructed Strategic Hamlets (concentration camps) where they could be more easily controlled by Diem's police. Thao pushed this program to the hilt:

> Ngo Dinh Nhu, Diem's nervous, calculating younger brother, was anxious to fence the countryside from the guerillas, and he wanted to see rapid progress. Albert more than fulfilled his boss's wishes in this. Construction moved fast... Albert's real goal was to sow confusion...[and] under his supervision the strategic hamlets created even more hostility than had the Agrovilles [a milder attempt to accomplish the same objective] before them. After a time this program also withered away, adding to the government's record of failure.

A second example is Tang's praise of Albert's role in his job "to investigate army officers...suspected [by Diem] of disloyalty."

> Officers with field commands drew special attention from the ubiquitous Albert Thao, whose bloodhound position made him the object of universal *fear and respect* [emphasis added]. Albert capitalized on his role by developing relationships with many of the most prominent military figures.

Some, who were of no use to him, he turned over to Diem's secret police; others, who were equally tyrranical, he helped to rise in Diem's hierarchy. The deciding factor for Albert was whether he thought that their swollen ambitions made it likely that they would help overthrow Diem when the time became ripe for a top-of-the-heap coup by disgruntled generals.

These encomiums for Thao make clear the superficiality, at best, of Tang's own "progressive" and "humanitarian" politics.

Meanwhile, Tang was leading his own less spectacular double life, holding a series of ever higher positions under Diem and the regimes that followed him, and working surreptitiously for moderate reforms. First he served as

> chief comptroller for the Industry and Commerce Bank of [South] Vietnam. I...left my bank comptroller's job to become director general of the Societe Sucriere, Vietnam's national sugar company. With its plantations, mills, refineries, distilleries and import/export operations, the Societe was the South's largest conglomerate.

If one goes only by the text, one has to give Tang credit for having risked his personal privileges under the Saigon regime by working, if secretly and cautiously, with South Vietnam's mostly open and public Self Determination Movement. According to him, this led to his arrest and imprisonment in February 1965. This is certainly the type of history that characterizes some other people who have since turned against the present Vietnamese regime. It may very well be true of Tang as well. But here is where the second set of questions comes in.

If one knows a little about Vietnam at that time, one has to be somewhat cautious about accepting at face value the reasons Tang advances for his arrest. It was a time of coups and counter-coups, and a lot of people were arrested not for radical politics but for betting on the wrong general. In January 1964, General Nguyen Kanh overthrew the generals who had taken power after the assassination of Diem. And by February 1965, when Tang was arrested, rival generals, headed by Ngueyn Cao Ky and working with the C.I.A., were known to be maneuvering to overthrow Khan. A lot of people suspected of involvement in these maneuvers were arrested, including Albert Thao's brother Lucien. One has to consider the possibility that it was Tang's involvement in this plot that led to his arrest. It is a legitimate question because Albert was a key organizer of the plot, which finally succeeded on February 19, two weeks after Tang's arrest. Tang goes so far as to describe the coup, in a chapter completely separate from the one in which he tells of his arrest, as "Albert's coup against Nguyen Thanh."

To add to the legitimacy of the question, sometime after Khan's overthrow and the accession to power of the even more repressive Ky, Tang was released from jail and restored to a top position in the Societe Sucriere. On the other hand, Tang says that he received a suspended sentence because his wife paid a $5,000 bribe to the judicial tribunal's president.

Back in his old privileged haunts, he tells us that he resumed working with various reform movements while concealing his activities in the following manner:

> To further the image I was seeking to project as an unstable though essentially harmless political idealist, I began to mold my private life on the pattern of Saigon's fun-loving and frivolous upper classes... Weekends I would spend...at our beach house on Cap St. Jaques or in the mountain resort of Dalat, socializing, playing tennis, and swimming. Weeknights I joined my friends at nightclubs and restaurants, or helped arrange the surprise parties and "four color card game" evenings that were esssential fare on the social menu. My salary, almost three times that of a cabinet minister, barely covered expenses.

One wonders what kind of revolution Tang was organizing among the fun-loving and frivolous upper classes in whose lifestyle he sacrificially immersed himself.

Finally, in June 1967, Tang was arrested again, and again his arrest may have been caused by work he says he was performing for the Self Determination Movement. This time he was tortured and then released in a prisoner exchange with the National Liberation Front and transported to the NLF's jungle headquarters. Tang's arrival in the jungle leads to the final chapters of *A Vietcong Memoir*, which describe his disillusioning interactions with communists from the North.

Conflicts In The Jungle

Tang reports a series of instances in which Workers Party members from the North were manipulative or overbearing toward non-party people like himself. In almost every instance, these examples are balanced by reports of other more sensitive party members or by the intervention of someone in a higher party position who reprimanded or overruled the offenders. None of this sounds surprising, given normal human frailty and the extreme pressures of their life in the jungles. Tang eloquently describes these pressures, with graphic accounts of the frequent, terrifying raids by B 52s and the nervous breakdowns and near breakdowns that he and others suffered. However, as the difficult days and months go on, he begins to interpret the occasional examples of strained relationships between formerly privileged Southerners such as himself and the long-term communist fighters as communist perfidy, proofs of Northern totalitarianism. When a party member is overbearing, he interprets this as a true indication of the contempt of the Workers Party for its non-communist allies in the Southern resistance movement. When a higher official acts in a contrary manner, it is because the higher officials are more adept at hiding their true feelings.

No one who wasn't there in the jungles with them can form a final conclusion, but his case seems somewhat forced. From my own experience, I think, for example, of the strains among World War Two conscientious objectors under trying but far less harrowing circumstances, in a maximum security federal prison. In particular, I think of what happened during two long hunger strikes that a few of us engaged in against the prison's brutal treatment of inmates. In the first one, when we finally had a meeting with the warden, a Quaker inmate was in attendance, and on a signal from the warden launched into an attack on our hunger strike as a coercive method that violated nonviolent principles. In the second, a well known pacifist leader came in to mediate between the hunger strikers and the prison authorities. On the one hand, he urged us to abandon the strike. On the other hand he negotiated an agreement from the warden to recommend the release of a non-striker from his organization, under an arrangement whereby the released prisoner promised not to speak or write about either prison conditions or the war. In both instances we felt betrayed far beyond anything Tang describes from his jungle experience. But it would have been ludicrous for us to conclude that the Quakers or the religious pacifist organization for which the second person worked were supporters of the terrorist practices against which we were striking.

A Case History II:
Tang's Story After the Fall of Saigon

Tang's alienation from his Northern "comrades" became complete after the fall of Saigon. He charges that during the first year of reunification the victorious Northerners failed to provide adequate opportunities for democratic participation by their Southern allies. Up to a point he is undoubtedly right. It's one of the mistakes that supporters of the regime (and official party documents) have acknowledged for years, without implying wrongful intent or sectarian persecution.

But Tang seriously overstates the case. It was a difficult and confusing situation at best. The leadership of the resistance movement in the South had of necessity been almost entirely underground and localized. It had been decimated by the casualties suffered in the Tet uprising of 1968 and the village-by-village assassinations of the C.I.A.'s Phoenix program. To complicate the new period even further, some of the surviving better known members of the Southern resistance movement had been forced into their opposition by the arbitrariness, cruelty and instability of the successive Saigon regimes, motivated by frustrated personal ambition at least as much as by a broader concern for a more equitable society.

Leaving aside all these factors, Tang launches a simplistic attack and ends up shooting himself in the foot. He says

> Like me, most...veteran revolutionaries put up an initial fight, refusing to cooperate once they discovered they were involved in a farce.

But he cites by name only one of these veteran revolutionaries who refused to cooperate, Dr. Hoa. We know that Hoa is running a children's clinic in a Ho Chi Minh City hospital and says that this, not serving as a government bureaucrat, is her life work. The supposedly most damning evidence Tang can supply of her non-cooperation is the following: "'Let the Northern cadres make the wind and the weather,' growled Dr. Hoa as she stalked out of the Ministry of Health." When? Why? The context seems to suggest that it was during a conference with health department officials from Hanoi. I've been at lots of difficult coalition meetings in the American movement for justice and peace when tensions were high and someone stalked out with an irritated remark, only to have the problem resolved in a friendly discussion before the next meeting or at it.

Tang follows this with the names of five of the surviving top leadership of the South's Provisional Revolutionary Government who became *active* in the new reunified regime. This in itself would appear to be a denial of his major thesis, even without considering several other presently active former leaders of the Southern resistance whom he fails to mention but with whom I have been in personal contact. He explains the participation of three of them by saying that they "kept their mouths shut, frightened by the thought of deviating from the Party's will." Of the two very top leaders, both of whom have occupied key positions in the new government from the beginning, he has this to say:

> Meanwhile, NLF President Nguyn Huu Tho and PRG President Huyn Tan Phat took steps to secure their privileges by faithfully expounding the new line: *Forced reunification and the rapid socialization of the South.* [Emphasis added.]

This passage is one of many that makes it clear that these two aspects of post-war policy, reunification and socialism, were the bones that stuck in Tang's throat and provoked his exodus. Yet reunification was always the open aim of an overwhelming majority of the resistance fighters, North and South. The question of socialism was more complicated. It was the established practice in the North and the announced aim of the North and of many in the South. But there is no question that one of the unified government's most serious mistakes was to try to force through a speeded up and too narrowly conceived socialization of the Southern sector (see Chapter Twenty).

The jacket of the book misleadingly identifies Tang as one who as a student in Paris, met Ho Chi Minh [and] was personally inspired by Ho's *vision to unify Vietnam.* [Emphasis added]

This is perhaps implied, though never explicitly stated, in Tang's enthusiastic accounts of the spell Ho cast on him as a youth in Paris. But a careful reading of the rest of the book consistently reveals a different story.

From the beginning, the activities that he says caused his arrests and eventual deportation to NLF-occupied territory had been, by his own account, to reform, stabilize and perpetuate South Vietnam's *independent existence.* The more daring of the organizations with which he worked, South Vietnam's Self-Determination Movement, had as its objective:

America for Americans. South Vietnam for South Vietnamese. We demand that the NLF and the Government negotiate peace between the two brothers. South Vietnam must have the right to determine its own future.

To avoid any misunderstanding on the reader's part, Tang makes a point of underlining who "the two brothers" were. They were not the South and the North, as one might expect, given the fact that the South and the North were the artificially separated brothers, the two halves of an historic and patriotic whole. Rather he identifies them as "the Saigon regime and the NLF," both of them exclusively based in the South (if it can be said that the Saigon regime had a base).

Besides direct passages like these, Tang's opposition to reunification is also circumstantially supported by his complaint that when Vietnam was forced to choose between the two rival socialist superpowers, it chose friendship with the Soviet Union rather than China. As we have seen, China consistently opposed reunification and this was particularly clear during the period of which Tang is complaining.

The most outrageous of Tang's statements about reunification is a quotation he attributes to Pham Van Dong, the prime minister of North Vietnam at the time. He writes

"How could we have the stupid, criminal idea of annexing South Vietnam?" Pham Van Dong said to various foreign visitors.

But I was one of those foreign visitors, five times, and met with Dong every time. Never did he ever say anything to me of this kind. Always, he and every other official I talked with, inside and outside Vietnam, stressed the exact opposite: that Vietnam was one country and that a major goal of the war was to reunify the artificially divided sectors. This was asserted unequivocally not only by Northern officials but by every representative of the NLF with whom I talked, in Phnom Penn (Cambodia), in Vientiane (Laos), in Bratislava (Czechoslovakia) and in

Paris during the lengthy peace negotiations. It was also stated by underground leaders in Saigon with whom I talked in 1966. Further, through the happenstance of having been the first American visitor to North Vietnam after the U.S. war had entered the stage of its full fury, I helped arrange many American trips to North Vietnam during the crucial years from 1966 'til the end of the war. I always met with these visitors on their return to the United States. All of them reported hearing the same story: Vietnam was an artificially divided country that was fighting to be liberated from American occupation and made whole again.

At various times and in various circumstances, the government may have envisioned and spoken of a longer transitional period, with more concessions to non-socialist institutions in the South than it permitted when it responded to the unexpected, complete collapse of the South. It definitely rushed some aspects of the attempted transition to socialism without sufficient sensitivity to some in the southern resistance movement and to the pragmatic realities. But it did permit a mixed economy with both public and private sectors. (See Chapter Twenty-One.) Under emergency conditions and intoxicated both by its sudden complete victory and its war-time habit of centralized decision-making in the North, it made many mistakes. Dr. Hoa, Xuan Oanh, Ngo Ba Thanh, Nguyen Ngoc Dung, among others, all say that it took several years for the party to rid itself of its unfortunate war-induced "commandism." But particularly in view of the self-criticism it has made and the new economic policies it has instituted, this is far different than the coldly calculating perfidious totalitarianism of which Tang accuses it.

The reality is that it was the U.S. that created the emergency conditions to which Vietnam reacted. Noam Chomsky reminded me

> Kissinger announced very clearly, the day the Paris Accords were signed, that the U.S. intended to violate every crucial segment of them, and the White House confirmed this in the clearest possible terms. The point has been obscured, even in the peace movement, because the media, without exception, took Kissinger's version of the Accords (which rejected every crucial principle) to be the actual version, followed by virtually all scholarship, one of the most amazing examples of servility to the state that I've ever seen.[2]

John McAuliff discusses the consequences of the U.S.-Saigon violations in *Vietnam Reconsidered*:

> The record demonstrates (and Frank Snepp [ex-C.I.A. operative in Saigon] confirms it) that it was the Thieu regime which was determined that the agreement would not be implemented politically or militarily, and the Communist side which initially favored and honored it... Had the agreement been

implemented, it is likely that several things would have come about:
1. A more gradual transfer of power;
2. a more complex balance of forces within the South, and between Northern and Southern parts of the country;
3. an opportunity for an orderly and safe departure of people who could not fit into the new Vietnam.

The precipitate collapse of South Vietnam surprised the Vietnamese revolutionaries. In their own planning, they expected the war would go on another year—and they were not politically prepared to administer the South. To their credit, the bloodbath that the U.S. government so often predicted (and which had happened in China after its revolution, in Indonesia to the Communists, and in France to the Vichy collaborators)[3] did not occur. To their blame, tens of thousands of persons were detained without trial in re-education camps... Only the most extreme and suspect of refugee accounts describe postwar conditions of imprisonment and torture which approximate those that were routine and widespread in the [U.S.-sponsored] Republic of Vietnam.

In the end, Tang, despite his opposition to both reunification and socialism and despite his letters to Pham Van Dong complaining of Party insensitivity toward Southerners (or perhaps because of the letters), was offered and accepted a moderately high position. It was not in the cabinet but as director of the National Rubber Industry, a position that seems fitting in view of what he has told us about his earlier career as bank controller and director of the sugar conglomerate.

Perhaps the job directing the National Rubber Industry was not up to the kind of political post that Dr. Hoa and others say that Tang coveted. But it was not something to be given up lightly to emigrate as a boat person. That he did so seems to have been motivated at least as much by his opposition to reunification and socialism as by dissatisfaction with his high economic post. On the other hand, it is hard to separate his opposition to reunification and socialism from his desire to regain the prerogatives and perquisites he enjoyed as director of "the South's largest congolomerate." The evidence is overwhelming that government and Party officials under the new regime receive salaries significantly below the current level of most private entrepreneurs and certainly far below those that were rife under the Saigon regimes and had been enjoyed by Tang. After the example established by Ho Chi Minh, Party cadres and government officials lead a very austere existence close to that of the people. They may or may not live up to Ho's "Three Withs" for rural cadres and officials—"Eat with the peasants, live with the peasants and work with the peasants." But they live well below the standard to which Tang apparently would like to return.

Some Personal Conclusions About Tang

Based on his book, my guess is that Tang is a disappointed and disillusioned, mostly decent and definitely naive, political moderate, with an addiction to the privileged lifestyle he inherited from his wealthy parents. He was thrust by circumstances into waters beyond his depth, beginning with the tumultuous and corrupting situation in South Vietnam for which the United States bears a heavy responsibility. An unexpected prisoner exchange saved his life, sparing him the fate that befell thousands of opponents of Diem, Ky and Thieu. It also threw him beyond his depth into a close alliance with more thorough-going revolutionaries in the jungles in which they hid out and from which they conducted their campaigns for a unified, independent and socialist Vietnam which he was not prepared to accept. When victory came, he was not as prepared to continue the alliance as they were. They offered him an important job in line with his talents. He used it as a base from which to arrange a flight to the greener pastures of Paris.

For all this, Tang has written a book that is often both honest and useful. Unintentionally, it reveals more of himself and, by implication, some of his fellow critics of Vietnam than he intended. It is marred by his self-serving need to justify his inability to accept a regime that is committed to a unified country, and an attempt to institute the socialist society that he feared because of what it would do to his elitist privileges. Inevitably, some of his criticisms hit the mark, such as his laments about the failure of the regime to release with sufficient speed those who were sent to re-education camps. These included his two brothers, both of whom flourished under cruel dictators, one as head of the foreign exchange department of the National Bank, the other as director of the Saigon General Hospital. Yet even here, by all accounts the number imprisoned has fallen from perhaps a hundred thousand to somewhere between 8,000 and 10,000 and in a book published in 1985, Tang writes as if none have been released to this day. Sometimes his criticisms extend to outrageous complaints, such as his attacks on reunification as a betrayal of the goals for which most people struggled.

My own appraisal of the strengths and weaknesses of the current regime in Vietnam takes positive note of the regime's attempts to find a place for a person like Tang to play a useful role in the development of a new society. Unfortunately he appears to have reverted instead to the prejudices and conditioning of his privileged upbringing and earlier career.

If the regime had been more sensitive; if it had not fallen for a time into the trap of commandism; if it had not been confronted by the consequences of the U.S. failure to implement the Paris Agreement; perhaps Tang would have risen to the spirit of the new period. At least we can be thankful that Vietnam did not impose on him the fate that befell dissidents in other post-revolutionary countries. That doesn't tell us everything that we want to know, and should know about Vietnam today. But it tells us something that the media and Washington want us to forget.

Postscript

Although *A Vietcong Memoir* is written as Tang's first-person account of his own life, the book's jacket and title page tell us that it was written "with" two other persons, David Chanoff and Doan Van Toai. Neither is mentioned in the text or anywhere identified in any way. I happen to know some things about Toai and they all lead to the C.I.A. Perhaps this explains the book's odd mixture of seemingly honest revelations and crude fabrications.

Here is what I wrote about Toai in June, 1979:

> Huynh Tan Mam, former president of the Saigon Student Association [whom I know personally and consider reliable], writes that Toai was indeed arrested, as he claims, along with Mam himself, in December 1969, Mam says that

> Under the relentless pressure of the student struggle movement, the Thieu regime was forced to release us two weeks later. However, Toai's life changed a great deal after that; he went to work in a private car and lavishly spent money... Students began to let it be known that he had been bribed and now was in the pay of the Thieu-Khiem clique, while pretending publicly to be enthusiastically involved in the struggle... In 1970, Toai travelled to South Korea, Japan, Thailand and the Philippines... organizing an "Asian Student Anti-Communist League."

> In 1970, Toai also visited the United States. Doug Hostetter and other activists in the U.S. National Student Association [NSA] suggested at the time that he might be a C.I.A. agent. Hostetter, who is New England regional secretary of the American Friends Service Committee, tells me that he had concluded that this was the case, because of the speeches Toai made and also because he found out that Toai's trip was not paid for by the Saigon Student Association, which he claimed to be representing. Later the NSA learned that Toai had been expelled from the association and denounced as an informant. Mom writes, "Toai betrayed many students... Many were arrested, disappeared mysteriously, all because Toai and the secret police infiltrated our student association."

> In 1979, Toai was the main source of Joan Baez's widely publicized attacks on Vietnam for having smashed human rights in Vietnam and thereby betraying the American anti-war movement. Her "Open Letter to the Socialist Republic of Vietnam" appeared in full-page advertisements in five major newspapers. Part of my response in the article I have been quoting from seems relevant here.

I won't accuse [Jack] Newfield, Baez, or most of the signers of intellectual dishonesty [as Newfield had accused me in the *Village Voice* for having refused to sign]. I believe that within their own understanding they were speaking out against a deplorable tendency in some sections of the left to shut one's eyes to crimes committed by countries...that are thought to be "progressive." But I do accuse them of failing to do their homework on either Vietnam or the C.I.A....

On the phone I explained to Joan that not endorsing her charges was not a question of my unwillingness to criticize the Vietnamese, publicly or privately, as the case may warrant. It is a matter of demanding a modicum of accuracy and reliability. The material circulated by Baez includes reprints from *Le Monde*, the *London Observer*, the *Washington Post* and *Newsweek*. But all four stories originated from interviews with one individual, Doan Van Toai, who also visited Baez in her home. Two of the most widely known individuals whom Toai claims have been arrested have specifically denied it. They did so personally to Paul Quinn Judge, a Quaker relief worker who returned to Saigon in August 1978 and, two months earlier, in an indignant letter to the Association of Vietnamese in Paris. One is Nguyen Van Hieu, one of the commanders of the 1968 Tet offensive, whose arrest was falsely reported in *Le Monde*, courtesy of Toai. The other is Ton That Duong Ky, identified by Toai as former vice president of the NLF.

Toai lists Ky as one of the eight signers of "The Disinherited Vietnamese Manifesto on Human Rights," a key document in Toai and Baez's arsenal. The *Washington Post* has pointed out that Toai claimed that he had smuggled it out of Vietnam in his rectum but "lost it...and had to rewrite it from memory." Ky calls the document "a cruel and stupid trick, for its cruel but stupid C.I.A. style."

...Last month, Murray Hiebert of the Mennonite Central Committee showed Toai's charges to Mme. Thanh in Vietnam. Her response? "If even half of what he says was true, I'd be out demonstrating myself." Thanh is a member of the Paris-based International League for the Rights of Man.[3]

I do not believe that the C.I.A.'s probable involvement should lead to an oversimplified view of *Vietcong Memoir* or its author. After all, just as counterfeit money must bear some relationship to real money or it won't pass, so counterfeit history must bear some relationship to real history. And I think we have seen that *Vietcong Memoir* does provide us with some interesting insights into some of the people who once worked together and now are in opposing camps. It furnishes some valuable case histories of the complicated and changing relationships that take place in the world of oppressive regimes, the coalitions that form against them, and the strains put on those relationships by the overthrow of the regimes and the decisions that must then be made by all the individuals and groupings involved. And the role of the C.I.A. in these shifting relationships is also part of the case history of our times.

17

Nguyen Ngoc Dung and Ngo Bha Thanh on the Rights of Citizens

Besides being Deputy General Secretary of the Fatherland Front, Nguyen Ngoc Dung is on the National Executive Board of the Women's Union. Much of her work is with women. She says

> We emphasize that women have equal rights with men. We work to educate them about their rights after years of sub-servience. And we tell the men not to be subservient either. They should be active for women's rights and for everyone's rights, including their own.
>
> We teach everyone to work together for the common good and to challenge officials who violate the law or act in any way contrary to the people's interests. The Fatherland Front educates the masses to nominate and vote for good candidates, to have lively debates and discussions on the candidates and issues. Without active participation by the people, democracy doesn't mean much. And we work for real democracy by controlling the officials who apply the laws.

Dung told me that both the Fatherland Front and the Women's Union have the right to draft and submit proposed laws to the National Assembly. When I checked the constitution in an English language version, I found that this privilege extends to the Confederation of Trade Unions, the Peasants Association and the Ho Chi Minh Communist Youth Union as well.

Dung's description of the functions of the Fatherland Front and the Women's Union does not satisfy my reservations about a one-party state, but it does indicate some attempts to minimize or counter some of its historic abuses. It also fits in with some things that Ngo Ba Thanh had said a few days earlier about attempting to deal with the problem head-on:

> I was trained in Western concepts of freedom and democracy and was uncomfortable with a constitution that said that the Communist Party runs the country without any opposition parties. That was the approach of the constitution of North Vietnam, as we understood it, and many people assumed that it would apply to the whole country after reunification. But I was elected to the National Assembly and I got the constitution changed to make it clear that many organizations can participate in the political process. The people participate through their mass organizations and through the Fatherland Front. The mass organizations nominate candidates for office—grass-roots, district and national—and they stand up for the rights of their members. The people must be protected from governmental abuses.

I was impressed by her words, but somewhat skeptical about how successfully they get implemented. So I asked her to spell out how this works in practice. She explained that

> Any citizen has the right to subject the Party to the rule of law. I do it as a non-Party member of the National Assembly, but anyone can do it. Anyone can get up a petition with complaints and present it to the mass organization to which they belong or to the People's Inspectors. There are local, regional and federal Inspectors. Every mass organization has the right to speak in the public hearings that are instituted as a result of these petitions, and in any court trials of officials that may result.
>
> I myself am a member of the Legal Rights Commission of the National Assembly and go to the provinces to see if the officials are carrying out the law properly, without abuses of human rights. Recently, I found a case in which the Director of Police was abusing the power of his office. He was brought to trial and sent to prison. Anyone could have instituted similar proceedings, though I'm sure it helped that I am on the Legal Rights Commission.
>
> One of the most active mass organizations is the Women's Union, which is constantly bringing cases concerning the abuses women suffer from, everything from violence at the hands of men to long established denials of equal rights. Men convicted of brutality against women are assigned to re-education classes or, if necessary, to six months in a re-education camp, a year in extreme cases.

When Thanh used the buzz words (for Americans) of "re-education camps," John McAuliff seized the opportunity to challenge her about sending *new* people to the camps, "when there are already ten thousand who have been there for ten years." I'm glad that he raised this question, but at the moment I was thinking along slightly different lines: If the Vietnamese are sending *new* people to the camps for such things as offenses against women, and holding them there for periods as short as six months, how many of the ten thousand have been there for ten years and how many are relatively new short-timers? All the critics, myself included, have been assuming that all ten thousand are leftovers from the immediate post-war years. If this is not the case, it might put the camps in a new light.

Unfortunately, Thanh's answer to John's question only touched indirectly on this aspect, when she mentioned that some of the original people had been released and then sent back for new crimes—including the crime of extorting bribes from people who wanted to leave as boat people. And, to my regret, I never returned to this important question—either then or in later discussions about the camps with Le Duc Tho and others. It was only after I got home and was going over my notes that I recognized a lost opportunity.

Thanh's response to John was to say that most of the long-termers are there because

> They are criminals who refuse to face up to their crimes, and be re-educated. A lot of them are people who were released once and have been sent back because of new crimes they have committed.
>
> In the United States, as in every society, Americans keep sending people to prison. What is so strange about the Vietnamese sending people to re-education camps? They are part of an international trend in the criminal system, an attempt to avoid the harshness of prison and the failure of prison to get at the roots of the personal and social problems that cause criminal acts.

I raised Amnesty International's charge that people are held in the camps without the "due process" of public trial in regular courts. To this, Thanh replied that no one was sent to the camps without going through "scrupulous administrative procedures." Knowing how few effective safeguards an indigent person of color has in our "public trials" in the United States, despite a bevy of constitutional and other "safeguards," I started to ask further about the effective rights of the accused in such "scrupulous" proceedings, but the discussion involved several people and the subject got changed back to Vietnam's attempts to educate and empower the people to participate more fully in the day-to-day political processes and to stand up for their rights against governmental abuses:

> Anyway, our main problem is not criminals but how to educate the people after forty years of slavery to assert their rights against authorities who violate the law. They are not used to this kind of freedom.

I offer the testimony of Dung and Thanh in this area without coming to any conclusions as to how vigorously and effectively the democratizing procedures are carried out.

On the cautionary side, I remember observing, way back in 1936 or '37 when I was a student at New College, Oxford, the impact on some of my fellow students and other English "progressives" of a report by the highly regarded Sidney and Beatrice Webb, after a trip they had made to the Soviet Union. From analyzing the New Soviet Constitution and talking with their hosts, the Webbs concluded that the Soviet Union was the most democratic country in the world. Even then I doubted it, on the basis of contrary evidence. But by now, no sane person could argue that the Soviet Union under Stalin was a functioning democracy, no matter what the theoretical provisions of the Soviet Constitution.

On the hopeful side, both Thanh and Dung (as well as Oanh and others whose integrity I respect, after checking it out for twenty years) make a generally positive case without minimizing the problems. They speak of the extent to which people in South Vietnam are beginning to stand up for their civil liberties, as they are encouraged to do by the mass organizations and the amended constitution. But they also speak of the difficulty of outgrowing old habits in the South, after years of governmental corruption and popular subservience. And Oanh made a point of calling my attention to a recent article in the press that he summarized as follows

> National leadership is in the hands of an older generation that is out of touch with modern developments—with the new situation and new ideas. We need to supplement the old leadership with a new leadership that is more abreast of a changed world.

"Before," he continued on his own,

> a minority ran everything, because of the necessities of wartime, and they are not used to the complexities of the new period. That is why we are working through the mass organizations to make openings for new, younger grassroots influences.

His summary and personal comments are typical of something I noticed in many of the people I probed these questions with. They made strong criticisms unhesitatingly while expressing confidence in the soundness of their system and form of government and talking about efforts they and others are making to improve things. They sounded a lot like civil libertarians in the United States who emphasize both that "power corrupts" and that "eternal vigilance is the price of liberty." But they sounded a lot more optimistic than a lot of our weary civil libertarians who have been fighting an uphill battle against the Reagan administration.

Civil Liberties in Context:
Vietnam and the United States

There are obvious differences in the context in which the struggle for civil liberties takes place in the two countries. In Vietnam, civil liberties are automatically linked to other basic human rights and freedoms—the right to the product of one's labor, for example, and the right not to live substantially below the level of others; freedom from want, for example, and freedom from economic exploitation.

A few excerpts from the Constitution suggest this:

> The rights and obligations of citizens reflect the system of collective mastery of the working people, a harmonious combination of the requirements of social life and legitimate individual freedoms...on the principle: each for all, all for each. [Article 54]
>
> Citizens enjoy freedom of speech, freedom of the press, freedom of assembly, freedom of association, and freedom to demonstrate in accordance with the interests of socialism and of the people.The State shall create the necessary material conditions for the exercise of these rights. [Article 67]
>
> The State is responsible for the protection and improvement of the people's health; combines modern and traditional medical and pharmaceutical practices; combines prevention and cure with the emphasis on prevention; and combines State-run health services with people's health services at the grassroots level. [Article 47]
>
> The State provides free medical examinations and treatment. [Article 61]
>
> Women and men have equal rights in all respects—in political, economic, cultural, social and family life.
>
> The State and society are responsible for raising the political, cultural, scientific, technical and professional standards of women, and constantly improving their role in society.
>
> The State establishes work conditions suited to women's needs. Women and men receive equal pay for equal work. Women are entitled to pre- and post-natal paid leaves...or to maternity allowances if they are cooperative members.
>
> The State and society ensure the development of maternity homes, creches, kindergartens, community dining halls and other social amenities to create favorable conditions for women to produce, work, study and rest. [Article 63]
>
> Collectives of working people at offices, factories, cooperatives, population centres and other basic units participate in State and social affairs, including the planning of economic and cultural development... [Article 11]

Within this context, there is a list of freedoms and rights, including the following:

> The right of ownership of lawfully earned incomes, savings, housing, other personal possessions and the means of engaging in authorized private work;
> the right of inheritance;
> freedom of worship and [to] practice or not practice a religion;
> [freedom from arrest] except on authority of a People's court...of the People's Control Commission or on a decision subject to ratification by the latter; and in accordance with the law;
> strict prohibition of all forms of coercion and torture;
> the right to protection by law with regard to their lives property, honor and dignity;
> the right of inviolability with regard to place of residence;
> privacy of correspondence and telephone and telegraphic communication;
> freedom of movement and residence.

Guarantees on paper are important, but we know that all governments tend to encroach on the proclaimed rights of their citizens unless they are held in check by dynamic citizens' movements to assert and protect them. Even apart from this, the Vietnamese approach, for all its attractiveness in adding inalienable human rights denied by the American system, creates two significant dangers: The first is that the government that sets out to implement these indispensable economic rights, health rights, women's rights etc. has a lot of power, becomes corrupted by it, and, in the interests of its own power, violates the rights of freedom of speech, assembly and protest, the guarantees against arbitrary arrest, etc. A second, related danger is that both the government and the general population put the economic and social objectives ahead of their commitment to civil liberties. The society's need to defend itself against those who would re-establish the old unjust order can serve as a coverup for suppression of opinions inimical to the government and repression of those who advance them.

During wartime, most governments of whatever kind restrict civil liberties and de facto press freedom. In the United States today, during peacetime, there is an increasing tendency to use "national security" as an excuse for classifying and witholding information vital to a genuine exercise of democracy. An artificially promoted Cold War serves as a cover for this. At another level, concern with muggings and other crimes committed by those growing up as losers in our society's class warfare has led to experiments with "preventive" arrests, denials of the right to bail, and other erosions of the rights of persons suspected of crimes or considered dangerous to the status quo. Obviously, it is not difficult for Vietnam's authorities to argue that their present besieged and "temporary" transitional state justifies similar, equally dangerous restrictions, or worse ones.

Despite these negative features, from what I could observe Vietnamese civil libertarians are buoyed by their belief that their state is organized on the principle of actively promoting the full welfare of all its citizens, with the underlying aim of creating a classless society. To them, this means that any violation of civil liberties (or of any other human right) is a violation of the society's accepted principles and can be challenged by any citizen or mass organization, as is their explicit constitutional right. But they are also very conscious that they have to struggle against the tendency of the society to put power into the hands of fallible officials who periodically encroach on civil liberties and need to be kept in check through the kind of active vigilance that Thanh and Dung emphasize and promote.

By contrast, civil libertarians in the United States are buoyed by the society's commitment to civil liberties, in the Bill of Rights and in a long tradition of court cases that periodically (if erratically) reaffirm this commitment. But they have to struggle against the tendency of the society to treat different categories of people unequally when they attempt to exercise these liberties. This is a direct consequence not only of the country's heritage of slavery and persistent racial prejudice, but also of the society's commitment to the principle of inequality of reward and status according to one's supposed talents, abilities, hard work, capital investments, etc.

We make a theoretical commitment to "equality of opportunity," but emphatically reject "socialistic" concepts of even a rough "equality of access" to the basic necessities of life and dignity, such as food, clothing, shelter, medical care and useful, gainful work. Civil liberties and freedom are inextricably linked not to the right of everyone to live on a level close to that of one's fellows, but to the right of the winners in our proudly competitive society to live substantially above the level of other people; not to everyone's freedom from want but to the freedom of those who accumulate or inherit capital (both individuals and corporations) to hire and fire and buy and sell in the pursuit of private profits—even if it causes other people to live in abject poverty.

On the positive side, all residents have the legal right to complain about (speak, write and demonstrate against) the resulting privations and injustices—and against the economic and political system that produces them. On the negative side, the rich and well established have tremendous power over the operations of the government and all its agencies that deal with such complaints, including administrative agencies, the Congress, the courts and the police. The results are often disastrous for the de facto civil liberties of the poor, people of color and those victimized by other prejudices. The white-collar crime of the rich and well established is treated entirely differently than the crimes of these people. All ten of the country's major arms manufacturers have been convicted of fraud involving millions or hundreds of millions of dollars—and possible loss of human life in military training exercises, let alone the consequences in actual warfare—but none of the perpetrators have gone to jail. At most they have to pay back, in fines, a portion of the money they have stolen.

I won't explore, here, the complicated matter of comparing Vietnam and the United States with respect to the existence, and impact on civil liberties, of other actual or potential prejudices, such as those concerning gender, sexual orientation, age, religion and physical, mental and emotional disabilities. We all know that all of these prejudices are rife in the United States. And we know, from the history of Cuba's treatment of homosexuals, that a society that dedicates itself to the attainment of economic democracy, as Vietnam has, can still hold to one or more of these social prejudices, with painful consequences for those against whom they are held.

Vietnam suffers from a one-party press and partially offsets this by the ability of the mass organizations (women's groups, producers' cooperatives, religious groups, youth groups, etc.) to publish their own materials (and carry on other activities of an educational nature) concerning matters affecting their members. In the United States, we benefit from legal guarantees of press freedom, and the importance of this should not be underestimated. But this is substantially undermined by the fact that, as A. J. Liebling once pointed out, in reality "We have freedom of the press for anyone with enough money to own one." Nowadays, this limits the ability to achieve a mass audience to mostly billionaire corporations that own television networks, newspaper chains and, increasingly, book publishing companies and chain book stores. The rest of us have more freedom to speak and write than we do to be heard and read, particularly if we are raising basic questions about either the morality or viability of the capitalist system.

Vietnam explicitly champions the right of the government to ban publications that challenge the dominant economic and political system by name. I find this offensive. But there is a surprising amount of free debate arguing for more or less private property, for more or less emphasis on state industries, for and against voluntary or compulsory membership by farmers in agricultural cooperatives—and of material of all kinds against both governmental bureaucracy and Communist Party Commandism. (See Chapters Nineteen and Twenty.) In addition, contemporary novels and short stories probe deeply into the combined human and political problems of the postwar society. Robert Shaplen, in the *New Yorker*, tells of a best-selling novel by a young Southerner named Nguyen Manh Tuan: .

> [It] is about the quarrels that take place in a fishing enterprise, first between the pre-Communist management and the workers and then between the Communist management and the

workers...in angry but sometimes humorous scenes of confrontation.

Shaplen also reports a proliferation of works dealing with bureaucracy and links this with the emphasis of governmental leaders on combatting both bureaucracy and subservience to the Party line. He quotes Le Duc Tho, "generally considered to be the No. 2 man in the Politburo," as saying in an important speech:

> It is necessary to eliminate the practice by certain localities of granting Party membership only to yes-men. District and precinct Party Commmittees and local-level Party Committees must find outspoken people who have, out of their concern for the common good, dared to denounce shortcomings and defend the truth.

Finally, he quotes Nguyen Dinh Thi, the head of the Writer's Association as follows:

> The older generation has a wider cultural canvas. Many of them know French and English, and they have read more. They... know about the past as well as the present. The new writers are mostly grass-roots types. Their weak point is that they have no perspective, no background, no basis of comparison. But they benefit from considering the new regime as their own, so in some ways they feel freer to criticize it frankly, and to attack its weaknesses. They have no complexes or hangups, so they show a greater freedom of spirit.[1]

In contrast to Vietnam, the U.S. government does not have the right to ban books because they oppose the dominant economic or political system or the country's foreign policy. And this, of course, is as it should be. But once again it is the rich and well established who control the institutions that can either circulate these arguments fairly to a mass audience or can ridicule them, distort them or ignore them altogether. Every night most Americans turn on the TV and have their news filtered for them through one or more of three networks and a cable news system, all of which are owned by giant profit-making corporations with substantial investments in the armaments industry.

One cannot discount Thanh or Dung and their optimism concerning de facto civil liberties in Vietnam lightly, given Thanh's history and both women's sincerity and readiness to exercise their freedom of speech concerning the failings of the Communist Party and its leadership. Thanh was beaten up and imprisoned without trial under the U.S./Nguyen Cao Ky regime; after a substantial period in prison (a year and a half, as I remember it), she was released, continued her criticism and opposition and was again imprisoned under the Thieu regime. In the end she spent six years in prison for her opposition to the totalitarian methods of the U.S. puppet regimes. I know less of Dung's history than of Thanh's, though I saw quite a bit of her when she was a member of the Vietnamese Mission to the United Nations for several years, and she impressed me then, as she did during this Vietnam trip, with her honesty and courage.

At one point, Thanh summed up her attitude toward the Party and government leaders by saying

> For forty years we had nothing but war. The people who lived through that are now running the country. It's not surprising if they don't know how to run it.

Present when she said it was a member of the Communist Party of Vietnam. This hardly fits with American images of a totalitarian society and a cowed population.

18

More on Reeducation Camps: Treatment of American and Vietnamese P.O.W.s

Arguing for Release of Prisoners Held in the Camps

I did have an argument with Ngo Ba Thanh about re-education camps. When John McAuliff and I challenged her about the presence of eight to ten thousand prisoners in the camps, at least some of whom have been there for ten years, she said that the camps are not prisons. I responded that that was ridiculous and no excuse for their continued imprisonment. "I served a year and a day," I told her, "in a federal facility in the United States that was called a Rehabilitation Center, but no one who was forcibly sent and held there would call it anything but a prison. If you can't leave and someone controls all the major aspects and petty details of your life, it's a prison."

I was a little happier with her report that inmates in the camps are allowed conjugal visits, a rare phenomenon in the United States and one of our demands, always denied, in any of the long-term prisons I have been in. In the hectic days following the end of the war, many of the prisoners were taken to camps in the North, but now most, perhaps all, have been transferred to camps in the Southern part of the country in order to facilitate family visiting.

On the fundamental question of holding or releasing the remaining inmates, Vietnam offered in June 1982 to release them all to the United States, if the United States would have them. But the United States refused the offer, saying that it would have to consider the prisoners on a case-by-case basis. Vietnam continued its offer for the next two-and-a-half years without ever getting a positive answer from

151

the United States. Apparently Washington thought it would better serve its propaganda objectives to let the prisoners remain in the camps as an example of Vietnam's repressive policies.

Finally, in December 1984, Vietnam's position changed. The change followed the arrest of 21 Vietnamese nationals on charges of sabotage and spying in behalf of the United States and its allies, Thailand and China, both of which border on Vietnam. Le Duc Tho told me, in May 1985, that they still want to release the re-education camp detainees to the United States, but that now they require assurances that none of them will be smuggled back into Vietnam to be used in such a role. In the United States, the spy trial was mostly presented as another example of Vietnamese political repression, but given the U.S.'s long history of sabotage, disinformation and spying in Vietnam, it doesn't seem unreasonable to think that Vietnam's charges are true and their current reservations justified.

Other Vietnamese I talked with mentioned not only this case and other cases of alleged spying and sabotage but also the murder, inside the U.S., of Dr. Ed Cooperman, director of the U.S. Committee for Scientific Cooperation with Vietnam. Cooperman had been working for normalization of relations between the two countries and had organized several trips of American scientists to Vietnam. He had received numerous death threats from right-wing gangs of Vietnamese refugees, who have committed a series of assaults on Vietnamese defenders of the current regime and are thought to have been responsible for some assassinations of Vietnamese in this country who advocate normalization of relations. No direct connection has been established between the young Vietnamese man who assassinated Cooperman and these gangs, but, not surprisingly, the Vietnamese are additionally concerned by this case and the other assassinations.

I don't have much doubt that some opponents of the regime have been imprisoned unjustly or for too long for their own good and the good of the society. But in discussing this with Than, Le Duc Tho and others, I was always conscious of the hypocritical nature of most American objections, even apart from Washington's refusal to agree to Vietnam's offer to release them for resettlement in the United States. Politicians, editorial writers and columnists berate Vietnam for holding people who, in many cases, are known war criminals, former collaborators with an invading foreign government that ravaged their country and killed about three million of their countrymen. Some of the puppet soldiers took suspected members of the Vietcong up in helicopters and threw them overboard; others worked with such American outfits as Colonel Lansdale's SMM teams, the C.I.A. and the Green Berets in activities that any civilized country would condemn. Although for a short time in the United States there was significant condemnation of such activities, their full extent was never brought out and today this background to the camps is all but forgotten. Our moralists one-sidedly condemn Vietnam for holding some of the Vietnamese participants in such crimes in prisons called re-education camps—and almost in the same breath call for vengeance against Nazi war criminals. Many of these critics demand that the United States throw teen-aged muggers into jail and throw away the key. Some of them support the death penalty and call for its extension to Americans who collaborate with a foreign power by spying for it. But these same people describe Vietnam as a totalitarian country, because of the re-education camps.

I certainly don't want Colonel Lansdale or his governmental sponsors (people such as Robert McNamara, my old college friends W.W. Rostow, William and McGeorge Bundy, and others) thrown in prison. And I want the Vietnamese prisoners released. But it's hypocritical for Americans holding the views I have mentioned to condemn Vietnam for having re-education camps.

In 1965, Quaker anti-war activist Norman Morrison was appalled by U.S. actions in Vietnam and decided to focus on the responsibility of Robert McNamara, then Secretary of War, a man thought to be more ambivalent than some of his colleagues about the legitimacy of the massive death and destruction the U.S. was imposing on that country. Norman didn't go to McNamara's office with a gun to try to kill him. Instead, he poured gasoline on himself, lit it and burned to death outside McNamara's Pentagon window. He did this as a dramatization of what was happening to Vietnamese victims of American napalm and as an appeal to McNamara (and presumably others) to come to his senses and reassert his humanity.[1]

It was an extreme act and not one that I recommend. But Norman Morrison was right in seeing that the proper response to criminality is not to fight lies with lies, murder with murder. He understood that the only way to break the vicious cycle is to find ways of bringing out and nurturing the repressed and atrophied instincts of love and universal unity in those who lie and kill. He was a disciple of Gandhi, and Gandhi had said that we should not allow our opponents to choose the methods by which we fight but should develop our own methods.

Fortunately, I had a revered Vietnam source to quote in my pleas for the release of those held in the camps, someone who had told me of his admiration for Norman. Always I cited a conversation I had had with Ho Chi Minh in 1966. Speaking of the American P.O.W.s, Ho had said:

> I don't have to tell you of the terrible things they have done. You have seen...the death and destruction they have rained on our people, on our towns and villages, schools, hospitals and churches. But we feel sorry for them because they have come thinking that they are helping the Vietnamese people, saving

them from some terrible thing called Communism. [At this point he gave a little laugh, that sounded to me as if he were a little self-conscious, perhaps even embarrassed at some of the crimes that have been committed in the name of communism. Maybe I was projecting my own sentiments, but if so they seemed to fit his mood and words.] We don't want to punish them and we don't want to keep them here. We want only that they be able to return to their homes better informed and better citizens of their own country and the world than when they did these things.

The Vietnamese always made a distinction between the American people and the U.S. government. Ho emphasized that this distinction included those who did the American government's dirty work as bombing pilots and foot soldiers. He spoke feelingly of his sympathy for the G.I.s who arrived in Vietnam convinced of their noble mission, only to be disillusioned by finding out that "even most of the anti-Communist Vietnamese don't want them here, don't want their help and want them to go home." I don't know if he knew, as we know now, that the South Vietnamese "invitation" to Washington to intervene in Vietnam had been drafted by U.S. officials in Washington. But he accurately read the sentiments of the South Vietnamese population, as I myself had been astonished to observe them in my visits to Saigon.

Always, in my pleas for the release of the people confined in the camps—in personal conversations and in a newspaper interview—I drew a parallel between the prisoners Ho Chi Minh spoke of and the Vietnamese prisoners, many of whom had also done "terrible things." Always I argued that if Ho could call for forgiveness of invading foreigners and for their return to "normal, useful lives," certainly they could forgive their fellow Vietnamese and release them.

Sometimes the Vietnamese response was to say that more than 90 percent of those who were originally subject to re-education processes are now free, with only hardened, recalcitrant criminals remaining in custody. Sometimes it was to point out that some of those they had already released had linked up with "foreign agents" to accumulate arms and engage in subversive plots. Thinking about what I knew from the *Pentagon Papers* and other sources of U.S. complicity in activities of this sort, I had no reason to doubt what the Vietnamese said. When Colonel Lansdale's team was polluting the bus company's oil reservoirs in Hanoi in 1954 and drawing up a list of targets for paramilitary attacks, none of us outside the government knew about it. It took seventeen years before it became known, and then only because Daniel Ellsberg courageously risked his freedom and released the secret *Pentagon Papers*.

One of the persons I talked with who had been subject to re-education processes and is now free is General Nguyen Huu Hang.

Hang is the former top figure in Saigon's anti-communist military and political efforts whom I mentioned earlier in connection with wartime collusion between the U.S. and China. He told me that after the regime's surrender he had been forced to attend two months of re-education classes but had not been confined in a camp. Later, still living at home, he participated in 18 months of additional classes. I think he said that the second classes were voluntary, but I would be surprised if he were not under considerable pressure to attend. He says the classes were conducted by the Fatherland Front and included examinations of Marxism-Leninism and other systems.

> "Let us compare the various systems," they said, and I did. But I still am not a Marxist Leninist. Now I am myself a member of the Fatherland Front and we no longer discuss capitalism and communism, only what is in the best interests of Vietnam.
>
> My son was killed by the N.L.F. We killed on both sides, we killed each other. Now we must put all that behind us and work together for the people of our country and for the future. When the Communist forces were overrunning the country and on the point of capturing Saigon, many of my colleagues fled. But many of us were patriots and stayed. We are nationalists. Now we are working for the good of our country. We have to put old hostilities behind us. Today it's not a question of communism and capitalism but of crucial matters such as how to improve the economy.

Listening to General Hang, I thought of how difficult it proved, after the U.S. Civil War—and how long it took—for Americans to "put old hostilities behind us."

Earlier in our conversation, General Hang had spoken about the Americans and his role in working with them.

> I thought that with the Americans we could have independence. But I found out that everything was under their control. They overthrew presidents and changed other officials. I experienced this myself when I commanded the ARVN forces in the delta, in the area near the Cambodian border. My American advisors told me to call for B52 bombers. But I flew over the designated territory and saw that it was populated by civilians and I said "No." They had me demoted to a Deputy Commander and filled my position with someone who agreed to the bombing. The B52s came in and it was a massacre of civilians. It was horrible.

Abuses Suffered by U.S. P.O.W.s

Of course the historical reality with respect to the P.O.W.s was never as simple or positive as quoting Ho's words would suggest. The Vietnamese held most of the prisoners as long as the war continued, holding out the promise of release without trials for war crimes as an inducement for the United States to end its invasion. Some of the P.O.W.s were beaten and tortured.

From time to time the Vietnamese released three P.O.W.s as a sign of good will and an indication of their eagerness to release them all. The first release came shortly after my 1966 visit, during which I had confronted Vietnamese officials with U.S. reports that the prisoners were being abused and were going to be tried as war criminals. A month or so after my return, I received a telegram asking me to come back to Vietnam to facilitate a prisoner release. Wanting others to have a first-hand experience of North Vietnam, I consulted with other anti-war leaders and we selected Father Daniel Berrigan and Howard Zinn to go.

The spirit of the first release was violated when the United States intercepted the three released P.O.W.s before they could get closer to home than U.S.-controlled Laos, returned them to an Air Force base in Thailand and reassigned them to new bombing missions in Vietnam. No one knows how many P.O.W.s this callous act caused to be held unnecessarily for many months or years. But after a delay, the Vietnamese government resumed the practice of limited releases, eventually arranging with me and other anti-war Americans that the P.O.W.s fly back through Peking, Moscow and Copenhagen. In all, four groups of three P.O.W.s were released between January, 1967 and August, 1972 with Cora Weiss, Reverend William Sloane Coffin, Richard Falk and I escorting the last three home.

Some P.O.W.s did suffer brutality at the hands of their guards. Besides the testimony of a few P.O.W.s, some of which is clearly genuine and some just as obviously exagerrated, my friend Oanh and others in Vietnam have admitted this to me. But they all assert that this was in clear violation of government policy and determined efforts to prevent it. They say that, not surprisingly, some individual guards took out their anger and resentments in terrible ways. Unwitting but impressive confirmation of this explanation comes from a recent article by Jack Anderson and Dale Van Atta. Writing about a spectacular U.S. commando raid on a purported P.O.W. camp at Son Tay, they write:

On Nov. 21, 1970, a force of 60 elite commandos landed in a secluded compound 23 miles west of Hanoi, deep inside North Vietnam. The men were told their mission was to liberate as many as 80 American P.O.W.s being held there.

Not a single P.O.W. was found...

The chief planner of the raid, Gen. Donald T. Blackburn, told our associate...years later: "We knew they [the P.O.W.s] had been moved. But we didn't want to give up the demonstration of power." The real purpose of the raid, he said, was to show the North Vietnamese how vulnerable they were.

According to this story, one of several positive results was that P.O.W.s were moved to Hanoi, where they received better treatment:

The treatment of American P.O.W.'s improved dramatically as they were moved into Hanoi for security. *It was "less likely that some sadistic sergeant out in the sticks" would mistreat them.* [Emphasis added][2]

Nothing can justify what some "sadistic" (or enraged) guards did. But we can be thankful that none of the P.O.W.'s were tried and executed for the war crimes that some of them clearly committed by carrying out orders in violation of the Geneva Conventions and the Nuremberg Principles, not just in many of the bombing targets and the use of outlawed types of bombs but by strafing civilians.

It is worth thinking about what would have happened if, during either the Vietnam War or World War II, an Asian had parachuted down in the United States after dropping napalm, anti-personnel fragmentation bombs or a gigantic explosive on a U.S. city, school or hospital. Or after strafing civilians. I wonder if he would have gotten to prison before he was lynched by enraged ("sadistic?") Americans, even if the official government policy was as enlightened as that voiced by Ho Chi Minh and the Vietnamese government.

For additional perspective, any long-term inmate in almost any American prison has experienced or knows of brutality by guards or officials that is comparable to that experienced in Vietnam's prisons by some of the P.O.W.s—or worse. In Lewisberg Federal Penitentiary, where I did two years as a war resister, it was a common practice of the guards and of the captain who was in charge of them to offer anything from parole to other favors to inmates who beat up other inmates who were giving the authorities trouble. While I was there, several were killed—at least one while guards were watching and egging on the killers. To cite only one of several instances in which I was the intended victim, at the conclusion of a sixty-five day hunger strike against prison racism and other abuses, I was taken, weak and dizzy, to a "fuck-up" dormitory of predominantly white Southern prisoners who had been convicted of violent crimes in the military—rape, murder, etc. The two guards who took me there told the prisoners that I was a "nigger-lover" who had been on strike to make them eat and sleep with "niggers" (the dining hall and dormitories were segregated), and was "a Nazi who spits on the flag." They then said that they would go away and not come back "until you take care of him." So I don't have a lot of difficulty believing Oanh and the others that individual guards did the things that Captain James Stockdale and a handful of other P.O.W.s say happened to them—and even believing that some individual prison authorities condoned such things.

Abuses Suffered by Vietnamese P.O.W.s

When I mentioned these incidents of prison abuse to Le Duc Tho, he said

> If some did suffer abuses, we regret it. We don't condone such things. But none of them were killed, no matter what they had done. But on Phu Quoc Island [a notorious South Vietnamese prison supervised by American "advisers"], our prisoners were tortured and mistreated to death. Today there are five thousand graves of such victims on Phu Quoc island.

Tho's comment about Phu Quoc Island is supported by the courageous testimony of three American G.I.s at the Bertrand Russell War Crimes Tribunal in Copenhagen, in 1967—and by many conscientious veterans today, including some I work with myself.[3] At Copenhagen, each of the three—Peter Martenson, a trained interrogator of Vietcong prisoners, David Tuck, a black infantryman, and Donald Duncan, a sergeant in the Green Berets—gave gruesome testimony concerning the treatment of NLF prisoners by their American and South Vietnamese captors and interrogators. One has to recognize that the types of treatment they reported had to be common knowledge among the Vietnamese, undoubtedly contributing to the anger and contempt that some of them took out on the P.O.W.s. Of course its a terrible two-way process. Some on each side use the brutality of the other as a reason for exploding into brutality themselves. Veterans invariably testify, as these three did in Copenhagen, that whatever reservations they arrived in Vietnam with about killing in cold blood, after they had seen their buddies blown up by a mine or killed in combat, they were ready to pull out all the stops.

The Tribunal heard more than a hundred pages of testimony that made it clear that torture was commonplace. I'll only mention a couple of examples. Private David Tuck testified:

> I happened to be on a work detail at a place called Camp
> Holloway, which is right outside the town of Pleiku, and while
> I was there I saw a V.C. being tortured by the South Vietnamese
> under the direction of U.S. forces. When I got there they had the
> man tied on the ground; he was spreadeagled. They were using a
> knife to sort of pry under his toenails and the soles of his feet.
> When this got no results they went on to other more sensitive
> parts of the body. Well, this still got no results, because
> evidently this man was, as we say in America, a tough nut to
> crack. So then after that they put the knife under his eyeball in
> another endeavor to make him talk, and he still wouldn't talk.
> So then what they did, they put him in a barbed-wire cage in
> which he was on his hands and knees. And if he made any moves
> the barbs of the barbed wire would press into his flesh, so they
> kept him there for two days. And I had to go back on another
> detail, and when I got back the man was gone. I assume that they
> had turned him over to the South Vietnamese to execute him.[4]

Tuck continued with another instance of a different sort:

> Now it was the practice of our outfit to rotate men back and forth
> to base camp to give them a few days rest. So on that day, I
> believe it was about at 1400 hours, on that day I boarded a
> "Huey" helicopter. On this helicopter there was the pilot, the
> co-pilot, the machine-gunner, myself. There were also two dead
> American soldiers and two North Vietnamese prisoners. Well,
> while we were on there, one of the North Vietnamese pointed to
> one of the U.S. dead and started to laugh about it, see. So the
> shotgunner, he saw this, and he told the pilot about that, and
> the pilot said: "Throw the S.O.B. out." So he picked up the
> man, the man was tied anyway, bound, and threw him out of the
> helicopter... So then when we got back to base camp, you know,
> such a thing is an everyday thing. You know, we did not think
> too much about it.
>   ...Our officers, they told us that would be our policy ["to
> execute prisoners"]. That we weren't going to take any prisoners
> unless we happened to capture an officer and then there was an
> American officer there to decide that he should be saved;
> otherwise we were to get rid of him... But this is very common,
> the shooting of prisoners. Like I said before, the only time our
> officers wanted us to keep a prisoner was if it was an officer,
> because we figured that he can tell us something. But we figured
> that if he's just an enlisted man, he really can't tell us anything,
> so if he's wounded and we're in a hurry to move on, then we just
> executed him anyway.

I don't want to string this out with details of other, similar acts of torture or of G.I.s who "just go over and shoot him [the NLF prisoner] in the head to be done with it." Instead, I'll fill out the picture with a couple of quick references to what happened away from the field of battle in prisons similar to the one at Phu Quoc Island. For that, here are a few sentences from the testimony of a Vietnamese woman, Mrs. Pham Thi Yen, together with the corroborative testimony of "dissident" Truong Nhu Tang, in *Vietcong Memoir*.

Yen said that she was arrested "right in the streets of Saigon [by] the U.S.-Diemist security police."

> They tied my two arms behind my back, then hauled me up to the ceiling by strong cords attached to my wrists. They beat me with sticks, stopping only when I fainted. Then they let me down, throwing cold water over my face. Little by little I recovered consciousness... This was repeated I don't know how many times. They called this operation: "ride in a Dakota."... After a moment's rest, they applied the "ride in a submarine." They undressed me and tied me, face upward, to a plank. A towel was used to tie my head to the plank, a rubber tube led from a 200-liter barrel, fixed to a stand. The water fell drop by drop onto the towel, soon flooding my face. To breathe, I sucked in water through my nose and mouth. I was suffocating, my stomach started to swell like a balloon. I could no longer breathe and I fainted.

Yen says that when she regained consciousness, two commandos stamped on her chest and stomach to get the water out of her, causing her to vomit through her mouth and nose, "with blood pouring out. This was repeated several times." After that she suffered three other forms of equally horrible "treatment." Then she was tied to a kaki tree, covered with poisonous yellow ants and finally, "after ten hours of torture" and threats—"your children will be tortured in front of your eyes; your parents, your brothers and sisters will be imprisoned"—she was finally thrown into a cell.

Yen's descriptions are corroborated by Tang, who tells of being shackled to a bench, face up, having a compress put over his eyes and nose, his mouth wrenched open and soapy water poured down his throat until he lost consciousness.

> When I came to, one of the guards was pressing heavily on my stomach, forcing me to vomit... (Although I didn't know it then, the soapy water kills all intestinal flora, leaving a permanently damaged digestive system.) I jerked my head around, struggling to avoid drowning in the flow of my own vomit.[5]

Tang says that he would not have lived except for a fortuitous prisoner exchange which led to his being transported to rebel headquarters in the jungle.

I conclude by quoting Peter Martinson, a former Prisoner of War Interrogator with the 541st Military Intelligence Detachment in Vietnam, who was trained at the U.S. Army Intelligence School in Fort Holabird, Maryland. He added his own descriptions of brutal prisoner interrogations that he had either observed or conducted. In some of them, the prisoners had survived; in others they had not. He summed up his experiences as follows:

> I can't think of an interrogation that I saw in Vietnam during which a war crime, as defined by the Geneva Conventions, was not committed. I cannot think of one without harassment or coercion. Even where force was not used, coercion, such as beating, torturing and harassment...was used... All of our interrogators had participated in actual torture...
>
> Then you realize, because everybody participates in the torture—unless we have a special group of sadists working as interrogators, which I don't believe; I believe they are just normal people—you realize that there is an innate capability to do harm to your fellow man in proper circumstances, and these circumstances are provided by the war in Vietnam. It's so horrifying to recall an interrogation where you beat the fellow to get an effect, and then you beat him out of anger, and then you beat him out of pleasure. That is what is horrible to say.

Two wrongs don't make a right, but I think it's clear why the Vietnamese resent self-righteous accusations from Americans that whatever abuses of P.O.W.s did take place are indication of the barbaric nature of the Vietnamese Communists and the system they espouse, reasons enough for the U.S. intervention and for continued hostility and economic warfare today.

For Americans to accept this self-righteous approach, as promoted by the government and media, will not help us come to terms with either our past or our present. We can't undo the past, but we can change the present. We can insist on an end to the government's punitive treatment of Vietnam and the opening of normal diplomatic relations as a long overdue first step toward "healing the wounds of war." And we can insist that the government stop replaying its Vietnam crimes, in one form or another, in Central America, Angola, South Korea, the Middle East and too many other places around the world.

Behind the Problems in Vietnam's Economy: A Further Look at the Boat People

According to their own accounts, the Vietnamese made serious mistakes in their early efforts to speed up the transition from a wartime to a peacetime economy. These interacted with the lingering effects of an unprecedented wartime destruction of the country's productive resources and a number of geopolitical factors beyond Vietnam's control to produce a grim economic situation from which the country is only gradually and partially emerging. Let us look at all three problem areas, in reverse order, before examining some of the changes Vietnam has made to undo its mistakes and the mixed economy that currently exists.

When the Americans left, Vietnam automatically lost an average of a billion and a half dollars a year that the U.S. had been spending in the South. It was money that had seriously corrupted major elements of the population and had turned South Vietnam into a non-productive, consumer society, but it had artificially kept a bankrupt economy afloat. At the same time, China made drastic reductions in the material and technical aid that it had been providing the North (climaxed in July, 1978, by cancellation of that year's promised aid package of 300 million dollars).

After World War II, the United States had supplied humanitarian assistance and massive funds for reconstruction and development to Germany, Italy and Japan. But Vietnam was different. As John McAuliff has written

A poll in the *New York Times* of July, 1977 showed that two thirds of Americans supported sending food and medicines to Vietnam, and a majority favored economic assistance which would have helped the country rebuild. The failure [to do so] lay in the political leadership of our country—perhaps no surprise, since their defeat in war had not driven them from positions of power. Besides having an understandably vindictive feeling toward the uppity people who had successfully defeated the world's greatest power, they needed to ensure that postwar Vietnam was as terrible a place as possible...as a retroactive justification for the U.S. war effort [and] as a basis for attacking opponents of the war.[1]

So, despite the precedent and the commitments the U.S. had made in Article 21 of the Paris Peace Agreement, it supplied none of the help that might have contributed to "healing the wounds of war," economically as well as spiritually. Instead it placed an embargo on trade with Vietnam and imposed severe restrictions on private humanitarian assistance, including food, medicine and agricultural equipment. Finally, it used its influence to stop the World Bank and the International Development Fund from making loans to Vietnam and brought pressure on its Western Allies to withhold assistance, pressures that kept their financial aid at a minimum and in some cases eliminated it altogether.

As if these obstacles were not more than enough for Vietnam to deal with after forty years of war, Pol Pot's Cambodia, with arms supplied by China, began making sporadic raids on Vietnamese border towns as early as May of 1975, a few weeks after the collapse of the Saigon regime. The attacks gradually increased in frequency and intensity, destroying properties, creating refugees and diverting scarce Vietnamese resources. Finally, in December 1978, Vietnam responded by invading Cambodia and overthrowing the genocidal Pol Pot.

Vietnam compared its action to the Allied invasion of Nazi Germany and fascist Italy to get rid of Hitler and Mussolini. But neither the U.S. nor China saw it that way. And less than two months after the Vietnamese invasion, China launched its own four-pronged invasion of Vietnam, with a hundred thousand troops, "to teach it a lesson." Besides killing approximately 20,000 Vietnamese (and suffering similar losses of their own) the Chinese troops, before being driven back to China, succeeded in completely destroying over 300 villages, four sizeable towns, all the factories in the area, a railroad line, a power plant and a phosphate mine that was the country's main source of fertilizer for Vietnam's all-important agriculture. Six years later, Robert Shaplen wrote that

Vietnam will have to import more than a million tons of fertilizer a year until the phosphate plant destroyed in the 1979 war with China is once again able to function at full capacity.

> And restoring it requires other resources the country lacks... In both fertilizer and cement production, as well as in other industries, oil is needed, for which the Vietnamese are now totally dependent on the Russians.[2]

Totally dependent on the Russians because of the U.S.-sponsored embargo by non-communist nations.

Justified or not, the invasion of Cambodia saddled Vietnam with a costly occupation, without putting an end to border attacks. The main difference is that since 1979 the attacks have come from the Thai border with Cambodia and have been against Vietnamese troops stationed in Cambodia and against the Vietnamese-supported Cambodian regime, not against Vietnamese civilians in their own country. As before the attacks have been carried out by Pol Pot's Khmer Rouge armies, with arms and advisors supplied by China, but now with the addition of political and token military support from Prince Sihanouk, Son Sen and other aggrieved anti-Pol Pot, anti-communist, Cambodian nationalists. It's not clear how early the C.I.A. began supplying assistance to anti-Vietnam forces, but it would be surprising if U.S. agents were not involved from the beginning, in the attacks on Vietnam itself. By now it's an open secret that the U.S. is aiding the Cambodian contras. To add to Vietnam's problems, the invasion (combined with Chinese and U.S. pressures) caused the withdrawal of more than two hundred million dollars a year of Western European and Japanese aid.

The Boat People

Is it any wonder that by 1979 the Vietnamese economic situation had become catastrophic? This was the period of the massive exodus of the boat people, an exodus that was hailed in the United States as proof of its two major theses: that communism doesn't work; and that Vietnam is a totalitarian country from which its people flee to Western freedom. An interesting sidelight on this is that when Salvadorans and Guatemalans flee from the air attacks or death squads of U.S.-supported regimes, the U.S. insists that they are coming to the United States for purely economic reasons—and ships them back to face a double risk, as identified opponents of the regime.

Some comments about the boat people's plight are relevant, beginning with the obvious point that the U.S. wept crocodile tears for them without ever offering to work out arrangements with Vietnam to provide asylum and send ships and planes to transport them in a safe and orderly fashion (or even to rescue them from the perils of the ocean and of pirate attacks). It could have done so without absolving Vietnam from its failures to handle the crisis better. But Washington preferred to let the sufferings of the boat people serve as living proof that Vietnam was indeed "a terrible place," without ever mentioning that its own punitive actions had helped make it so. Here are some additional observations from an article I wrote during the height of the exodus:[3]

It is amazing how selective the media's indignation is. When Malaysia tows overladen boats back to sea, many to sink or fall prey to marauding pirates, *Time* says that "Malaysia insists, fairly enough, that it simply cannot afford to take care of so many exiles." *Time* doesn't stop to ask, with equal "fairness," whether Vietnam can afford to take care of so many exiles from U.S.-devastated areas in South Vietnam and China-invaded areas in the North...

Chris Mullin, a British journalist with Southeast Asia credentials and formerly employed by the BBC, reminds us of the numbers and backgrounds of the internal exiles Vietnam has to cope with:

"When the Vietnamese Communists took power in Saigon ...because the suddenness of their victory was unexpected, they captured nearly the entire ruling class of South Vietnam. The Americans had time to take with them only about 20,000 of their most committed friends. Behind they left a South Vietnamese army and police force of 1.2 million men...over 300,000 civil servants, and a huge community of rich merchants and wheeler dealers—mainly of Chinese origin—none of whom could expect to maintain their old lifestyle under the new order. Many...had already fled South from the Communists in 1954, but this time they had nowhere else to run... There were large numbers of prostitutes, drug addicts, and refugees from the countryside, none of whom had any means of supporting themselves."

...Nor are Vietnam's boat people Southeast Asia's only refugees. Besides the unfortunates fleeing Vietnam, Chinese citizens, displaced or displeased by China's recent moves to the right, have been flooding into Hong Kong at the rate of 40,000 or more a month for the last six months.

...We read in the June 29 [1979] *New Statesman* that: "Behind Mrs. Thatcher's decision to send 1,000 more troops to Hong Kong [to police its border with China] lies *a deeper tragedy than the well-publicized plight of the Vietnamese boat people*... [Emphasis added.]

Asia Week states that: "In Vietnam...the West has a direct accountability, stemming from the wars it fought there, for the situation that has produced the refugee crisis... U.S. reluctance to normalize relations with Hanoi is perhaps the most important factor behind the current predicament..."

In support of this interpretation, a U.N. official surveying the situation in Vietnam told an American delegation headed by David Stickney of the American Friends Service Committee that "if Vietnam were to receive sufficient economic aid, the refugee problem would disappear."

"In a brutal Catch-22 manner, the government is charging even those people it wants to exile for the privilege of leaving. The price apparently averaged about $2,000 per person, payable in gold or hard currency." So charges *Time* magazine, but Chris Mullin of the Pacific News Service reports that: "Syndicates based in Los Angeles and Hong Kong are said to be charging around $2,000 a head for passage. They are assisted by corrupt officials—many of them former servants of the Thieu regime who are now back in their old jobs after a spell in re-education camp."

...Mullin's account makes more sense. Corruption aside, there are few if any boat owners or brokers who offer free passage. And interviews with a number of refugees support this version. One refugee told the *Hong Kong Star* that: "I owned my house, had two cars, and my children went to an upperclass French-language school. [However] the Communists introduced policies for increased production and equality among the people. Before they could asssess my property, I sold it and bought gold as I knew there were syndicates operating to get people out of the country illegally."

So what some people consider "Communist Tyranny" may be necessary steps to increase production in a desperately poor country and establish rough "equality" among the people.

"Necessary steps" perhaps, but as we now know, poorly planned and without adequate sensitivity to either the human or the pragmatic economic factors involved. However, before looking at this aspect, let us continue with our examination of externally imposed factors that were essentially beyond Vietnam's control, except through a long, drawn-out process of remedial action.

Some Little Known But Economically Disastrous Effects of the War

There are some long-term physical effects of the war that seriously interfere with economic recovery, but are virtually unknown by the American public and, for probably obvious reasons, are never mentioned by the U.S. critics of Vietnam.

Before the U.S. war, Vietnam's major export was rubber. In all, approximately 350,000 acres in the South were occupied by rubber trees. Long before the war's end, virtually all of these had been destroyed. Those that had not been killed by bombing and chemical defoliation had been systematically uprooted by U.S. bulldozers as part of the effort to force the peasants out of the countryside and into concentrations where they could be more easily controlled—Strategic Hamlets and, later, a few major cities; Saigon's population, for example, tripled in a few years.

The Vietnamese have been slowly replanting rubber trees and currently have about 200,000 acres under cultivation, but it takes five to seven years before a tree can be tapped and begin to produce.

Tea, coffee and jute are also traditional Vietnamese export items but here too virtually all the plantations were destroyed and the soil polluted with chemicals. They are being slowly and painfully reclaimed.

Much of the other agricultural land was rendered unusable by chemical spraying, mines and unexploded bombs.

The Vietnamese say that before the U.S. left it dropped special small bombs that require two impacts before they explode. The first impact activates the trigger when the bomb hits the ground and, if it is fertile soil, buries itself. The second occurs when a farmer is plowing his field, with the assistance of a water buffalo or by hand. Several thousand peasants have been killed by such bombs in the last ten years and thousands of others have lost a limb or suffered other serious injuries. In 1975, one of the former negotiators of the Paris Peace Accords told me with real bitterness (rare in most conversations with Vietnamese[4]) that there had been an understanding with Henry Kissinger that the U.S. would supply bulldozers or other heavy equipment to clear the fields of unexploded bombs—as part of its commitment to Article 21—but of course it never happened.

In 1977, a U.N. report estimated that a million-and-a-half water buffalos and oxen had been killed during the war. One of my saddest experiences during my wartime visits was to hear of the U.S. policy of strafing the water buffalos from low flying airplanes. It was more than the slaughter of the animals and the destruction of an important agricultural force in an industrially undeveloped country in which tractors were virtually unknown. On my very first visit, I met a young woman whose younger brother had been killed while tending the family's water buffalo. After that I noticed that around every water buffalo's neck was a rope, and at the end of every rope was a small child. There was no fencing in rural Vietnam and it was the duty of a child to lead the animals from one pasture spot to another, keeping them out of the rice paddies. On all my subsequent visits I met others whose children or siblings had suffered a similar fate. In 1967, a badly scarred nine-year-old boy, Do Van Ngoc, was brought by Vietnamese doctors to the Copenhagen session of the International War Crimes Tribunal. He had been dive-bombed with napalm while tending his family buffalo.[5]

All of these acts conform to guidelines established by the U.S. Airforce. A manual used by the U.S. Air Force ROTC, Air Force University, entitled "Fundamentals of Aerospace Weapons Systems'

Manual" was introduced into evidence at the same Tribunal. Here are a few excerpts:

> a military target is any person, thing, idea, entity, or location selected for destruction, inactivation, or rendering nonusable with weapons which will reduce or destroy the will or ability of the enemy to resist.
>
> Targets within a nation fall into four categories, military, economic, political and psychosocial.
>
> The psychosocial structure of a nation includes the moral strength of the people... For purposes of target study, the psychosocial structure of a nation or people is often reduced to terms of morale.
>
> Some of the conventional targets for morale attacks have been water supplies, food supplies, housing areas, transportation centers, and industrial sites. The objectives of these attacks in the past have been...to create unrest, to reduce the output of the labor force, to cause strikes, sabotage, riots, fear, panic, hunger...
>
> While the use of toxic chemicals is closely controlled at a high level, chemical warfare is very much the business of the Air Force.
>
> Both biological and chemical attack may be made against crops. Crop destruction would affect the food supply of both man and domestic animals, and destroy sources of essential oils, medicines and industrial raw products.

Perhaps this is the place to mention one type of terror "Aerospace Weapon" that does not apply as directly to Vietnam's current economic difficulties but was extensively used in Vietnam to create "fear," "panic," etc. in the civilian population—the anti-personnel or fragmentation bomb. A huge "mother bomb," as the Pentagon called it—with a strange sense of motherhood—carried 640 smaller, "guava" bombs, each of which released between 240 and 300 tiny pellets (depending on the type of bomb). Each large bomb, therefore, released between roughly 150,000 and 190,000 of these deadly pellets. They were useless against wood, stone, cement, sandbags, earthworks, even thatch, but could penetrate human flesh with terrible results.

The Russell Tribunal heard extensive evidence concerning these bombs at its first session in May 1967, evidence from military and medical experts and from on-the-spot observers. (I myself had been present, some months before the Pentagon's denial, when a few unexploded guava bombs had been gathered in a civilian bombed-out area and had brought one home with me. At my first press conference I passed it around and it mysteriously "disappeared," evidently appropriated by an efficient government agent posing as a reporter.) Because of the public interest and press inquiries that resulted from the

Tribunal's proceedings, the Pentagon issued a public denial that it had ever used any such bombs. But by the time the second Tribunal met six months later, we had copies of Pentagon documents sent out to major weapons's manufacturers requesting bids for the contracts to manufacture these bombs.

"Conventional" Bombing

Besides these lesser known human tragedies and economic costs of U.S. war policy, there are the more obvious costs of the better known massive bombings with high explosives. But even here, the full extent of the bombing was never quite grasped (for all the temporary indignation it aroused in the United States and around the world). By now, it has faded from public discussions and rarely enters into media accounts of why Vietnam is not better off than it is, ten years after the end of the war. Robert Muller, National President of Vietnam Veterans of America, and a paraplegic U.S. victim of the war, supplies some important information:

> In the Second World War, we dropped 2.5 million tons of bombs in Europe and the Pacific; in Vietnam, by air alone we dropped over seven million tons. When you add to that naval artillery and other explosives we dumped on that country, it totals more than fourteen million tons of explosives dropped on Vietnam— the most heavily bombed country in the history of the world... One out of thirty people in all of Indochina was killed. One out of twelve was wounded. And one out of five was made a refugee. Add to that what happened after the war—natural disasters, flood, famine, typhoons—and you can start to appreciate just what kind of rubble and disaster confront the efforts to begin rebuilding Indochina.[6]

I won't try to add up the physical toll of all this, and couldn't if I wanted to—the number of factories and quantities of industrial equipment destroyed, the costs in human labor and materials of replacing homes, schools, hospitals, churches, rail lines etc. But I will mention one crippling factor that has a lot to do with Vietnam's years of post-war poverty: the almost total destruction of its electrical power plants and the years it takes to replace them with modern new ones. As Robert Shaplen wrote in the *New Yorker*,

> Along with the shortage of oil, there is a dire need for electric power... A huge hydroelectric power plant being built by the Russians at Hoa Bin...is scheduled for completion in the early nineteen-nineties...and no one knows whether the Russians may run out of patience or money... And even when Hoa Binh is finished, it cannot function without vast reconstruction of the

country's run-down electricity-distribution grid...and the Russians insist that Vietnam will have to bear part of the cost. The Vietnamese hope that they will eventually be able to obtain aid for the reconstruction from the West, including the United States, which is still regarded as having an obligation to "heal the wounds of war," though the phrase is heard less often these days.[7]

On top of all these immense problems, the Vietnamese made serious mistakes, especially in the early post-war years, as they are the first to tell any open-minded visitor. What were some of these mistakes and what have they been doing to try to correct them? What is the economy like these days?

Vietnam's Economic and Political Mistakes and the Nature of Its Marxism-Leninism

Le Duc Tho's analysis of Vietnam's mistakes in the immediate post-war years can be summed up as follows: We tried to go too fast with too little peacetime experience, too few management skills, too much emphasis on rapid industrialization, and too much reliance on the centralized decision-making that had been a wartime necessity.

Virtually every Vietnamese I talked with agreed with this diagnosis. I heard it from government officials, from bitter opponents of the regime, and from a range of people in between. I heard it from a dissident former English translator for a U.S. general, who initiated a lengthy conversation with me in a cafe, and from a waiter, in another cafe, who readily told me that he had tried to flee in a boat, had been stopped, held for two days and released without penalties to return to his old job. I heard it from enthusiastic supporters, such as Oanh, Thanh, Dung and many others. And I heard it from people such as Dr. Hoa, Nghi and Phan, who spent a lot of time complaining about the mistakes but made it clear that the present government and situation were incomparably superior to anything that had existed under the cruel and corrupt U.S.-Saigon regimes.

The differences came mostly in the degree of emphasis different people placed on the centralized and bureaucratic decision-making (or "commandism," as some officials candidly called it), and whether they thought the party had shown itself capable of moving seriously away from it. Neither the waiter nor the former translator was willing to concede that there has been any move away from centralized, authoritarian controls. But most of the people I talked with, in and out of the government, felt differently.

171

Le Duc Tho spoke to me much as he had spoken to Robert Shaplen a few months earlier:

> Our management during the war was bureaucratic; that is, the government directed and supplied everything. You can call it conservative. After liberation, this method was no longer applicable. We have had to find ways of combining unified leadership from the center with extending to the provinces and districts the right to solve their own problems, to become more dynamic by themselves.[1]

Le Mai, one of the younger high officials, told me that

> After 1975, we were too much centralized and attempted too quick an industrialization. It was unrealistic. For example we lacked the electricity required for industrialization. All of our power stations had been bombed out. We managed to get some smaller ones into use by 1978, but the major ones take ten to fifteen years to complete.

And the official Party historian, Nguyen Khac Vien, in a published interview in 1980, gave another example:

> In some cases people have tried to go too fast and set up cooperatives which were too large for the equipment available and the managerial ability of the present cadres.[2]

The new cooperatives he referred to were were mostly set up in the newly liberated South. Yet, as the *Far Eastern Economic Review* recently reminded its readers, by 1975, after the losses suffered in the 1968 Tet offensive and the C.I.A.'s Phoenix program of political assassinations,

> Few of the surviving Party members in the South had skills which were relevant to the new period, and none of them had experience in administration.[3]

(Incidentally, this appraisal has to be borne in mind when considering the claims by American critics and people like Trung Nhu Tang that the North pushed aside the Southern leadership after reunification.)

The *Review* explains the unrealistic attitude as follows:

> [They] wanted to tackle socialist development with a speed and daring to equal the final campaign of the war. The result of their overconfidence was chaos and a near catastrophe for the country.

Like Dung, Vien labels this attitude "utopianism" and he spells out some of the consequences:

> Utopians want to skip stages, with no heed for reality, from there to the belief that human will by itself can overcome all

obstacles is only a short step. A short step too to the belief that those who don't think as you do are backward or reactionary. And a short step to the economic errors which lead to artificial shortages and avoidable conflicts. The food shortages and the lack of consumer goods, which were caused by the long years of war and the natural disasters were aggravated by such errors.

This is a remarkably forthright description of the trap that Vietnam's leaders fell into after the war, thereby compounding its already stupendous post-war problems. At the same time, it coincidentally provides an uncanny description of what is currently happening in the United States under far different circumstances. Here too there is an illusion that the human will by itself can overcome all obstacles without taking realistic stock of what they are. It is central to the Reagan administration's cheery propaganda that an unquestioning commitment to a vague and highly romanticized American way (and leave the details to us) will provide the capital investments, the military strength and above all the *will* to overcome all our problems by evading them. And the belief that "those who don't think as you do are backward or reactionary," can be seen in the administration's notion that all our difficulties in Third World countries are caused by reactionary Marxist-Leninists in Cuba and Moscow and all our domestic problems by reactionary, big-spending politicians who advocate non-military governmental programs to promote the minimal health, safety, dignity and wellbeing of our people.

And there is another parallel. In addition to the problems caused in Vietnam by the early post-war utopianism of the Vietnamese leaders, it wasn't long before they had to deal with a different sense of reality, in their own ranks and throughout the populace. The following analysis by a Western diplomat in Hanoi seems realistic, at least until things began to change in the last couple of years:

> Everything since the war here has been anticlimactic. What kept people going for so long, against the French and then against the Americans, was the siege mentality, and it provided a remarkable drive and force. But now that the big wars are over there is no substitute for its elan, and this accounts for the malaise... And for...an unfocussed discontent among the younger cadres... They're missing something, but they don't know what it is or how to get it.[4]

This sense of missing something and not knowing how to get it was widespread in the United States after a war that stimulated a lot of adrenalin and domestic conflict but for most Americans provided no elan, not even when they thought the U.S. was winning. Only in sections of the anti-war movement was there elan, mixed with anguish. For many of the latter, the period of post-war let-down is now past, but they face new problems. Today, activists for justice and peace must struggle against the dispiriting phenomenon of working in competition with a President who is amazingly successful at concealing the brutality of his policies behind the attractiveness of a down-home style of what appears to be blunt talk and personal integrity. He accomplishes this with mirrors—the concealed teleprompter from which he reads his "simple, heart-felt" words, as written for him by skilled speechwriters. And the illusion is perfected by a consummate acting ability and perfect type-casting. Clearly Reagan's personality fits the role. It's not important to speculate on whether he is totally sincere, a skillful liar or something in between. Perhaps he just doesn't care about the words he reads so long as he is getting the programs he wants and enjoying the glory of his office. What is important is that the image he presents is about as relevant to the content of his programs as the carefree, smiling singers and dancers are to the products they advertize in today's commercials. For millions of Americans, the illusion is created that at long last we are finally on the right track, getting the things that we were missing and that neither Reagan's high-level political rivals nor any of the grassroots resistance movements can provide. The United States, at last, is fighting victoriously on the side of justice, liberty and traditional American values.

Fortunately, Vietnam has no such shallow, dominant leader to sing siren songs of enchantment in behalf of programs that are leading step by step to disaster. Instead, it has a combination of national and local leaders who speak openly about the complexities and mistakes, and, at least for now, are responding positively to grassroots initiatives that seem to work and offer possible solutions to the country's difficulties (See Chapter Twenty-One).

Vietnam's Ambiguous Heritage of Marxism-Leninism

The question remains, however: How deep does the tendency to commandism go in the Vietnamese Workers Party and the government? For in addition to the government's post-war overconfident eagerness to skip stages and make an unrealistic "great leap forward," for which they lacked the material resources and the managerial skills, one has to remember the extension into the postwar period of the wartime habit of "commandism."

In my view, the Vietnamese make a mistake when they blame this grievous violation of sound politics and healthy human relations exclusively on habits created by war-time necessities. I think it also stems from their leaders' tendency to identify their drives for freedom and justice with the doctrines of Marxism-Leninism. Yet, I am convinced that this identification is both largely accidental and in conflict with the more compassionate (and pragmatic) commitment to basically egalitarian attitudes that keeps asserting itself. I originally drew this conclusion about the accidental and contradictory nature of their espousal of Marxism-Leninism from my extended conversations over the years with Vietnam's "Marxist-Leninists," about their views not so much on theoretical ideology as on concrete down-to-earth questions. But recently I came across a statement made in 1983, by Roger Hilsman, a former Kennedy official, that expresses the same view:

> I think that most people who have studied Vietnam deeply would agree that the principle force at work was not "worldwide Communism" but an anti-colonialist, nationalist movement... whose leaders happened, by a quirk of history, to be members of the Communist Party.[5]

And recently I received a letter from Noam Chomsky, in which he makes the same point, despite taking a more severe position than I do on the degree of innate rigidity and centralization in the Vietnamese society.

> I don't think they cared much about Marxism, beyond slogans... My impression in discussions there was that apart from the western-educated, who had gone through the usual rigamarole and remembered the slogans, the whole tale was largely for show...

In support of this idea, how many Marxist-Leninist parties in other countries admit publicly to having succumbed to the self-righteous attitude described by Vien and take measures to correct it? All too often they consider it utopianism to think that all those who don't think as they do are *not* automatically backward and reactionary and deserve to be treated with respect as legitimate participants in the national dialogue. Yet, historically, Vien's approach reflects the Party's persistent concern to avoid this narrow, dogmatic attitude and its willingness to take remedial action when it has yielded to it. Besides its present self-criticisms and policy changes, we have seen that as early as 1930 the Vietnamese communists emphasized that the land revolution should be carried out with sensitivity toward the rights of "rich peasants, middle and small landlords and...the national bourgeoisie." This concern was denounced by the Soviet-dominated Comintern as unprincipled and reformist. (See Chapter Two.) But when the 1954 land revolution in the North failed to reflect this broad sensitivity, the Party engaged in self-criticism and acted to halt the abuses.

The Vietnamese nationalists' espousal of Marxism-Leninism began with Ho. When he attempted, in Paris in 1920, to win support for Vietnamese independence from France's socialists and other partially progressive forces, he found that neither the socialists nor any other political group whom he approached was willing to emphasize putting an end to colonialism as a serious part of their ideology or program. But Lenin and the early Leninist Third International did! On this slender (but crucial) thread, Ho became "a Leninist." As he says,

> My only argument was: "If you do not condemn colonialism, if you do not side with the colonial people, what kind of revolution are you waging?"[6]

When Stalin, the later Third International and the French communists in Vietnam all showed themselves willing to sacrifice the Vietnamese independence movement to imagined Soviet interests, Ho clung to his belief in Lenin and Leninism. He wasn't the first, or the last, to consider betrayals of this sort betrayals of Lenin and inconsistent with genuine Leninism—and in this instance he appears to have been correct. From then until his death in 1969, Ho, in his humble, earnest way, influenced the Party in which he was the most inspiring and unifying force to continue as a self-proclaimed Marxist-Leninist Party. To this influence must be added the artificial division of the world, after World War II, into two Cold-War camps; the insistence of the U.S. and the Soviet Union on forcing all Third World countries into one or the other camp; and the military (and post-war economic) assistance that the Soviet Union, with its supposed Marxist-Leninist ideology, has provided a beleaguered Vietnam.

Pardoxically, during the period 1975-1978, when Vietnam was pursuing Soviet-style policies of centralized commandism and forced rapid industrialization, it held the Soviet Union at arms length, resisting Soviet pressures to enter COMECON (the Soviet-dominated Council for Mutual Economic Assistance), severely restricting Soviet uses of the deep-water port at Cam Ranh Bay, etc. When it began, in 1978 and 1979, to turn to more democratic forms of economic and political decision-making and expanded opportunities for small-scale private enterprise, it began to re-emphasize its Soviet ties and its supposed Marxist-Leninist ideology. It joined COMECON (June, 1978), entered into a Friendship Treaty with the Soviet Union (November, 1978) and adopted a Constitution (1980) that, in contrast to its many explicit provisions to the contrary, announced with a theoretical bow to Marxist-Leninist orthodoxy, that

> The Communist Party of Vietnam, the vanguard and general staff of the Vietnamese working class, armed with Marxism-Leninism, is the only force leading the State and society... [Article 4]

Besides the provisions to the contrary that I have already mentioned (see Chapter Seventeen), this frightening statement is almost immediately followed by the following more hopeful provision:

In the Socialist Republic of Vietnam, all power belongs to the people. The people exercise State power through the National Assembly and the People's Councils at all levels, which are elected by and accountable to the people. [Article 6]

And then page after page provides the details of how the people can lead the state, the society and the Party, beginning with "the right to recall National Assembly deputies and deputies to People's Councils at all levels who lose the confidence of the people." [Article 7]

In my mind there is a rough or at least partial similarity between the Vietnamese leaders' loyalty to Marxism-Leninism and the selective loyalty of Catholics who live by the tenets of liberation theology to the Catholicism that initially nurtured them, despite the hierarchy's long history of authoritarianism and bleeding of the poor. At the very least, there is in Vietnam, contrary to the way Marxism-Leninism often works, a significant strain of down-to-earth commitment to the poor, to serving them, to sharing their burdens, and to recognizing their right to participate in decision-making. Ho and most of the top leadership of the Lao Dong Party have always been fervent patriots with a strong emphasis on international solidarity. They found ideological support for their patriotism not only in Lenin's "Thesis on the National and Colonial Questions" but in his theoretical emphasis on being sensitive to indigenous conditions (national and local), and to respecting and learning from grass-roots initiatives. This gave them a green light to consider themselves Marxist-Leninists while pursuing their own policies, independent of and usually different from the Soviet practices. And, unlike the practice in many other Leninist countries, they have never gone very long without asking: If we do not condemn elitism —even within ourselves—if we do not side with the most oppressed members of the country and respect their initiatives, what kind of nationalism are we fighting for?

Leninist theory (and Vietnam's new Constitution) embrace "democratic centralism." Too often, beginning with Lenin himself, the centralism crowds out the democracy. In Vietnam, the "Leninists" succumb from time to time to unfortunate centralist tendencies, as they now say they did, in the immediate post-war years. But the more democratic tendency remains strong and receives support from the democratic practice and life-style of its premier "Leninist," Ho Chi Minh. It is clearly reasserting itself at the present time.

I consider Le Duc Tho a contemporary example of this historic and continuing tension. Tho was a leading actor in the post-war commandism and now he emphasizes the importance of "extending to the provinces and districts the right to solve their own problems, to become more dynamic by themselves."

So far no country, whatever its presumed ideology, has worked out a fully satisfactory relationship between the areas and occasions in which a degree of relatively centralized leadership and decision-making may be necessary or appropriate and the basic imperative for decentralized input and control. And Vietnam is no exception. But as we shall see, beginning in 1978 and continuing ever more strongly today, it has made significant adjustments to strengthen individual and local initiatives and control in the all-important area of the economy.

21

Correcting the Mistakes:
The Economy Today

The Vietnamese economy hit rock bottom in 1979. A number of factors, discussed in previous chapters, combined to do it in. But the problem that concerns us here—and the one to which the Vietnamese responded with drastic changes—was the economic bungling by an overcentralized and "utopian" command structure and a sometimes corrupt and mostly inexperienced bureaucracy. At the height of the two-front war with China and Cambodia, close to half the national budget was going to military expenditures. Besides the direct costs, over a million men and women were not available to engage in reconstruction or productive labor. But it was clear that the economy was floundering independently of these strains, which made it all the more necessary to take corrective measures.

After an intensive period of self-criticism and outside consultations, a Plenary of the Lao Dong Party's Central Committee passed a resolution, in September 1979, with profound economic and political implications. It emphasized the importance of the decentralizing measures I have already quoted from Le Duc Tho ("extending to the provinces and districts the right to solve their own problems [and] to become more dynamic by themselves"). But it did much more. When Khac Vien was asked "What are the resolution's most important points in the economic domain?" he replied:

> Firstly, to fight against the tendency which seeks to bring all sectors under State control... In particular, individual production should not be treated as "condemnable."... There is no

chance that capitalism will rear its head again in the present conditions of Vietnam. Individual and family production do not necessarily lead to capitalism.

In a similar vein, Le Mai spoke to me of encouraging "small private enterprises." When I asked him what he meant by small, he replied that

> Normally the enterprise should not employ more than about fifteen people. But there are no limits on the numbers in co-operatives and other joint state-private enterprises.

However, I gathered from my conversations with Mai and others that even in strictly private enterprises there is no exact fixed limit, but a rather flexible policy based on the nature of the enterprise, its usefulness to the economy and the political climate of the area in which it is located. Vien, for example, stresses that

> One of the key factors by which "the form of an organization should be determined...[is] the understanding and support of the people."

And Le Duc Tho told Shaplen that

> Fruit orchards on peasant holdings are rare in the north, but in the south they are often very big and the income from them is considerable. We have decided not to worry about this... We may never tax these orchards, unless a landlord gets to be too rich.

On corruption and bureaucracy, Vien had this to say:

> The real problem is not how to replace bureaucrats with non-bureaucrats, because each official is from one point of view a devoted militant and from the other a bureaucrat. We have to struggle against the tendency to bureaucracy, not against bureaucrats...
> Underdeveloped Vietnam cannot pay high enough salaries to its civil servants and a certain number of them who cannot make ends meet accept bribes from time to time. But socialist Vietnam has no ministers, generals or top executives with fat bank accounts and private villas, who do business with national and international companies, as they do in capitalist countries.

Writing about the September 1979 decision and its reaffirmation by a Party Congress in April 1982, the *Far Eastern Economic Review* stated that the new plan

> advocated greater initiative for local planners, lifting of some restrictions on the open market, and material incentives for workers and peasants... It represented an attempt of the central leadership to catch up with the grassroots with measures that had already been spontaneously initiated locally.[1]

The willingness of the central leadership to respond positively to spontaneous local initiatives is the typical counterpose to its Leninist tendency to overstress the vanguard role of "unified centralism." All through Vietnamese history since the early days of Ho, one sees this tension and alternation between the two impulses. In this case, it is generally agreed now that the new freedom got out of hand for a while in the South, especially in Ho Chi Minh City. But the pendulum did not swing back. Instead the central government dealt with the specific problem without reversing its basic program.

The problem was that profiteers trained in the old Saigon, including some returnees from re-education camps, took advantage of the new freedom by drawing on colleagues in Singapore for capital to buy up scarce goods either to sell them locally at exorbitant prices or to ship abroad. The central leadership stepped in to deal with the corruption and scarcity, mainly by setting up a General Export and Import Company to coordinate and monitor foreign trade. But it continued to permit and encourage local initiatives in domestic production and in both domestic and foreign trade. In fact, about a year after it had taken these remedial measures, the government put its official stamp of approval on a new "Contract System." Local areas had experimented with this method as early as 1979 or 1980, but in 1983 it was extended countrywide. This is an example of what the *Far Eastern Economic Review* was talking about when it referred to the central leadership adopting measures that had been spontaneously developed in the grassroots. And it is an example of the central government's respect for local initiatives that I observed in my frequent travels through North Vietnam during the war.

For all the attempts at centralized control during the war years and the immediate post-war period, Vietnamese peasants and local officials always found their own ways both of interpreting Hanoi's wishes and of using their own common-sense initiatives to deal with local realities. Like rural people most everywhere, the only thing that could stop them would be heavy-handed, overly zealous pressures by the central command structure or its bureaucratic representatives. But I remember well that during my travels in rural areas of North Vietnam in 1966, 1967, 1969 and 1972, the local projects I visited were always under the control of local officials. The government official who accompanied me always explained in advance that this would be the case, saying that the people in the local areas were the ones who had to deal with local problems and knew best how to do so. This was confirmed, in 1972, by A.P. correspondent Peter Arnett, who had travelled more extensively in the South during the war years than most American reporters. He told me, in Vietnam, that "The emperor's writ ends at the village gate." And I knew exactly what he meant. In April 1985, in Ho Chi Minh City, he told me that his current travels of more than a month, this time as a reporter for Ted Turner's *Cable Network News*, had convinced him that the Emperor's writ *still* ends at the village gate. This time I had less experience to go by but had already suspected that this was the case, based on my conversations with government officials and with ardent southern advocates of the south's unique vitality and special role (people such as Ngo Ba Thanh, Mme. Nguyen Thi Phat and Mme. Nguyen Thi Dinh, former deputy commander of the NLF's armed forces).

The "Contract System"

The contract system, as my friend Oanh and others described it to me, came about primarily in response to the failure of Southern agriculture to return to the high-level of productivity that had characterized the years before the American occupation. A cooperative (or individual farmer) and a local government committee negotiate a contract under which the enterprise agrees to produce a certain amount for sale to the government. Anything produced above the requirements of the contract can be sold on the free market at whatever price the farmers can obtain. The contract includes the amount of taxes to be paid on the product. The percentage of the tax is more for good soil, less if the soil is relatively unproductive and requires expenditures for fertilizer, irrigation etc., even though the state undertakes to supply these needs. Apparently the reason for this is the state's interest in increasing overall production, restoring relatively unfertile and war-damaged land, and keeping alive the principle of "from each according to his (or her) ability; to each according to his (or her) needs," even as it is modifying it to some extent by the principle of "to each according to his (or her) work."

In the case of agricultural co-operatives in which the land remains in private ownership and is worked by the owner (or renter), the contract system is extended to relationships between the individual farmer and the cooperative. The individual farm family contracts to supply a certain amount to the cooperative and is free to keep any excess for its own use or to sell in the free market. The co-op then negotiates its contract with the government in accord with its expectations from its member families.

These are the aspects of the contract system that have been reported in some Western publications. What I have not seen reported is what the government does with the produce that it buys under the contract system. According to the Vietnamese I spoke with, it provides these goods to the general population at a price below the one it has purchased them at, and even further below the free-market price. This is done under a system of rationing, which has been cited in the U.S. as an indication of Vietnam's lack of freedom. But what it accomplishes is to guarantee that every Vietnamese receives a basic minimum of necessary staples at less than free-market costs. When I discussed this with Oanh and others, I told them that a very similar program exists in Nicaragua—not the contract system but the provision of minimal amounts of the basic necessities to every Nicaraguan at below market costs. None of the Vietnamese with whom I talked knew about the Nicaraguan parallel. In Vietnam, there are ten basic necessities that are rationed and made available in this manner—rice, sauce, sugar, beans and other vegetables (as available), salt, cloth, soup, kerosene or fire wood, meat and cooking oils. The amounts are small but it is an important step toward seeing that no one is unable to purchase these necessities.

According to all accounts, the contract system was almost immediately successful. In some localities in the South, the total production of rice was doubled—and for the first time since before the U.S. occupation the country became self-sufficient in rice. These successes have to be measured against two factors. One is that the contract system was introduced to replace Hanoi's misguided post-war attempts to force a rapid collectivization of agriculture and a curtailment of the free market. This had provoked significant passive resistance by the peasants. The second, according to Oanh, is the habit some Southern peasants had developed during the U.S.-occupation of working the farms mostly for home and extended-family use while getting their cash from other, anti-social activities.

The contract system gets at a problem in the cooperatives in the North as well, one that Vien mentioned in 1980:

> During the war years, in order to assure minimum rations for everybody, particularly families with children in the army, war invalids and the sick, there was an egalitarian distribution of food; everyone received a fixed quantity per month, however much work they had put in. This mode of distribution doesn't stimulate productivity and able-bodied people sometimes refused to work for the cooperative in order to spend time on more lucrative occupations. The new regulations stipulate that after a portion has been taken aside for the truly needy, the share of each member will be strictly calculated according to work done... Individual peasants, like cooperatives, having made the required deliveries to the State, are free to sell the surplus either on the free market or to the State. The price is not fixed in advance, but is negotiated at the time of sale.

From this last observation, one gathers that the contract system was mostly an extension and sophistication of an earlier reform made in 1979.

In contrast to the days when Hanoi was bent on a rapid

collectivization of agriculture, membership in the cooperatives is now strictly voluntary. In 1985, two thirds of the farms in the South were still worked individually, either by their owners or by rent-paying peasants.

In addition to what I was told about the freedom to join or not join a cooperative, Shaplen writes as follows of his conversations with a number of people in the ancient city of Hue. The first speaker is Nguyen Van Luong, chairman of the provincial People's Committee of Binh Tri Thien Province in which Hue is located.

> "We believe that collectivization is necessary, but its form and the speed at which it takes place depends on current conditions. We do not force it either on peasants or on merchants. We let the people choose the way to follow..."
>
> I spoke with a seventy-three-year-old mason... He told me "I work by myself, mostly for people in the neighborhood. Some masons have joined the co-op, but...no one bothers me. I manage to make enough to live on..."
>
> Nguyen Minh Ky, the permanent chief of the provincial secretariat...explained, "We allow tailors to remain independent if they want to, but even those who do are assigned a certain amount of work by the government. We supply them with materials. There are some forms of business, like welding, that have to be organized cooperatively because what welders do complements what others do..." I asked Ky if he thought the country was developing a mixed economy and...he avoided a direct answer but agreed that "we are slowly working out our own system... Our policies represent the north's point of view, as set forth by the Central Committee in the recent Plenum, but we have our own interpretations of how these policies should be applied, and the government in Hanoi permits us to do things in our own way."[2]

Combined "State-Private" Enterprises

According to Vien,

> The [1979] resolution states that the national economy in the present stage is made up of different sectors: State, co-operative, individual, and in the South, capitalist and mixed [joint State-private]. Although the State sector plays the leading role, the contribution of other sectors should not be underestimated.

However, in May, 1985 I was told that there are also joint state-private enterprises in the North as well as the South, an example of the North learning from the South. Shaplen visited such an enterprise (in Ho Chi Minh City), something that I was unable to do during my short visit. His report confirms the general outlines of what I was told and fleshes it out impressively. He writes

> I was visiting the Second September Engineering Cooperative, which had won a record number of national and local awards as a model of its kind. Owned by the workers rather than by the government, the cooperative has been recognized by Hanoi for having initiated a new system of ownership and management, which falls between state control and private control. "We operate according to production contracts," I was told by Vo Sau...who had lost part of an arm in the French war and was a political worker in the Vietcong during the American occupation... "Our engineers go out and look for our own customers," he told me. "We go down into the Delta and up into the high plateau and ask the people what they need—what kind of water pumps, for example. Then we draw up the blueprints, get the approval of the local People's Committee, and buy our raw materials from the city...
>
> After the last war ended, he started the co-op with ten workers, including some who had served with the South Vietnamese and were unemployed and a few former small-factory owners who had access to some sort of equipment. The co-op now consists of eighty people, including a graduate engineer with a degree from Canada and one with a degree from Sri Lanka. Run by a council of workers, which elects the three directors from its members, it manufactures engineering tools of all sorts, agricultural implements, threshing machines, and small tugs and barges... Of the factory's total income...a third goes to the government for taxes, a third for repairs and expansion, and a third for wages. The co-op works closely with seventeen satellite production groups in the same ward of the city, including some that are government owned. "Our workers participate actively at all levels—in management, production, and the distribution of income," Sau said. "They make their own decisions. They are their own masters." Sau's Second September Engineering Cooperative is a particularly successful example of the kind of compromise between private initiative and state supervision of the means and mechanisms of production which the national government is currently trying to develop.[3]

"An Economic Turnaround"—but Population Control?

Vietnam is still a poor country. But virtually everyone in and out of Vietnam who is interested in facts rather than propaganda affirms that it turned an important politico-economic corner sometime after the low period of 1978 and 1979. From inside Vietnam, I'll only cite my friends Oanh, Phan and Hoa. Oanh says

> The living standard of the society is higher now and most people are better off, but the rich people do not have as many luxuries as they had in the U.S.-Saigon days—and for a while afterwards when they drew on their savings or sold off some of their superfluous possessions. In addition, more people are in control of their own lives now; before a minority ran everything.

Phan affirmed the economic improvement in strong terms, despite his ambivalence about the regime. Dr. Hoa, from her work in her private pediatric clinic in Ho Chi Minh City, states that signs of malnutrition among children are markedly less. According to her there was improvement even during the years of economic breakdown, owing to the government policy of making minimal necessities available to everyone, but now the improvement is far greater. She also stated that

> Although malnutrition is no longer a primary problem and yellow fever and plague have been wiped out, there is a serious shortage of vaccines and other medicines because of the medical blockade. Now, tuberculosis, dengue and malaria are the main problems.

Perhaps I should add that I also attended an industrial fair and found "ordinary" Vietnamese with whom I talked enthusiastic about the new products exhibited. I also visited an exhibit of Vietnam's achievements in the ten years since the end of the war. If the statistics in the charts that accompanied the displays are accurate, they are impressive in that they show a far superior situation at the end of 1984 than at any other time since the end of the war. On the other hand, I am always suspicious of such statistics. However, since these charts showed declines in 1982—and in some production areas in 1983 as well—after substantial rises in 1980 and 1981 and before even more substantial rises in 1984 and 1985, I am more inclined to believe them. This picture also coincides generally with reports in the *Far Eastern Economic Review* and by other foreign observers.

Among recent foreign visitors, my colleague John McAuliff, who has visited Vietnam in 1978, 1981, 1982 and 1985, says that each time he returns, there are more goods visible in the stores, more people buying and a lot more motorcycles and small buses on the streets. The buses are constructed by the Vietnamese, utilizing Honda motors. He adds that there is also "a more relaxed atmosphere now." Peter Arnett and Henry Truitt (of the *Baltimore Sun*) told me during a meal-time conversation that they had observed a noticeable improvement in agriculture under the contract system and that the stores are now selling radios and other things that were not available before. Robert Shaplen says that "an economic turnaround that began in 1979-80...did not gain real momentum until 1983." Even *Time*, which can't be accused of missing an opportunity to make anti-Vietnamese propaganda, writes that "Life may be better for most Vietnamese, but life is not good." One is tempted to ask by what standards it is not good? By the standards of the U.S. that tried to "bomb Vietnam back to the stone age" (in the words of General Curtis Le May, Air Force chief of staff during the early bombings of Vietnam)? By the standards of *Time's* more privileged readers in our consumer society, with our vast gulfs between rich and poor and the unclean wealth extracted from Third World societies?

The *Far Eastern Economic Review* states that "The economy has improved markedly since 1982 but...population growth is still outstripping food production." For those who think of Vietnam as an intrusive, totalitarian society, the comment about population growth introduces an interesting observation by Shaplen who writes:

> It's odd how an innate pragmatism, or peasant common sense, can overcome ideology in some respects, as with the agricultural reforms... There are certain things they are reluctant to, or refuse to, get involved with. Family planning is one... The [Vietnamese] leadership hasn't done what the Chinese have done... hasn't provided the discipline for family planning, which means direct interference at the family level to persuade people to have one or two children instead of three or four or five, and to impose penalites if need be.

When I read this in the *New Yorker*, I remembered my experience in Vietnam in 1975. Here is an excerpt from my report at the time:

> During all my previous visits, I had heard a great deal about the Three Don'ts, a program promulgated by the government because of wartime emergencies. The "three don'ts" were "If you are not engaged, don't get engaged; if you are engaged, don't get married; if you are married, don't have children."
> On my earlier visits, I had never had a real chance to gauge the success of the policy. Children had been evacuated from Hanoi to the countryside and my travels in the countryside had been mostly by night. Even so, I had been puzzled at the number of children I had seen in "evacuated" Hanoi. When I asked about this, I was told that "Parents like to see their children, and we are not very strict about such matters. It's really up to the parents."
> On about the third day of this trip...it suddenly hit me that I had never been anywhere in the world where there were so many children, especially children who were ten or eleven or younger and had to have been born during the Three Don'ts. (Later I found that the statistics supported my observation. During ten years of the American war, the population of North Vietnam

rose, despite all the casualties, from seventeen to twenty-four million.) It was as if a vast, primitive defense mechanism had been at work to counteract the sophisticated instruments of genocide employed by the Americans. Or maybe the people turned to sexual intimacy as an antidote to fear and privation— or as an act of faith in the future, despite the attempts of the U. S. government to destroy that faith and the urgings of the Vietnamese government to "don't."

"Quoc," I said, to the young junior official with whom I was riding when I first realized what a colossal failure the Three Don'ts must have been, "Look at all those children. Everywhere we go there are hundreds of them, thousands of them. I've never seen so many young children in all my life. How do you explain the vast numbers of children conceived and born during the period of the "Three Don'ts"?

"We tried," he said, "but it's very difficult to educate the people on those matters. Besides, a lot of them don't have satisfactory methods of birth control. But we are teaching them."

A few days later, I was travelling with Quoc again. Without forethought I asked him how old he was. "Twenty-six," he replied—which would have made him somewhere between twelve and sixteen and presumably unmarried when the Three Don'ts became a serious campaign.

"Do you have a family?" I asked, not making the connection and thinking only to get to know him better.

"Oh yes," he said. "A wife and two children."

"How old are the children?" I asked, after a pause and this time not the least bit innocently.

"Six and three," he replied.

The Effects of the Cold War

Vietnam is still experimenting with ways of combining private initiative and limited material incentives with national safeguards and controls and with coordination and supervision by grassroots People's Committees, such as the one mentioned by Sau. But one of its continuing problems is the determination of the United States to punish it for its insistence that "Nothing is more precious than independence and freedom" and for its arrogance in working out its own form of society that deviates from the U.S. capitalist model. When Shaplen wrote about the "economic turnaround," he also wrote that

Serious questions remain about what kind of socialism, if any, the individualistic Vietnamese can adapt themselves to; and whether they can successfully get out from under the bleak domination of the Soviet Union, about which they have become disillusioned, while the doctrinaire Russians have grown increasingly fretful about them...

And later, he wrote that

With Vietnam all but isolated economically from the West, exports that could bring in much needed dollars to buy raw materials and Western machinery for the modernization of industry have been consistently low and behind target. This more than anything else, has contributed to the country's continued poverty...

In my 1975 visit, I found the top Vietnamese leadership, including Pham Van Dong, Le Duc Tho and Le Duan (First Secretary of the Lao Dang Party) enthusiastic about entering into friendly relations with the U.S., engaging in trade with it and opening up investments from U.S. corporations. They were so enthusiastic that I found myself warning them of the subtle corrupting power of such corporations. After all, they invest only in the interests of substantial profits and are not known for their concern for the welfare of the people in countries they invest in. Invariably, the Vietnamese response was that if they could defeat the U.S. military they would be able to handle the profit-seeking corporations.

Pham Van Dong with the author.

Shortly afterward, the U.S. decided that by turning its back on Vietnam and playing the China card it could simultaneously punish Vietnam, pursue its Cold-War politics by means of a China-U.S. anti-Soviet alliance and garner greater profits from China's massive potential markets and cheap labor. In 1985, I found the top Vietnamese leadership still interested in entering into "normal" relations with the U.S. and developing positive economic and trade relationships with it, but more guarded. Despite its economic needs, it appears anxious to preserve its dignity as a nation in its efforts to attain peaceful, friendly relations with the United States. This, of course, is the policy it has followed for years in its relations with the Soviet Union.

Meanwhile, Vietnam had reluctantly joined COMECON, the Soviet dominated Council for Mutual Economic Assistance and finally, after years of resistance, signed a Friendship Treaty with the Soviet Union. In part these steps had been a delayed response to the U.S. campaign to isolate Vietnam and drive it into the Soviet camp. They were also a delayed response to Soviet military and economic aid. But all indications are that the Vietnamese still desire to enter into "normal" diplomatic and economic relationships with the United States, both because they covet being a fully independent, "nonaligned" nation relating to both Cold War camps and because they need the trade and peaceful relationships. Independent support of this thesis comes from Le Duan's comments in 1982 when he visited Ho Chi Minh City to work out a solution to the crisis created by the runaway export-import activities of corrupt private operators who were taking advantage of the new economic freedoms. He said at that time that Ho Chi Minh City should indeed become an "export city," but without the corruption:

> Vietnamese workers in agriculture and industry...should devote a third of their time, or a hundred working days a year, to producing goods for export, and the goods should go to "nationalist, non-aligned and independent" countries, capitalist as well as socialist.[4]

One of the main arguments in the U.S. against restoring diplomatic and economic relationships with Vietnam is the continued Vietnamese occupation of Cambodia. Leaving aside the U.S.'s claimed concern for the welfare of the Cambodian people—the hypocrisy of which is revealed by its support for the genocidal and totalitarian Pol Pot—what are the chances for a Vietnamese withdrawal of its occupation forces from Cambodia?

22

Vietnam's Invasion of Cambodia

For many Americans, the most disillusioning news about Vietnam since the end of the war came in late December 1978—January 1979 with the Vietnamese invasion and occupation of Cambodia. Together with the flight of the boat people, which reached its height a few months later, it provided powerful ammunition to those in the U.S. who had been arguing that the Vietnamese communists were contemptuous of human rights, those of their own citizens and those of their neighbors. Many former members of the anti-war movement were won over to this view. Some went further. The year of 1979 also saw the Soviet invasion of Afghanistan. Perhaps Vietnam really was part of an international Communist Conspiracy to take over vulnerable countries and eventually the world.

Cambodia was a no-win situation for Vietnam from the beginning. In May 1975, less than a month after the fall of Saigon, the Cambodians began making sporadic raids on Vietnamese towns and villages in the Mekong delta and proclaiming that most of Southern Vietnam, including Ho Chi Minh City, belonged to them. For three years, Vietnam fought back within the border areas; meanwhile, inside Cambodia, Pol Pot was, step by step, ruthlessly eliminating his more moderate political rivals, including those who advocated peaceful relations with Vietnam. By 1978 he had consolidated his power and on December 22, launched a massive attack. Vietnam repulsed the attack, continued on into Cambodia, and overthrew the Pol Pot regime. Immediately, the United States condemned Vietnam as an aggressor nation out to take over all of Southeast Asia.

There was some historical rationale for Cambodian claims to

Vietnam's Mekong delta area, but it went back to a period before there was a United States, when Indians occupied all of the North American continent except for a few European enclaves. In the thirteenth century, an Angkor (Cambodian) king had twice taken over areas occupied by Vietnamese tribes. And in the 17th and 18th centuries, with the Angkor Kingdom having long since disintegrated, Vietnamese kings had repeatedly invaded Cambodian areas, overcoming the scattered tribes and annexing the lower part of the delta for what is now Vietnam.

Clearly the Cambodian claim had less historical basis than any claims that American Indians might make to the continental United States, based on prior occupancy by their ancestors of all the areas that now constitute our cities, towns and rural areas. But the main problem with all such claims is that they ignore generations of subsequent history. One can imagine what the American response would be if the American Indian movement (armed and supported by a foreign power) decided to lay claim to its former territories and began launching military attacks on American cities and towns and killing the inhabitants. Or if Mexico, armed to the teeth and with support from the Soviet Union, began to attack border towns in Texas, New Mexico, Arizona and California, while announcing that it was laying claim to these areas that had been illegally taken from it in the Mexican-American war.

Neither of these parallels is realistic in terms of today's power realities. But it is worth remembering that in 1776, when North American power realities were different, the U.S. Declaration of Independence did accuse King George III (and by implication his more loyal Canadian stronghold) of stirring up the Indians against the American colonists. With this in mind, let us look more closely at China's role in stirring up the Cambodians to attack Vietnam.

From 1972 to 1975 China had actively colluded with the United States in efforts to force Vietnam to accept a permanent division of Vietnam into North and South. (See Chapter Twelve.) In 1974 it invaded and took over the disputed Paracels Islands, to which both Vietnam and China claimed ownership. And, beginning in 1975, it supplied the arms and advisers that made it possible for Cambodia to attack towns that had been Vietnamese for the better part of three hundred years.

According to Khac Vien,

> In 1975 Pol Pot possessed six divisions of five to six thousand men each, with no artillery, armor nor aircraft. Beijing furnished arms and advisers to bring this army up to twenty-three divisions, providing it with heavy armaments and aeroplanes...[1]

This assertion is backed by articles in the western press. For example, Agence France Press reported a non-refundable Chinese grant of one billion dollars in August, 1975 for economic and military assistance over the next five years.[2] And in 1978, prior to the massive Cambodian attack of December 22, the *Far Eastern Economic Review* reported that

> Through the port of Kompong Som, China is stepping up the transfer of weapons to Kampuchea, including long-range 130-millimeter guns and Chinese made MiG-17s, to the tune of two shipments a week.[3]

A month later, the *Los Angeles Times* reported that

> The Chinese military presence in Kampuchea has developed into a significant force. Kampuchea has been receiving more Chinese personnel than it needs; China controls the activities at Pochenton airport and has established an airlift starting from China's southern coast and flying to Kampuchea through the southern tip of Vietnam.[4]

Vien's account continues:

> In December, 1978 after the great floods which ravaged our country, Beijing thought that Vietnam was completely worn out and set the Pol Pot troops at the attack, while Chinese troops were being concentrated at Vietnam's northern border. The Pol Pot attack would oblige the Vietnamese forces to look to the South and give Beijing a pretext to attack Vietnam on the northern border. Deng Xiaoping received Washington's sanction for this.

Vien did not give any source for his claim that Washington gave its sanction for the Cambodian and Chinese attacks. But it fits in with the long history of U.S. covert and diplomatic warfare against Vietnam. And in this particular period we can note the following sequence of events: In May, 1978 the U.S. National Security adviser, Zbigniew Brzezinski, visited China and met with the Chinese leaders, a sign that the U.S. had decided to reject Vietnam's request for normalization of relations and to play the China card instead. In December, the U.S. and China signed documents establishing formal diplomatic relations. On December 22, 1978 Cambodia massively attacked Vietnam along the entire length of the frontier. Vietnam repelled the attackers, invaded Cambodia and, on January 7, 1979 overthrew Pol Pot. On February 17, China invaded Vietnam.

We need a latter-day *Pentagon Papers* release by some new Daniel Ellsberg to let us know the exact U.S. role in relationship to the Cambodian and Chinese attacks. Meanwhile a leading official of Pol Pot's Khmer Rouge forces, Thiounn Mum, perhaps lifted the veil of secrecy a little in 1980 when he made an apparent reference to the

Khmer Rouge's value to U.S. covert-action efforts *inside* Vietnam:

> If there are no DK [Democratic Kampuchea or Khmer Rouge]
> forces, then how can the forces which these Americans support
> in Vietnam and Laos develop? Kampuchea is the key...[5]

In 1985, Le Mai gave me his version of China's rapprochement
with the U.S. and its subsequent attacks on Vietnam:

> In 1979, China took decisive action to open all doors to the West
> by opposing the Soviet Union as strongly as possible. It wanted
> U.S. funds for modernization. Deng Xiaoping was anxious to
> show the United States that China and the U.S. had parallel
> interests. He did this by attacking Vietnam. Obviously this was
> preferable to attacking the Soviet Union directly. For one thing,
> in the 1969 border clashes between the Soviet Union and China,
> China was hurt badly. Better to attack it through its ally. In the
> process, it lost Cambodia.

"Like the Invasion of Nazi Germany"

During my 1985 visit, Le Duc Tho told me that Vietnam compares
its invasion of Cambodia to overthrow Pol Pot with the Allied invasion
of Germany during World War II to overthrow Hitler and the Nazis.
The logic behind this comparison goes beyond the Khmer Rouge's
attempted expropriation of Vietnam's most fertile lands and largest
city, in the manner of the Nazis' earlier revanchist policies. It extends to
the genocidal internal policies of the Khmer Rouge, especially after a
series of internal purges in 1977 and early 1978.[6] A fanatical Pol Pot and
his colleagues viewed and treated any of their country's occupants
whom they considered tainted by Western influences or addicted to the
"curses" of the old society (religion, the arts, science, Western
medicine, and the other "bourgeois professions") the way Adolph
Hitler viwed and treated Germany's Jews, Gypsies and homosexuals.
And by the lowest estimates, hundreds of thousands of "impure"
Cambodians suffered the fate of these victims of the Nazis. The C.I.A.
puts the figure killed at 1,200,000 and the Vietnamese say 3,000,000.
Vickery makes a fairly convincing case that the number may be as
"low" as "740,800 deaths in excess of normal... over half...from hunger,
exhaustion and illness, leaving, say, 300,000 to be attributed to
executions." By most ordinary considerations that would be enough to
justify the Vietnamese intervention, even apart from the invasions of its
territory.

It took the revelations of the G.I.s who liberated the German death
camps and the subsequent evidence of the surviving inmates to bring
home to the American public the full horror or what had happened

under the Nazis. But the Cambodian mounds of bones were discovered by Vietnamese liberators, and the testimony of Vietamese "invaders" did not play well in Washington or Peoria. Washington in particular was more interested in finding retroactive justification for its own earlier attacks on an "expansionist" Vietnam than in acknowledging evidence that might make the Vietnamese invasion even remotely comparable to the Allied invasion of Germany. By the time that the popular movie *The Killing Fields* dramatized the horror of Pol Pot's Cambodia, most Americans had made up their mind that the Vietnamese invasion was a clear-cut case of unprovoked aggression. The film did not counteract this by making clear that the forces that liberated the Cambodians in this Hollywood-style movie were Vietnamese.

The United States was not blameless in its approach to Adolph Hitler and the Nazis. During most of the Thirties it colluded with them, for comercial reasons and because of Hitler's fanatical anti-communism. And after it had begun to turn against Hitler, it still refused to lower its immigration barriers to admit the mass of anti-Nazi refugees, turning away whole boatloads of them at U.S. ports. There are some indications that Vietnam may not have been entirely blameless in its early relations with Pol Pot and the Khmer Rouge or in its response to an influx of early refugees from the Cambodian killing fields. Nayan Chanda of the *Far Eastern Economic Review* has written that the Vietnamese government

> forced back hundreds of Khmer refugees to Cambodia—to certain death. Hanoi started denouncing the Cambodian massacres only after the Pol Pot regime broke diplomatic relations with Vietnam, charging it with aggression.[7]

I don't know how to evaluate this, but include it here because I have valued Chanda's work throughout the years, and because it provides a cautionary note about Vietnam's otherwise seemingly blameless role vis-a-vis Cambodia between 1975 and 1979. If the charge is accurate, perhaps the reason was Hanoi's attempts to achieve peace with its neighbor and former ally. Even so the picture of forcing back the refugees to almost certain death is not a pretty one. For an additional cautionary note of a different sort, when John McAuliff and I were in Ho Chi Minh City in April-May 1985, we asked the Vietnamese about reports that Chanda had been denied a visa to attend and report on the tenth anniversary events—because of reporting unfavorable to Vietnam. At the time I did not know of this particular article. When Le Mai confirmed that Chanda had been denied a visa "because of fabrications," we spoke against his exclusion. For whatever it's worth, when I saw Le Mai in New York during the October, 1985 U.N. meetings, he told me that "My government has issued an invitation to Nayan Chanda to visit Vietnam. If you are in touch with him, please urge him to accept."

In Hanoi in September, 1975 I was introduced to one of Pol Pot's closest allies, a smiling Khieu Samphan. Samphan was soon to become Cambodian head of state, with Pol Pot as prime minister. Perhaps this coziness at the time between Vietnam and the Khmer Rouge was understandable. It was early in the regime and they had worked together to oust the Americans from Indochina and to overthrow the pro-American Lon Nol regime—as the U.S. and the Soviet Union had worked together thirty years earlier to get rid of Hitler.

Prince Sihanouk

The mercurial Prince Norodhom Sihanouk was in Hanoi at the same event, telling me of his joy at Cambodia's newly restored independence and praising the Vietnamese for sending troops to aid in bringing it about. Both Sihanouk and Samphan had been in China, Sihanouk in exile for five years, Samphan on a diplomatic visit for the Khmer Rouge, during which he may have negotiated Sihanouk's return to Cambodia. After Sihanouk's return, several of his children and other family members were executed by the Khmer Rouge, while he was kept under house arrest until the Vietnamese liberated him four years later.

Despite what happened to Sihanouk and his family under the Khmer Rouge, and despite his earlier expressions of gratitude for the help of Vietnamese troops in liberating his country, he has consistently condemned Vietnam for sending troops to overthrow the Khmer Rouge. Behind this is his fear that this time Vietnam will not withdraw its troops, as it did in 1975. Also, one has to suspect his personal ambition to become Cambodia's top ruler once again, as he was, under one title or another (king, premier, head of state), from 1941 to 1970. Meanwhile, he is playing a sleazy role in an opportunistic alliance with the Khmer Rouge. He serves as a convenient fig leaf for U.S. support of the genocidal Cambodian "contras," a support that it provided diplomatically, and probably militarily through Thailand (Indochina's equivalent of Central America's Honduras), even before Sihanouk agreed to serve as technical head of the anti-Vietnamese coalition.

Paradoxically, and I am sure unintentionally, Sihanouk recently provided two conventional justifications for the Vietnamese invasion. His testimony is important because, as the statement indicates, he has a lot of anti-Vietnamese feelings. Ethnically the Vietnamese and Cambodian peoples are very different and there has always been considerable prejudice in both countries against nationals of the other—a factor that complicates, and might shorten, the present occupation by the Vietnamese. Sihanouk has always reflected and played on the Cambodian's anti-Vietnamese prejudice in order to advance his own ambitions. In addition he is a long-term anti-communist who banned all communist parties and publications during his terms of office. Here is his testimony:

> As far as the Vietnamese...are concerned, if I could have remained head of state, then I'm sure that I could have prevented them from invading Cambodia. But Pol Pot and his Khmer Rouge made provocations against the Vietnamese from when Pol Pot took power in 1975 to 1977. In 1978 Pol Pot and his Khmer Rouge had more and more clashes with the Vietnamese...

In August 1978, four months before Vietnam took matters into its own hands, Senator McGovern called for an armed intervention by an *international* force to overthrow Pol Pot and the Khmer Rouge.

> You know there is a problem about human rights. Senator McGovern wanted an intervention [in 1977] by the U.S. into Cambodia to save my people.
> Your government rejected the proposal...under the pretext that a state has no right to cross the borders of another sovereign state. So the question is this, must we reject this law consisting of not violating the borders of a sovereign state even if a people is dying and the government...is practicing a policy of genocide? Personally I think that we must reject such a law.[8]

With respect to both international law and concern for the human rights of the Cambodian people, there has been a lot of hypocrisy on the part of the United States. Michael Vickery points this out and simultaneously raises a question that must currently concern those who see through that hypocrisy:

> "International law" has been invoked *ad nauseam* in opposition to Vietnamese actions in 1979, but the...Cambodian attacks in areas clearly Vietnamese...justified, in traditional international practice, a military response.
> ...[However,] if almost everyone agrees that the destruction of the DK was in some measure a humanitarian act, and even though it is easy to argue that Vietnamese military intervention was to some extent justifiable under international law and practice, the legitimacy of the regime which resulted from that intervention has been and still is strongly contested.[9]

The longer that Vietnamese troops remain in Cambodia, the more serious and valid will be the questions about the legitimacy of that regime, no matter how humane and constructive its policies may be. It's not enough that virtually all independent observers report positively on the combined accomplishments of the regime and its Vietnamese supporters, as Vickery accurately notes in the following passage:

> [Stephen] Heder's research...concurs with my own impressions, and with the reports of most journalists and aid personnel within the country—but in contrast to the propaganda churned out by DK [and its anti-Vietnamese allies] and retailed via a number of Bangkok-based journalists—that the policies of the...regime and its Vietnamese backers have been humane, pragmatic, and unoppressive, with the Vietnamese gradually withdrawing and leaving the administration in the hands of the Cambodians themselves.

I might add that in addition to the propaganda of Bangkok-based journalists, which is aimed at non-Cambodians, the Voice of America has been broadcasting "destabilizing" propaganda into Cambodia. Besides painting seductive pictures of the freedom enjoyed by those who flee to Thailand (most of whom are in fact confined to crowded refugee camps), it has been making inaccurate broadcasts about the Vietnamese siphoning off vast quantities of foreign aid sent for distribution to needy Cambodians.

Leaving aside all questions about how to distinguish between truth and propaganda, one truth is as real for Cambodians as for Vietnamese, Americans and everyone else: "Nothing is more precious than independence and freedom." So let us focus now on the following questions: What are the prospects for an end to the current occupation? What is the Vietnamese position? What can Americans do to speed up the process of withdrawal?

Prospects for an End to the Vietnamese Occupation

In the past there have been mixed signals from Vietnam concerning its openness to working out an international solution that would permit the withdrawal of Vietnamese troops. During my recent visit, officials seemed very eager to do this and I asked about some of their more negative earlier statements. In diplomatic language, Le Duc Tho said that some of the statements that might have seemed intransigent were necessary responses to the hypocritical rhetoric of the Chinese and Americans as they excoriated Vietnam for its "colonialist" and "expansionist" takeover of Cambodia.

Dignity is very important for most individuals and peoples, and especially perhaps for newly independent countries under attack by their former colonial masters—or in this case by their former occupiers and would-be masters. This might still be a diplomatic factor to be taken into consideration, leading to a cooling of U.S. rhetoric similar to the one that occurred when Ronald Reagan temporarily stopped talking about the Soviet Union as "the evil empire" and the "focus of evil in the modern world." If Reagan could do this in order to satisfy the public's demands for a summit meeting with Gorbachev, the U.S. ought to be able to focus its Cambodian policies on negotiations to resolve the conflict rather than on continuing to exacerbate it by inflated and non-productive rhetoric.

After talking with Le Duc Tho, Le Mai and others, there is no question in my mind that Vietnam is anxious to work out an international settlement that will permit the withdrawal of its troops. It was obvious in their analyses and proposals, and it was unmistakable in the enthusiasm with which they described a few hopeful international developments. They spoke of the conflict as a problem that is draining their resources and standing in the way of broader international accommodations. One of their hopes is that a positive resolution of the Cambodian problem will create diplomatic and economic openings in the non-Communist world, including the West, Japan and the ASEAN countries. (The members of ASEAN, the Association of Southeast Asian Nations, are Indonesia, Malaysia, the Philippines, Thailand, Brunei, and Singapore.[1]) Better realtions worldwide would benefit the economy and would help them become the non-aligned state that they have always wanted to be. Beneath and beyond all this is the ardor of their yearnings for peace, after generations of almost unbroken warfare. As Le Duc Tho said, in reference to who started Vietnam's two-front war with China and Cambodia,

> What country after forty years of war would go and provoke a war against a country of a billion-and-a-quarter people? Only a *madman* would do that.

Tho and others know that peace is something they won't have as long as Vietnamese troops are in Cambodia fighting the U.S.-and-China-sponsored "contras"; and as long as China can use the occupation as an excuse for massing its troops on Vietnam's northern border, shelling border towns, making periodic raids into Vietnam, and threatening to "give Vietnam a second lesson." They don't have to be told that it is in their self-interest to end the occupation. The question is whether the U.S. power elites and the Chinese leadership think it is in *their* interests. The solution lies in the ability of the U.S. public— Vietnam veterans, anti-war veterans and everyone worried by U.S. interventionism and the nuclear threat—to persuade our power elite to enter into serious negotiations to eliminate this arena of unnecessary conflict and danger.

Vietnamese Efforts and Proposals

Le Duc Tho said that Vietnam is seeking realistic discussions with all the concerned parties, including the United States, China, the Soviet Union and the ASEAN countries.

> The object of the discussions is to prepare the way for an international conference at which all the interested parties will work out an agreement that will guarantee a peaceful, independent and non-aligned Cambodia. Included in the conference would be all of the Cambodian forces except Pol Pot.

Tho specifically emphasized that the Cambodian participants would include Sihanouk and Son Sen, two of the three leaders of the present anti-Vietnamese forces, and Heng Samrin, the present Cambodian head of state.

> Everyone should sit down and discuss what kind of Cambodian regime they favor, what kind of constitution and what kind of elections there would be. Afterwards there would be international guarantees for internal peace and security in Cambodia and for the security of all the Southeast Asian countries from external attack.
>
> If any formula for a satisfactory settlement of the Cambodian problem is to come from the United States, we must begin by sitting down and having talks together. When we sat down together at Paris, no one knew what the outcome would be. But we agreed on the importance of sitting down and trying to work out a solution. Now we must try again, without knowing in advance what the details of the solution will turn out to be. It is time for us to sit down together again.

Concerning the exclusion of Pol Pot, Tho said that in advance of bi-lateral discussions and the international conference,

> There are differences on this question among the ASEAN countries; China says include him and the U.S. seems ready to exclude him. Exclusion of Pol Pot is our one demand.

He also said that Vietnam has already entered into preliminary discussions with—or made overtures to—a number of the countries involved. Independent confirmation of this comes from the *Far Eastern Economic Review*, in two articles and a letter to the editor from a Southeast Asia expert. The first article is by Nayan Chanda:

> Observers believe that Hanoi wishes to gain ASEAN agreement for a political solution built around Prince Sihanouk as leader of a new coalition in Phnom Penh, which in practice would amount to legalizing Hanoi's domination of Cambodia.
>
> While launching the early dry-season offensive late last year [1984], Vietnam also stepped up efforts to establish contacts with...Sihanouk, a personality who would be acceptable to both sides in the Cambodian conflict... Hanoi has been telling diplomats and journalists that Sihanouk and Son Sen would be allowed to play a role in Cambodia if they left the coalition [with Pol Pot].[2]

I have trouble with Chanda's contention that Sihanouk's leadership would amount to legalizing Hanoi's domination of Cambodia, both because of Sihanouk's personality and history of nationalism, and because he wouldn't be acceptable to both sides if this were the case.

But the *Review* clearly affirms that the process mentioned by Tho is underway.

The second article in the *Far Eastern Economic Review* says:

> Vietnamese foreign minister Nguyn Co Thach wrote a letter to his Chinese counterpart, Wu Xuegian, calling for secret talks on normalizing relations, which would include discussion on Vietnamese troop withdrawals from Cambodia. "We have not forgotten," Thach wrote, "all that China has done for us in the past, especially during the war."[3]

The letter was from Ben Kiernan, formerly at the Yale University Southeast Asia Research Center and now working in Victoria, Australia. Kiernan wrote:

> Since late January [1985], Vietnam has been proposing to withdraw its troops from Cambodia in return for the exiling of Pol Pot and Ieng Sary [Pot's Khmer Rouge colleague] and the disarming of their followers. Indonesia's foreign minister Mochtar Kusumaatmatja stated on 18 March 1984 that Hanoi's diplomacy has made "a significant step forward" and then on 19 March 1985 that Hanoi had again made "an advance in substance." Not a bad year's work for Indonesia (and Australian Foreign Minister, Bill Haydon). Perhaps now it is time to make a reciprocal advance and drop ASEAN demands that Pol Pot's Khmer Rouge forces share in power and keep their weapons.[4]

The reference to Australian Foreign Minister Haydon refers to a recent visit Haydon made to Hanoi and his announcement that Vietnam was ready for a positive settlement that the Western countries should take seriously.

I didn't get to talk with Foreign Minister Thach in Vietnam during my 1985 visit, but Le Mai, the number-two person in the Foreign Ministry gave me the following optimistic analysis:

> The time is now arriving for a political solution. The people in the region think that the problems interfering with a solution are minor and should not be allowed to forestall the Bangdung type rapprochement that was signalled at the recent meetings on the thirtieth anniversary of that conference [of non-aligned nations]. They are hungry for cooperation in the mutual economic development of the area.

This assessment has subsequently received support from non-Vietnamese sources. M. R. Sukhumbhand Paribatra of Thailand, in a paper prepared for an ASEAN conference on "ASEAN in the Regional Context" wrote in the Winter of 1986 that

> Indonesia and Malaysia...hold less rigid positions. Because they perceive China as the greatest long-term threat to the region,

and because they appear to be committed to the ideal of transforming Southeast Asia into a Zone of Peace, Freedom, and Neutrality (ZOPEAN), Indonesia and Malaysia take a more balanced view of...the Vietnamese threat than Thailand does. ...Indonesia and Malaysia reject the notion that Vietnam is an instrinsically hostile state. They argue instead that Vietnam has legitimate security concerns and, if allowed to become truly independent, has an indispensible part to play in the containment of China and in the fulfillment of the ZOPEAN ideal.[5]

And Richard Falk, of the Center of International Studies at Princeton, writes that

Several ASEAN countries, including Indonesia and Malaysia, have recently encouraged trade relations and diplomatic contacts with Vietnam—a departure from earlier efforts to isolate Vietnam in the region. Even Thailand has recently seemed more inclined to reassess the utility of its aggressively anti-Vietnamese approach. Vietnam possesses a considerable market for exports and, if given a stake in normalization, could well contribute to the first real stabilization of Southeast Asia since the end of World War II.[6]

Both of these optimistic assessments of the changing situation echo earlier sentiments expressed by Le Duc Tho and Le Mai in Vietnam when there was less public evidence to support them. In fact, at the time, Le Mai said that

Although some of the ASEAN countries still make negative public statements under pressure from China and the United States, they assure us that they agree with us on the basic principles of a settlement. Those principles are democratic elections in Kampuchea and the withdrawal of Vietnamese forces, without the return of Pol Pot.

Within the area, only China and Thailand are holding out in opposition, but there are pressures in Thailand for a less bellicose position and China's current policy is a promising sign.

A key reason for Thailand's "rigidity" (Sukhumbhand Paribatra) and "holding out in opposition" to its ASEAN partners (Le Mai) is the influence of the United States. Sukhumbhand Paribatra points out that

U.S. bilateral aid to Thailand has increased in recent years, and now totals over $100 million a year. Moreover, U.S. arms to Thailand have been qualitatively and quantitatively upgraded, and have included completed or pending deliveries of Harpoon ship-to-ship missiles, an integrated, computerized air defense system, and a squadron of F-16 fighter aircraft. The...U.S.-Thai military relationship is also reflected in the growing number of calls made by U.S. Seventh Fleet units to Thai ports, and in the upgrading of the annual Cobra Gold military exercises, conducted jointly by Thailand and the United States. In 1985, these exercises involved not only amphibious forces, as in previous years, but also land-based F-15 fighters, a U.S. infantry battalion, and six Green Beret Special Forces teams.[7]

All in all, Thailand seems to be undergoing a process of combined internal militarization and growing foreign policy domination by the United States. The U.S. is using it as it uses Honduras in Central America. And in Thailand, as in Honduras, this is creating considerable uneasiness among Thais who want to maintain civilian rule and develop in a democratic direction. Thus Sukhumband Paribatra warns:

> The Kampuchean problem seems to have given the military just the opportunity it needs to play an increasingly dominant role. Generally speaking, an external conflict is capable of making civilians grow accustomed to the requirements of a national security state—namely a growing defense budget, the centrality of the military's position in the affairs of state, repressive laws and suppression of internal dissent, growing paramilitary and territorial defense formations, and the perception that there is no alternative but to accept restrictions for the sake of "national security" or "national unity." ...The persistent involvement of some military leaders in all issues of political significance has become readily evident, and paramilitary formations are being expanded and strengthened... The main "beneficiaries" have been those in charge of weapons procurement policies, arms shipments to the Khmer Rouge, and security on the Thai-Kampuchean border.[8]

When Le Mai came to the U.N in October, 1985 we talked further about Cambodia. He began by saying that "the problem is near a solution." But when I asked him, "How near?" he said, "It will be resolved within a few years." This didn't make me as happy about the situation as he appeared to be. However, since then Vietnam has announced that although it hopes for a political solution earlier, it will withdraw all its forces unilaterally by 1990, even if the concerned international parties have not come to an agreement by then. Its position is that by 1990 the Cambodians will be strong enough to defend themselves against any attacks that the Khmer Rouge might still be able to mount.

Le Mai explained that his optimism was based on discussions Vietnam has been having with a number of the concerned countries and indications of a coming together on the major principles of a settlement. The main reason for his thinking that it might take a few years to put the principles into practice was the apparent lack of seriousness by the United States about resolving the Cambodian issue.

According to him,

> There is less open hostility today than there was previously, especially in 1979 and 1980. But the U.S. keeps tieing a solution of the Cambodian problem to other issues, such as the M.I.A.s. Yet if the U.S. would cooperate more seriously in resolving that problem, by giving us more documentation, such as the coordinates of airplane crashes, we could solve that problem earlier. Anyway, at least things are still moving.

A few weeks later, the U.S. did supply the coordinates of at least one B52 crash, which is a beginning.

Signals from China

On China, Le Mai had this to say:

> We have received some positive signals from China, but there are still military pressures on the border (shellings, etc.) and public expressions of a continuing hostile policy. For example, the Foreign Minister made recent statements at the U.N. that are hostile to Vietnam.
>
> On the positive side, China sent a warm message on Vietnam's Independence Day, in September. And some of us went to Beijing recently and were well received by the Chinese authorities. And although China threatened at the beginning of the year to give Vietnam "a second lesson," and mobilized hundreds of thousands of troops on the border, they did not act.
>
> We think there are three important reasons why they did not.
>
> First, Vietnam is better prepared militarily. We feel that we would give *them* a second lesson.
>
> Second, among the Chinese themselves there are internal differences and the leaders do not want to add another source of discontent. The subject of Vietnam is not one of their major internal difficulties, but even so another invasion would add another difficulty that they do not want.
>
> Third, and most interesting, is the changes in China's international relations. In 1979, the ASEAN countries automatically supported China. Now they would go against it. They don't want war and instability because of the effect on foreign investment into their countries. Also, Chinese-Soviet relations are improving. Before they wanted to attack the Soviet Union by attacking one of its allies. Now they desire improved relations and partially have them. They don't want to do anything to interfere with this.
>
> Because of these changes, if China stays outside of the developing consensus, it will not be to her interests.

Le Mai said that there are five principles of settlement that are agreed on by most everyone. They are

1. *Withdrawal of the Vietnamese forces without allowing Pol Pot to return.* Even the U.S. seems ready to agree to this. China does not object openly, but there are indications that it is not happy with it.
2. *National reconciliation among all Cambodian factions on the basis of the elimination of Pol Pot as a military and political force.* He is genocidal, so there can be no reconciliation with him. But this does not mean eliminating all of Pol Pot's followers. The leaders yes, and no continuation as a military force.
3. *Peaceful co-existence of all the countries in the region.* Thailand says that its security is threatened. So does China. So we must establish together the principle of peaceful co-existence.
4. *Non-intervention of foreign powers into Southeast Asia.*
5. *International guarantees of the agreements by the big countries.*

Conclusion

This is a reasonable program. The time is ripe for Vietnam to withdraw its occupation forces from Cambodia. At this point Vietnam is not the problem but China and the United States are. To a lesser extent, Thailand is a problem, too. But China and Thailand are not in a position to hold out if the United States decides to join with Vietnam in working out a solution. The problem is that the U.S. government wants to see Vietnam bogged down in a Cambodian quagmire, as it was once bogged down in Vietnam itself:

> The humiliating character of the American defeat encouraged the U.S. leadership to do whatever possible to discredit and inflict pain upon the victor. In a sense, U. S. policy...over the past decade reflects our country's inability to come to terms with the psychological aftermath of the war... In this regard, the new movement to honor America's war casualties through war memorials and public acknowledgement is long overdue and to be welcomed, provided it is not used to falsify the character of the war or to encourage a militarist mood... We are still struggling toward a political understanding of the Vietnam experience—an understanding that rejects the official policy of military intervention, yet remembers both those who were killed or injured doing their national duty...and those who refused to participate in a war of which they disapproved... U.S. policy, preoccupied as it is with disgracing and punishing the Vietnamese appears to be out of step with the times.[9]

Now is the time for a joint healing action by those who fought in the war and those who fought against it. Together with everyone else who is concerned for the future of the United States and of its surviving victims in Vietnam and Cambodia, we can join in a campaign to stop the U.S. government's punitive interventions in Cambodia, Thailand and Vietnam. Together we can help bring peace at last to Southeast Asia. A first positive step in this direction would be to press for the U.S. to end its support for the Cambodian guerillas and to sit down in an international conference to bring peace to that troubled land. This should be accompanied by calls for a normalization of relations between the U.S. and Vietnam.

It's hard to add another activity to the struggles for economic and racial justice at home, for an end to imperialist interventions in Central America, Angola, etc., for an end to U.S. support for apartheid in South Africa. But Vietnam has a special place in our history. Its ghosts still haunt us and exert a negative influence on all our country's policies. By helping to put the Vietnam war behind us, we can help bring peace to the United States. We can help change the climate in favor of a more constructive foreign policy in other sections of the world as well.

Afterword

From the Villages of Vietnam to the Halls of Montezuma and the Shores of Tripoli

The war in Vietnam was not an isolated incident in the history of the United States. The attitudes, drives and policies that produced both the war and the anti-war movement have been with us a long time and have continued into the present.

In 1954, the C.I.A. installed Ngo Dinh Diem as premier of South Vietnam. In 1963, it conspired to have him assassinated. In 1969, the C.I.A. supported a coup in Libya that brought Colonel Muammar al-Qaddafi to power. Now it is trying to kill him.

The U.S. backed Qaddafi, like Diem, because of his anti-communism. When he failed to support the totality of American policies as anticipated, Washington turned against him and tried to be rid of him by coup or assassination. In both South Vietnam and Libya, the U.S. turned against a former ally, not because of hypocritical charges of tyranny and terrorism, but because of the lack of consistent subservience to their sponsors. Each in his turn had grown too big for his britches, desiring a degree of political independence that ran counter to Washington's purposes and conflicted with some of its policies.

On March 24, 1986, the war against Qaddafi took the form of an attack on Libyan radar stations and patrol boats in the Gulf of Sidra. We are told now, as we were previously told about the Gulf of Tonkin, that the "enemy" fired first. If so, the Libyans were responding to a provocation on Washington's part that was aimed at producing exactly that result.

As in its disagreements with Nicaragua, the U.S. refused to submit the dispute concerning the limits of Libya's territorial waters to the World Court or to any other form of international mediation or arbitration. European nations that failed to support our taking the law into our own hands were condemned as disloyal or cowardly, as selfishly concerned that our war to end terrorism would cause more terrorist attacks on their citizens. We expect unequivocal support from our European allies, without joint planning, in return for stationing our nuclear missiles on their soil—to "defend" them, we say. Margaret Thatcher's government displays such loyalty. But when I was in England recently there was a Fourth of July demonstration demanding that England declare its independence from the United States. The demonstrators were protesting the presence of 147 U.S. military installations on their soil plus a U.S. intelligence facility that can listen simultaneously to 30,000 private British phone calls.

Apparently at least sixty Libyans were killed in the Gulf of Sidra attack. But the U.S. reported that Qaddafi did not immediately announce their deaths to the Libyan public and used this to counteract any feelings of sympathy that might have been expressed for these hapless victims.

On April 14, a terrorist bombing of a West German nightclub frequented by American soldiers killed a black G.I. (Join the Armed Forces and get a job.) This disgusting act may or may not have involved a direct or indirect response to the first American attack on Libya, but the U.S. announced that its intelligence services had traced it to Qaddafi. Neither the media nor the "opposition" party in Congress raised any serious questions about the possible unreliability of the claim. Yet Manfred Ganshow of the Berlin Staatschutz, head of the 100-person unit investigating the nightclub bombing, told *Stars & Stripes* after two weeks of investigation that they "had no more evidence that Libya was connected to the bombing than...two days after the act—which is none... We are still tracking down other leads that are totally non-political."[1]

On top of this, both the media and Congress know that the C.I.A. routinely fabricates such information to justify potentially unpopular acts by the U.S. And even the stupidest of them knows something even more disturbing: that President Reagan or his speechwriters regularly lie when it suits his (or their) purposes. Indeed, even while the Libyan crisis was coming to a temporary head, he was caught in a number of flagrant untruths about Nicaragua.

Here are five of Reagan's Nicaraguan assertions, all solemnly and convincingly stated, all exposed in their falsity, and none of them retracted:

1.) "Nicaraguan government officials are deeply involved in drug trafficking." But the Drug Enforcement Agency said, both before and the day after he said this, that it has "no evidence" to support the charge.

2.) "The Sandinistas are training and arming guerillas that are active in Central and South America, including El Salvador and Brazil." The day after the president said this on national television, the Brazilian government pointed out that no guerillas have been active in Brazil for the past ten years. Reagan was repeating something Secretary Shultz had told Congress a few weeks earlier and that had already provoked an official Brazilian protest. According to the *New Yorker*, "Elliot Abrams, the Assistant Secretary of State for Inter-American Affairs, had been obliged to retract the claim in an 'explanatory letter.'"[2] As for El Salvador, former C.I.A. operative, David McMichael once again repeated his denials that the C.I.A. had evidence that the Sandinistas have sent any arms to El Salvador since a small shipment in early 1981. It had been McMichael's job to coordinate the effort to find any such shipments.

3.) The President ridiculed those who say that the Contras are led by former members of Somoza's National Guard. He did this despite a congressional study that had revealed that 12 of the 13 top Contra military leaders are former guardsmen and that their commander-in-chief was Somoza's former military attache in Washington.

4.) The president explained the documented Contra atrocities by saying that "Communist operatives dress in freedom-fighter uniforms, go into the countryside, and murder and mutilate ordinary Nicaraguans." Here he was repeating a governmental claim that was made by an earlier administration about the known atrocities of the U.S.-supported regime in South Vietnam which no one would dare repeat today.

5.) The President accused the Sandinista government of anti-semitism. He "proved" it by saying that they had firebombed a synagogue in downtown Managua, but the damage to the synagogue had taken place years earlier, during the bombings and mortar attacks of the civil war.

None of this mattered to those who rallied behind the President's call for punitive action against the obviously "insane" and untruthful outlaw, Qaddafi. Nor did it matter that Israel said that Syria, *not* Libya, had trained the terrorists who attacked the Rome and Vienna airports. At that point the U.S. wanted to attack Libya, not Syria, so it continued to insist that the attackers had been trained and directed by Libya. To the tune of resounding cheers from the Democratic opposition, the U.S. bombed the Libyan mainland, causing more than a hundred civilian casualties.

II. The Black Response

The U.S. G.I. killed in the Berlin nightclub bombing may have been black, but the black experience in the United States is such that most black leaders knew better than to join in the cheerleading. What follows are a few examples of what they said.

Representative Micky Leland, chairman of the Congressional Black Caucus, said that the Reagan administration:

> "sought a military option before exhausting all peaceful means of settlement," a move that indicates a disturbing preference for violence.[3]

The Reverend Hycel B. Taylor, president of Operation Push, protested that:

> This administration is not only wrong in Libya, it is wrong in Nicaragua, in Angola, in South Africa and in the Middle East in general... Black Americans see terrorism in the context of American history. We remember the terrorism of being kidnapped from Africa and the terrorism of slavery. When slaves revolted, we remember that they were often called terrorist. We saw the terrorism of taking this land from the Native Americans who were slaughtered in the process. We recall the terrorism of the lynch mobs and the Ku Klux Klan.

Congressman John Conyers complained that, "Our reaction to Libyan terrorism is isolating us in the region. It was questionable from a legal standpoint and it will increase further rather than decrease international terrorism." Conyers said the U.S. should be working instead on the Palestinian issue, which is the root of the Mideast crisis.

Rev. E. Randel Osburn, program director of the Southern Christian Leadership Conference observed that, "We don't equate patriotism with war mongering because we know that time and time again this country has violated human rights in the name of patriotism." Conrad Worrill, chairman of the Black United Front, said that the Libyan bombing was a direct assault on "black people's ancestral homeland" and feared that black American soldiers will soon be ordered to fight against blacks in Africa:

> The stage was set with the ruthless invasion of Grenada in 1983, when most of the invading ground troops were blacks and Hispanics. The Reagan administration is using the fear of terrorism to build an awesome war machine that is sucking blacks into it to be used as cannon fodder.[4]

Finally, Jesse Jackson received a standing ovation at the founding convention of the National Rainbow Coalition when he condemned the action.

> We have entered a period of unconventional warfare whose end we cannot control or predict. When a rock is thrown into the water, one must be concerned with the resulting concentric circles. In the midst of the euphoria over the initial military

success, we dare raise a serious question: has such a calculation been adequately made? The street corner rhetoric and the "eye for an eye and tooth for a tooth" approach that is passing for this administration's foreign policy could leave the world blinded and toothless.

III

Libya invited the U.S. media to view the civilian destruction but most of the American press buried reports of the damage and casualties in minor stories in inside pages. In one case, after a TV camera in Tripoli presented a panorama of dead civilians, the commentator in New York made a point of saying that the U.S. television crews were permitted access only to what the Libyans wanted them to see—as if that somehow denied the reality of the horror broadcasted.

For its part, the U.S. government stonewalled by attributing the civilian damage to Libyan anti-aircraft missiles. When this was seen to be patently ridiculous, it conceded that some of the damage came from a few stray bombs, but continued to insist that the rest came from Libyan anti-aircraft missiles. Once again, this was a repeat of claims an earlier administration had made in Vietnam. In that case, after it had become impossible to deny that U.S. bombing raids had been accompanied by extensive damage to hospitals, schools, churches and civilian housing, the U.S. said that such damage was caused by Vietnamese anti-aircraft shells falling back to earth. In Vietnam, we know from Air Force documents that the bombing of such places was intentional—under the mistaken notion that it would weaken public morale and undermine the will to resist (see Chapter Eight). In Libya we have no such information. What we now know is that one of the targets, the headquarters of the Libyan intelligence service, is "in downtown Tripoli and hard to hit without causing heavy casualties among Libyan civilians." *Time* magazine told us this in an issue published before the raid took place.

Qaddafi's daughter was killed in the second attack and two of his young sons were seriously injured, "one of them with serious brain damage."[5] Too young to have been responsible for anything that their father did or did not do, their sufferings—and the sufferings of others killed or wounded in the attack—did not evoke the sympathy or indignation in the American press that the death or wounding of civilians on "our" side had called forth. We were told that the Libyan's "claimed" that the baby girl was Qaddafi's daughter—and an "adopted" daughter at that. A number of articles reported that Qaddafi was mysteriously "silent," "depressed," lacking in his customary flamboyance. Some of them stated, and others implied, that he was depressed because the raid had successfully called his bluff and achieved the administration's objective of putting him in his place. I saw no references to the possibility that these symptoms had anything to do with what had happened to his children.

A report in the inside pages of the *New York Times* told us that

> American warplanes left a 300-yard row of bomb craters stretching from his [Qaddafi's] home to his office... [N]ormally reliable foreign sources have said the Colonel sprinted the roughly 100 yards [from a"Bedouin-style tent he favors for meetings"] to his fortified bunker underneath the office building when he heard the first firing as the American F-111 bombers came roaring in over the city.[6]

Despite this report, both President Reagan and Secretary of State Shultz denied that an object of the attack was to kill Qaddafi.

> When asked today if he would advocate revoking regulations ruling out assassination as a tool of American policy, Mr. Shultz said that he would not. "I think it doesn't fit our way of thinking on how to do things," he said.[7]

Did he say this because the regulations look good on the books and don't seriously restrain us anyway? Because we can do it covertly, without having to deal with the resistance of a queasy American public? If anyone doubts it, consider the following two news items:

> Assassination was first outlawed as an instrument of U.S. policy by President Ford, following disclosures that over the years the C.I.A. had plotted to assassinate or conspired with assassination attempts on Fidel Castro, former Dominican strongman Rafael Trujillo, leftist Congolese leader Patrice Lumumba, Che Guevara, Chilean Chief of Staff Renee Scheider and Vietnamese leader Ngo Dinh Diem.
>
> President Carter continued the prohibition, and so did President Reagan.
>
> "So what?" asks Clark Clifford, elder statesman of the Democratic Party; former aide to Presidents Truman, Eisenhower, Kennedy, Johnson and Carter; pillar of the Eastern liberal establishment.
>
> "...There are persons who can be bought in every country of the world. If a certain number of persons are liquidated, it would be a very useful way to go at it."
>
> ...Should the law be repealed? "No, no, no," Clifford said. "Leave the law on the books. Just get the job done and don't talk about it."[8]

Or as Secretary Shultz put it, in the interview quoted above:

> Covert action is something that we need to be using," he said, "...there are many things that need to be done secretly and we

have to have a greater capacity in our country to recognize the importance of being able to do things without having them publicized ahead of time.''[9]

Meanwhile, the government is stepping up its efforts to see that the "secret covert programs" of its intelligence agencies *don't* become known. It fears that such programs would cause a groundswell of public indignation and revolt, so it is classifying more and more material that falls within the public's right to know. And it is cracking down on anyone in the media or government who reveals it to the public.

Much of the censored material is information that the public *must* know if the exercise of our vaunted freedoms is to be more than a meaningless ritual. What does it mean to have freedom of speech and assembly, the right to petition for redress of grievances, and the right to vote, if we are denied the knowledge necessary to exercise these rights and freedoms intelligently? How can democracy function if the people are denied information about the decisions the government is making, the policies it is carrying out, and the methods by which it is doing so? What does freedom of the press mean if the government is able to prevent press access to vital information? If classification is not censorship, what is it?

Do I overstate the government's intentions and efforts? In addition to Secretary Shultz's revelations about the importance of secret covert action, consider the following back-pages item in the *New York Times*:

> The Administration's current discussions with the *Washington Post* about publication of an article based on classified information mark the sixth time in the last 12 months that Government officials have pressed the newspaper to withhold or alter an impending article, Leonard Downie, Jr., the managing editor of the *Post* said Friday.
>
> In two cases, Mr. Downie said, the *Post* complied with the Administration... [This] is occurring against the backdrop of what Mr. Downie termed the Administration's "increasingly aggressive" stance against officials who leak classified information and newspapers and magazines that publish it.
>
> The Director of Central Intelligence, William J. Casey, warned this month that he would consider prosecuting the *Post* if it published the article by Bob Woodward and Patrick Tyler about American intelligence abilities.

The *Times* doesn't mention that it was a series of articles by Bob Woodward and Carl Bernstein that opened up the Watergate scandal. These articles contributed mightily to the forced resignation of Richard Nixon and to opening the floodgates to a temporary spate of revelations about the government's covert actions. These revelations shocked the public and forced through the restrictions that are now being circum-vented. This information might have been thought "fit to print," as background or context for the present campaign. But even if the *Times* neglected this aspect of the story, it did continue with some very important information:

> Last month, Michael E. Pillsbury, an Assistant Under Secretary of Defense was dismissed... He was suspected of having leaked to the *Post* and the syndicated columnists Rowland W. Evans and Robert Novak information that Mr. Casey had gone to Angola to arrange for the covert shipment through Zaire of antiaircraft missiles to Jonas Savimbi's insurgent Angolan forces.
>
> ...Mrs. Graham [Catherine Graham, the chief executive officer of the Washington Post Company] wrote in the *Post* "Outlook" section in April: "I want to emphasize that the media are willing to—and do—withhold information that is likely to endanger human life or jeopardize national security."[10]

I wonder. Endanger human life or permit its endangerment through unpublicized covert-action programs? Jeopardize national security or allow the government's views of "national security" to take us further down the road to World War III, jeopardizing the future of life on the planet?

There are several contradictions in these efforts to keep the government's covert actions secret. One is that the claimed reason for indulging in the covert action programs is to defend American values, as exemplified by our free press and our democratic decision-making by an informed public. A second contradiction can be seen in the government's claim that its covert actions against the government of Nicaragua are justified, among other reasons, by that government's censorship of the anti-Sandinista newspaper *La Prensa*. How embar-rassing then that the indiscretions of our too free press (loyal and cautious as the media are) have acquainted careful readers with the fact that *La Prensa* is being subsidized by a combination of U.S. govern-mental and corporate funds:

> The National Endowment for Democracy, a private group, has channeled a total of $53.7 million in Government money to foreign political parties, labor unions, newspapers, magazines, book publishers and other institutions in countries where democracy is deemed fragile or nonexistent.
>
> The Federal money is being used for such undertakings as...buying materials ["newsprint, ink and other supplies"] for an opposition newspaper in Nicaragua... Money is also going to monitor and publicize human-rights abuses by Vietnam...
>
> "We're engaged in almost missionary work," said Keith Schuette, head of the National Republican Institute for Inter-

national Affairs, which conveys some of the money to foreign political parties that share the Republicans' views.[11]

I credit the *Times* with giving rather more publicity than usual to a story of this kind, starting it on the bottom of page one. However, it raises no questions concerning the Endowment's claims that this money is *a substitute* for C.I.A. covert programs of a similar nature rather than *an addition* to them.

The *Times* points out that the Endowment's chair is John Richardson, former president of Radio Free Europe in the 1960s, which was funded by the C.I.A. Its board of directors includes Henry Kissinger; Walter Mondale; Lane Kirkland, president of the A.F.L-C.I.O.; Representative Dante B. Fascell, Democratic chair of the House Foreign Affairs Committee; Olin C. Robison, president of Middlebury College; Frank J. Fahrenheit Jr., chair of the Republican National Committee; and Charles T. Manatt, former chair of the Democratic National Committee.

The president of the Endowment is Carl Gershman, an aide to Jeane Kirkpatrick when she was chief of the U.S. delegation to the United Nations. He is quoted as saying:

> It would be terrible for democratic groups around the world to be seen as subsidized by the C.I.A. We saw that in the '60s and that's why it has been discontinued.

I am grateful for his recognition of the public's distrust of the C.I.A. (which has always used both foreign and domestic groups as fronts for its activities), but I question his assertion that the C.I.A.'s current propaganda and disinformation activities are limited to those of the Endowment.

Even without knowing about the subsidy to *La Prensa*, some people might notice another irony in the government's self-righteous condemnations of Nicaragua for its censorship of that publication. The Nicaraguan government says that its censorship is necessitated by wartime considerations of national security. The U.S. scoffs at this argument, even while it is using *La Prensa* in its war to overthrow the Nicaraguan government. To heighten the irony, the U.S. now says that *our national security* requires censorship of efforts to inform the U.S. people about the methods by which it is carrying out this war.

IV

If it would be wrong to think that the attacks on Libya represented a principled attack on terrorism, it would also be a mistake to think that their purpose was solely an escalation of the U.S. war against Qaddafi. They were aimed even more at the American media and public, at the

European and Japanese allies, and at any uppity little nation that might be so foolish as to think that the U.S. does not have the will, the power and the public support to make them say uncle to Uncle Sam. At home, the attacks were part of a psychological and political war against the dreaded Vietnam Syndrome. That syndrome, strangely persistent despite the well-reported transformation of anti-war activists into Yuppies, makes the American public resistant to U.S. terrorism as foreign policy. As an editorial in *The Nation* described it,

> The decision to wage war against Col. Muammar el-Qaddafi was made many years ago, in the context of a global strategy and a regional campaign...to project American military power in the Middle East, to wreak revenge on the Moslem world for a long list of economic and political insults, and to assert the inalienable right of the president of the United States to strike "any part of the earth," as Reagan once said, in defense of the national interest as he defines it. The pretext could be found, provoked or supplied at any time.[12]

If Qaddafi did not exist, the Reagan administration would have invented him. Indeed, the U.S. did help invent him, by its early support through the C.I.A. Now it has invented much of the context in which he supposedly operates.

In particular, the attacks on Libya were clearly timed to rally public (and especially Congressional) support for the Administration's unpopular efforts to get approval for military aid to the Nicaraguan Contras. They were intended to provide a shot of patriotic adrenalin, to convince us that "standing tall again" can be accomplished by beating up on small nations. It was also hoped that those who have hesitated to support such ventures would be carried along by the anticipated wave of public enthusiasm. If they couldn't accept them in their heart of hearts, at least they would be cowed into silence. And many people were.

For months, the American public was systematically prepared for the attacks on Libya by a deluge of stories repeating and re-emphasizing old accusations that Colonel Qaddafi was a terrorist, a kook, a flake, a "madman" and finally, according to no lesser authorities than George Bush and Ronald Reagan, "a mad dog." Everyone knows what you do to a mad dog. Typically the "mad dog" epithet came originally from an honored commentator on one of the major TV "news" networks, George Will. According to Alexander Cockburn,

> George Will stated the theme back in 1981: "Can the Western world be taken seriously in its determination to survive [!], if a mad dog on the streets of the world, such as Gadaffi [sic], is allowed to go on like this?"[13]

The U.S. shot down two Libyan jets over the Gulf of Sidra in 1981 while the U.S. media raised no questions about the claimed circumstances. Instead, shortly afterwards, it was regaling the American public with a suspense drama starring a Libyan hit squad that had entered the United States from Canada on assignment to assassinate President Reagan. The information was supplied by the White House, on the authority of U.S. intelligence services. The only problem was that the stories were false. Eventually it was revealed that the suspects were Lebanese members of the Shiite Amal. Besides being sworn enemies of Libya and Qaddafi, the Amal have shown no interest in assassinating President Reagan. But the weeks of suspense had the desired effect. They lingered in the public subconscious and undoubtedly had an influence on the public's reaction to later reports, in 1986, that Qaddafi had threatened to send suicide squads to the United States. These reports helped create a public mood favorable to the subsequent U.S. attacks, particularly since the press almost never mentioned that Qaddafi's threat was in response to prior U.S. threats to attack Libya and was to be activated *only if the U.S. did attack militarily.*

None of this denies that Qaddafi is a tyrant in a world awash with them, some of them supported by the Soviet Union and some supported by the United States. Among other crimes, Qaddafi's agents have tracked down Libyan dissenters in foreign lands and assassinated them. Amnesty International has documented fourteen such assassinations or attempted assassinations. This would be a slow day's work for U.S. troops in Vietnam or the U.S.-supported Contras in their forays into Nicaragua. But such matters cannot be judged by statistics alone. Tyranny and terrorism are objectionable, whatever the statistics. As to whether Qaddafi is "mad" or not, the only certain thing is that he has succeeded in driving a lot of other people over the brink. He has intensified tendencies to a type of insanity that inflicts considerable harm on the American people as well as on the allies and "enemies" of the United States. As Pete Hamill pointed out in the *Village Voice*, "For Americans, comparing Reagan to Qaddafi is a form of blasphemy. Yet the parallels are unavoidable and spooky."

If other nations took seriously the idea that government-sponsored terrorism justifies bombing attacks on the guilty country, morally and as a method of putting an end to its terrorist activities, clearly they would be justified in bombing the United States. Fortunately, most of the countries and peoples who suffer from the U.S. policies (and from those of its ally and surrogate in the Middle East, Israel) do not have the power to respond in this manner, either against the U.S. or against Israel. So some of them take another tack, the small-scale but horrible terrorism that vents their bitterness, anger and frustration.

Like the early bombings of Vietnam, the bombing of Libya was explained as a measured and necessary response by a peaceful U.S. government. But there are important differences in the two situations. In Vietnam, the independence forces struck out directly and selectively against the U.S.-sponsored terrorists who were oppressing them. In the Middle East, some Palestinian groups have struck out in desperation against tourists and other civilians who happened to be in the wrong place at the wrong time, especially Jews.

These misguided acts have offended all decent people. My visits to Lebanon, the West Bank, Syria and Jordan convince me that at least as high a percentage of Palestinians have been offended by these actions as the percentage of Americans who were offended by the Reagan Administration's terrorist attacks on Libya, by its prior attacks on Palestinians, Syrians et. al. in Lebanon, and by Israeli terrorism in Lebanon, the West Bank, Syria and Tunisia.

Clearly, Palestinian terrorism is politically counterproductive. It has alienated countless supporters and potential supporters of the Palestinians' right to a homeland. It has strengthened the hand of those in Israel (and the United States) who advocate Zionist expansionism and the existing policies of economic and political repression in the illegally occupied territories, including collective punishment, arrest without warrant and political deportations. It has immensely complicated the task of the opposition forces in Israel who desire justice and a secure homeland for both Palestinians and Israelis. But neither the horror nor the folly of these desperate acts are an excuse for having the U.S. join Israel in multiplying and intensifying the terrorism in the Middle East. The terrorism of the strong is as offensive and self-defeating as the terrorism of the weak and dispossessed.

By focussing on Qaddafi's flamboyant behavior and attacking Libya militarily, the U.S. has played a major role once again in diverting attention from the legitimate grievances of the Palestinians, after having played a major role in creating and perpetuating them. It has chosen to ignore problems that have festered for years and that have produced terrible acts that cannot be justified but whose causes must be understood and eliminated.

V

One of the vocal cheerleaders of the United States attacks on Libya was my senator, Patrick Leahy of Vermont. But a few weeks later, Senator Leahy began to beat a retreat. In a speech on the Senate floor and at a follow-up news conference, he said that whereas he had endorsed the President's original strikes as reasonable and justified, he now cautions against any similar actions in the future. He pointed out that reliance on military action fails to resolve the underlying political problems in the Middle East. He was honest enough to say that he had come to this position as a result of having been deluged with protests from his constituents.

I draw two conclusions from this development and from the second thoughts of other enthusiasts of military action who are now sounding a different note. One is that educational campaigns and vigorous protests *do* make a difference. The second is that the American public was not as completely supportive as media applause and hasty, unreliable polls would have us believe. We have already taken note of the black response. As Michael Parenti pointed out in *Inventing Reality: The Politics of the Mass Media*:

> The media cannot mold every political feeling that we have, but they can fill the air with pronouncements about what our feelings allegedly are... The press may not be able to create a conservative mood within us, but it can repeatedly announce that a conservative mood exists.

It is time for us to stop allowing the media to intimidate us. It is time instead to pay attention to the feelings of sisterhood and brotherhood that keep rising within us. And it is time to assert our own common sense. Each in his or her own way can nourish those sentiments and express them by taking whatever steps seem either necessary or possible in the "protracted struggle" to be true to ourselves and to the rest of the human race.

Today millions of us allow the press to tell us what our feelings allegedly are. Millions of others know their true feelings but have been intimidated into thinking that "you can't fight the government." But as the history of the anti-Vietnam War movement demonstrates, flawed as that movement was, we don't stand alone and together we can accomplish miracles. As more and more of us break free from these patterns of paralysis and join the millions who have already done so, wonderful things will begin to happen.

Notes

Introduction

1. *New York Times*, April 30, 1985.

2. Apparently one of his sources was *Black Box* by Alexander Dallin (University of Chicago Press, 1985). A scholarly book by a respectable investigator, it tells us that "aviation industry professionals as well as civil aviation administrators rather unanimously dismiss as exceedingly small the likelihood of simultaneous malfunction of all 3 independent navigation systems (INS) which had previously worked without noticeable error... Assuming the very unlikely combination of circumstances by which all three INS had suddenly malfunctioned...the crew still had available to it the weather radar system, which would have shown clearly when KAL 007 was flying over or near land—such as Kamchatka and Sakhalin—at a time when the flight plan (and the flight crew's position reports to Anchorage and Narita) had it over water."

Chapter 1

1. Quoted in Edgar Snow, *The Other Side of the River: Red China Today*, p.686. Also, see *Vietnam: History, Documents, and Opinions on a Major World Crisis*, Marvin E. Gettleman, ed.: Fawcett, 1965, p. 46.

2. Founded in 1939, it had operated underground under the slogan "Neither the French nor the Japanese as Masters. Independence for Vietnam."

3. Harold Isaacs, *No Peace in Asia*, New York, 1947; excerpted in Gettleman.

4. The U.N. was established at a conference in San Francisco that was convened by the U.S., Soviet Union, Britain and China and attended by 50 countries, from April 25 to June 26, 1945.

5. The first tentative approach from within Japan came in September 1944. Others came with increasing intensity from then until the end of the war. On May 28 (1945), Harry Hopkins, President Truman's special envoy to Moscow cabled Truman that "Japan is doomed and the Japanese know it. Peace feelers are being put out...and we should therefore consider our joint attitudes and act in concert about the surrender of Japan." (quoted in David Horowitz, *The Free World Colossus*, Hill & Wang, 1965.) But the United States was anxious that the war not end until it could drop the A Bomb, which it thought would insure its domination of the post-war world, ushering in what *Life* magazine hailed shortly afterwards as "The American Century." Sec. of War Henry Stimson says that on June 6 he told Truman that "I was a little fearful that before we could get ready [to use the bomb] the Air

Force might have Japan so thoroughly bombed out that the new weapon would not have a fair background to show its strength." (Gabriel Kolko, *The Politics of War: The World and United States Foreign Policy, 1943-1945*, Random House, 1968).

The technical reason given (ex post facto) for the U.S. refusal to accept the numerous Japanese proposals (which it kept secret at the time) was that the Japanese wanted the Emperor to retain his traditional ceremonial role; but the terms of the surrender that the U.S. "imposed" unconditionally, *after* Hiroshima and Nagasaki, permitted this anyway. It was a little like what happened in 1972-3, when the United States cut off negotations with the Vietnamese in the fall of 1972, carried out merciless military campaigns that involved tragic losses of American and Vietnamese lives, and finally signed a treaty that had been available to it before these campaigns. It was during this period of unnecessary warfare that the 1972 Christmas bombings took place, with the U.S. dropping more bombs on Hanoi and Haiphong than Germany had dropped on Great Britain during the entire Second World War.

Apparently the Soviet Union did not want the war to end "prematurely" either, until it could move its troops from the European theater to Asia and declare war on Japan (which it did not do until August 8, 1945) thereby strengthening (it thought) *its* post-war position. It failed to notify the United States of the earliest formal messages from Japan, which asked it to use its good offices to arrange a surrender.

6. The listing under "Annam" in the *Encyclopaedia Brittanica*, Fifteenth Edition, 1985 begins: "Annam (Chinese: *pacified* South) French-governed Vietnam... The term Annam was never officially used by the Vietnamese to describe their country, even during the French colonial period." [Emphasis added]

7. *Pentagon Papers*, Gravel Edition, Vol. 1, pp. 20, 50, 51; Vol. 5, p. 34.

8. Quoted in Isaacs; Gettleman, p. 47.

9. Transcript from *ABC News* of Show #1024, April 25, 1985.

10. Bernard B. Fall, *Last Reflections on a War*, Schocken Books.

11. *Philadelphia Inquirer*, Sunday, December 16, 1984. Here are some other excerpts from the article:

> Several (relatives of helicopter crewmen killed in 1983) mentioned ventures into hostile territory in Central America. One specifically mentioned Nicaragua. Another mentioned El Salvador. A third referred to "going south" to a region where "what they sent you on could kill you."
>
> The battalion-size unit had 17 aircraft fatalities in 1983—nearly half the 35 reported by the entire Army for that year...

The elder Alvey's recollection coincides with that of Linda Jennings, 30, of Key West, Florida. She is the widow of Warrant Officer Allen E. Jennings, 30, reported by the Army to have died on August 26, 1983, in a Black Hawk crash at Fort Campbell. "Everybody (in the unit) knew that if they were lost, nobody would know," Jennings said during an interview. "They knew if they got grounded or caught, they were on their own."

Another woman widowed in the August 26 crash, Brenda Jordan, 32, of Tampa, Florida, said her husband, David, a warrant officer, had told her the same thing days before his death...

Current task force members would say almost nothing... "That's in the top-secret category, so I'm not going to talk about that," said one Army airman who is close to the unit and who was asked about the Task Force's Central American missions. Another, just out of the unit, said, "I don't want to go to jail."

"These were not training exercises," Alvey insisted. "Don said one time you could tell damn well they had been in a fight because a lot of them were wounded." Alvey also recalled that his son had spoken of ferrying troops into Nicaragua from an offshore container ship. Press reports in 1984 indicated that the C.I.A. was using a so-called mother ship off Nicaragua's Pacific coast.

During the Vietnam War, military personnel were often assigned to the C.I.A. for secret operations in Laos and Cambodia... These roles created a problem when personnel were killed while on secret missions in noncombatant nations, said a former Army officer assigned to the C.I.A. to plan such missions.

The solution, said the former official, who asked not to be identified, was "bodywashing." He explained, "If a guy was killed on a mission, and if it was sensitive politically, we'd ship the body back home and have a jeep roll over on him at Fort Huachuca." Fort Huachuca is a remote Army intelligence and covert-operation base in Arizona.

12. Ho Chi Minh, *Selected Writings*, "Answers to the Press on U.S. Intervention in Indochina," July 25, 1950.
13. "A Libertarian Analysis of Central America," interview with Noam Chomsky in *Kick It Over*, Winter 1985/86, Toronto, Canada.

Chapter 2

1. *Anatomy of a War*, pp. 26, 27.

2. Fall, *ibid.*

3. In 1945, Isaacs met with Ho ("my Shanghai friend from long ago") in Hanoi, where Ho made this comment directly to him.

4. Ho's "Address to the 6th Congress of Party Cadres," January 18, 1949; *Ho Chi Minh Selected Writings,* Foreign Languages Publishing House, Hanoi, 1973, p. 89.

5. "Elevate Revolutionary Ethics. Make a Clean Sweep of Individualism." Written on the 39th anniversary of the founding of the Vietnam Workers [Communist] Party, Feb. 3, 1969. *Selected Writings,* pp. 352, 353.

6. *Anatomy*, p. 56.

7. Ho Chi Minh, *Selected Works*, Vol. IV, Hanoi 1962, pp. 254, 257.

Chapter 3

1. Ho, *Selected Writings*, p. 91.

2. *Anatomy*, p. 14.

3. Jumper and Norman, "Vietnam, the Historical Background," Gettleman, p. 24.

4. Ho, *Selected Works*, Vol. IV, p. 33.

5. *Anatomy*, p. 57.

6. Ho, *op. cit.*

7. *Anatomy*, p. 58.

8. Nancy Wiegersma, *Peasant Land, Peasant Revolution,* forthcoming, p. 241. Gerard Chaliand, *The Peasants of North Vietnam,* Baltimore, Penguin Books, 1969.

9. *Anatomy*, pp. 66, 67.

10. Christine White, "Family and Class in the Theory and Practice of Marxism: The Case of Vietnam," Institute for Developmental Studies Conference, No. 133, University of Sussex, England, pp. 17-20; in Wiegersma.

11. Ho, September, 1954. *Selected Works*, IV, p. 33.

12. *Selected Works*, IV, p. 193.

13. *Ibid.*

14. *Nation*, March 6, 1954.

15. Article in *The China Quaterly* [London], January/March, 1962; Gettleman, p. 210.

16. Letter to the *New York Times*, dated April 30, 1985, published May 7. Hilsman was Assistant Secretary of State for Far Eastern Affairs in 1963 and 1964.

17. Wiegersma, pp. 310, 311.

18. *Anatomy*, p. 105, 106.

19. Henry Kissinger, *White House Years*, p. 31.

20. A case can be made that Lyndon Johnson was in the midst of a similar, secret strategy in 1968, which was intended to take him to

Moscow just before the Democratic Nominating Convention and bring him back to the United States (and the convention) just in time to turn the convention around and accept a draft to be re-nominated. If so, the Soviet invasion of Czechoslovakia made it impossible for LBJ to go to Moscow and frustrated the plan. See my *Revolutionary Nonviolence*, Bobbs-Merrill and Doubleday/Anchor, 1970; and Theodore H. White, *The Making of the President—1968*, Atheneum.

    21. *White House Years*, pp. 120-1.

Chapter 4

    1. Quoted in Michael Mott, *The Seven Mountains of Thomas Merton*, Houghton Mifflin, 1984; p. 415.

    2. Eddie Wright, Senior Thesis, Vermont College Adult Degree Program, February 1985.

    3. *New York Times*, April 17, 1954. Nixon went on to say that "The main target of the Communists in Indochina...is Japan."

    4. From the Final Declaration of the Geneva Conference (July 21, 1954). The Geneva accords are printed in Gettleman.

    5. The quotations are from pages 54, 59 and 60 of the *New York Times* edition of the *Pentagon Papers*.

    6. *Ibid.*, p. 55.

    7. Neil Sheehan's introduction to the *New York Times* edition of the *Pentagon Papers*.

    8. The Winooski 44 Trial, Burlington, Vermont, November 1984. Stockwell's disclosure was originally made a few years earlier.

    9. Robert Scheer, *How the United States Got Involved in Vietnam*, The Center for the Study of Democratic Institutions; excerpted both in Gettleman and in Judith Clavier Albert and Stewart Edward Albert, *The Sixties Papers*, Praeger, 1984.

    10. Quoted in Scheer.

    11. *Ibid.*

    12. *Ibid.*

    13. *Pentagon Papers*, NY Times edition, p. 57.

Chapter 5

    1. *Anatomy*, p. 87.

    2. Because of this indignity, not to international law and solemmn agreements, but to the flamboyant American party-giver and her wealthy guests, the story appeared in the *New York Times* more than once, beginning on July 21, 1955. Gettleman, p. 164.

    3. *Anatomy*, p. 86.

4. Gettleman, p. 117, quoting from a McNamara news conference on December 21, 1963.

5. Gettleman, p. 163.

6. Robert Manning, "Development of a Vietnam Policy: 1952-1965," in *Vietnam Reconsidered*, Harrison Salisbury, ed., Harper and Row, 1984.

7. See speech by Jeannette Rankin in the House of Representatives on December 8, 1941; Dellinger, *Revolutionary Nonviolence*, Bobbs-Merrill, 1970; Doubleday, 1971.

8. *I.F. Stone's Weekly*, March 8, 1965.

9. *Vietnam Reconsidered*.

10. *Anatomy*, p. 113. Also, see the *Pentagon Papers, NY Times* edition, pp. 83-124.

Chapter 6

1. Stanley Karnow, *Vietnam: A History*, Viking, 1983; p. 371. Karnow, who supported the war and has only partially modified his view of its history, writes that "Subsequent research by both official and unofficial investigators has indicated with almost total certainty that the...Communist attack...never happened."

2. *New York Times*, April 30, 1985.

3. As reported at the time in *Ramparts* magazine. The official slightly sanitized version, as printed in *Public Papers of the Presidents of the United States, 1966, Book II* (Washington, 1967) is: "There are 3 billion people in the world and we have only 200 million of them. We are outnumbered 15 to 1. If might did make right they would sweep over the United States and take what we have. We have what they want." Note that while raising fears of losing the ill-gotten gains that accrue to us from our foreign investments (and military power) President Johnson simultaneously slipped in the idea that it is not our "might" but our "right" to take our troops and bombers to Vietnam. That Johnson did not place too much emphasis on our virtue can be seen in an earlier speech in which he proclaimed that "without superior air power America is a bound and throttled giant; impotent and easy prey to any yellow dwarf with a pocket knife." (Quoted in Noam Chomsky, *Turning the Tide*, South End Press, Boston, 1985.)

4. Vincent Harding, *There is a River*, Harcourt, Brace, Jovanovitch, 1981.

5. In *Vietnam Reconsidered*.

6. *New York Times*, October 10, 1985.

7. *Anatomy*, pp. 72-73.

Chapter 7

1. Dellinger, *More Power Than We Know: The People's Movement Toward Democracy*, Doubleday, 1975; p. 11.

2. *Anatomy*, pp. 189, 190.

3. *Dear America: Letters Home from Vietnam*, edited by Bernard Edelman for The New York Vietnam Veterans Memorial Commission, W.W. Norton & Company, 1985.

4. *Liberation*, August 1966.

Chapter 8

1. *Liberation*, December 1966. This report also appears in Dellinger, *Revolutionary Nonviolence*, Bobbs-Merrill, 1970.

Chapter 9

1. *New York Times*, May 1, 1985.

2. Le Duc Tho is a senior Vietnamese official who was Vietnam's top negotiator at the Paris Peace Talks. He and Henry Kissinger were jointly awarded the Nobel Peace Prize after they negotiated a cease-fire agreement in January, 1973. Kissinger accepted the award, but Tho declined it.

Chapter 10

1. *New York Times*, May 1, 1985.

2. *New York Times*, April 28, 1985.

3. *New York Times*, May 2, 1985.

4. *New York Times*, May 1, 1985.

5. There was some speculation among other correspondents as to why the *Times* had sent a relatively inexperienced newcomer for this important occasion. Perhaps, to paraphrase the old saying, since the *Times* had already developed its line on Vietnam from a distance, it didn't want to be confused by the facts.

6. In the article I have quoted from earlier, John Corry wrote: "Contact between Vietnamese and foreigners is prohibited by law."

7. I say "her," because in the falsely "objective," impersonal reporting of American newspaperese, the reporter almost always writes "talked with a Western reporter," "told a visitor" or some similar phrase, rather than "talked with (or told) *me*." The press hasn't adapted yet to Einstein's insight that the object observed varies according to the observer. If this is true when the observed is an inanimate object (Einstein's field of scientific inquiry), imagine how great the variations

can be when the observed as well as the observer is a human being. So why camouflage (for the most part unsuccessfully) the identity of the observer? The press's little ritual here may be both minor and not particularly successful, but it tells us something about its efforts to convince the public (and perhaps itself) that it scrupulously expunges all biases from its reportage and tells us the true "facts," the objective "truth." Thus the *Times* tells us "All the news that's fit to print" rather than the news that the publishers of the *New York Times*, influenced by their religious, class, national and other individual conditioning—and by business considerations—think is fit to print.

Chapter 11

1. See Chapter 1, footnote 5.

Chapter 12

1. In *Vietnam Reconsidered*.
2. Since reading this transcript, I have come across an earlier statement by Haig which says that China advised the U.S. "not to allow yourselves to be defeated in Vietnam, and not to pull out your forces from Southeast Asia." *Christian Science Monitor*, June 20, 1979.

Chapter 13

1. John McAuliff, in *Vietnam Reconsidered*.
2. "U.S. Chemical Warfare and its Consequences," *Vietnam Courier*, Hanoi, 1980.
3. *New Yorker*, April 29, 1985.
4. Taped conversation with Frank Wilkinson, Executive Director Emeritus of the National Committee against Repressive Legislation (NCARL); *Indochia Newsletter* of the Bach Mai Hospital Fund, P.O. Box 129, Dorchester, MA 02122, July/August 1985.

Chapter 14

1. We could start by working out arrangements for having the first fruits of agriculture and industry go to provide all members of the human family with such elementary necessities as basic food, clothing, shelter and medical care. How can we say that providing milk and

medical care for every child, for instance—or meaningful work and adequate shelter for every adult—is less of a community responsibility than providing fire protection, or, in a city, running water, toilets and public sanitation, for every resident.

Chapter 16

1. Truong Nhu Tang, with David Chanoff and Doan Van Toai, *A Vietcong Memoir, An Inside Account of the Vietnam War and Its Aftermath*, Harcourt Brace Jovanovich, 1985.

2. Letter to the author. Chomsky discusses this further in Chapter 4 of his *Towards a New Cold War*.

3. I wonder how many Americans have heard of the French bloodbath. I learned of it in Paris in 1950; and Simon de Beauvoir touches on it in her novel, *The Mandarins*.

4. *Seven Days* magazine, June 29, 1979.

Chapter 17

1. *New Yorker*, April 29, 1985.

Chapter 18

1. I talked with Norman about two weeks before he immolated himself—before, as far as I know, he had decided to do so. He was almost as upset with the failure of "ordinary decent Americans" and the traditional peace organizations to raise a determined enough challenge to what the government was doing as he was with the direct involvement of supposed "liberals" like McNamara. I have always felt that he died not just to challenge McNamara, but to challenge all of us.

2. "Washington Merry-Go-Round," *The Caledonian Record*, St. Johnsbury, Vermont, July 10, 1985.

3. For reasons of confidentiality, I prefer to cite the published testimony at the War Crimes Tribunal rather than that of other veterans.

4. This and all the subsequent testimony from the International Tribunal are from *Against the Crime of Silence, Proceedings of the Russell International War Crimes Tribunal*, ed. by John Duffett, O'Hare Books, 1968.

5. *Vietcong Memoir*, p. 112.

Chapter 19

1. In *Vietnam Reconsidered*.

2. *New Yorker*, April 22, 1985.

3. *Seven Days* magazine, August 14, 1979.

4. After supplying some grim statistics on the total bombing (which I will include later) Robert Muller, National President of the Vietnam Veterans of America wrote about a visit he made to Vietnam in December 1981: "We were particularly nervous about the reaction of the Vietnamese to us, since we arrived on the ninth anniversary of the 1972 Christmas bombings—the celebration of which was announced on posters around town. (It should be remembered that in those ten days, we, the United States, dropped on Hanoi and Haiphong more bombs than Germany dropped on Great Britain during the entire Second World War.) And yet, never once in all of our travels and all of our encounters with the Vietnamese people did we have one negative look, one negative comment and we were warmly welcomed and warmly embraced."

5. There is a photo of Do Van Ngoc and his wounds in *Against the Crime of Silence*.

6. From *Vietnam Reconsidered*.

7. *New Yorker*, April 22, 1985.

Chapter 20

1. *New Yorker*, April 22, 1985.

2. Nguyen Khac Vien, "Vietnam '80," *Vietnam Courier*, Hanoi, 1980.

3. From a retrospective article ten years after the end of the war, May 2, 1985.

4. *New Yorker, op. cit.*

5. In *Vietnam Reconsidered*.

6. "The Path Which Led Me to Leninism," Ho Chi Minh *Selected Works*, Vol IV. Also see Kolko, *Anatomy*, p. 26; and Bernard Fall, *Last Reflections*, p. 72. The more Fall opposed the U.S. war, the more he leaned over backwards to be critical of Ho and Vietnamese Communism, somewhat in the manner of Congressmen today who criticize some of the Reagan administration's terrorist activities against Nicaragua but cover themselves by coupling their criticisms with biased and inflamatory attacks on the Sandinistas. But he clearly confirms the significance of Ho's experience in Paris.

Chapter 21

1. *Far Eastern Economic Review*, May 2, 1985.
2. *New Yorker, op. cit.*
3. *Ibid.*
4. Shaplen, *The New Yorker*, April 22, 1985.

Chapter 22

1. Shaplen, *New Yorker*, April 22, 1985.
2. Agence France Press, Tokyo, September 13, 1975.
3. *F.E.E.R.*, March 17, 1978.
4. *Los Angeles Times*, April 14, 1978.
5. From an interview of Thiounh Mum with Stephen R Heder; quoted in Michael Vickery, *Cambodia: 1975-82*, South End Press, 1984. Both Heder and Vickery are Australian scholars who specialize in Indochina.
6. See Vickery, pp. 140-148.
7. *New York Review of Books*, Sept. 27, 1984.
8. Interview in the *New York Review of Books*, March 15, 1985.
9. *Ibid.* p. 196.

Chapter 23

1. ASEAN was founded in 1967, with encouragement and assistance from the United States. The U.S. has tried, against some resistance, to use it as an "independent," "indigenous" anti-communist bludgeon against Vietnam.
2. *Far Eastern Economic Review*, March 14, 1985.
3. *F.E.E.R* of April 18, 1985.
4. *Ibid.*
5. *World Policy*, Winter 1986, World Policy Institute, New York.
6. *Ibid.*

7. *Ibid.*
8. Sukhumbhand Paribatra, *ibid.*
9. Richard Falk, *ibid.*

Afterword

1. Alexander Cockburn, *In These Times,* May 28, 1986.
2. *The New Yorker,* "The Talk of the Town," March 31, 1986.
3. *In These Times,* May 21-27, 1986.
4. *Ibid.*
5. *New York Times,* April 24, 1986.
6. *Ibid.*
7. *New York Times,* April 28, 1986.
8. Lars-Erik Nelson, *New York Daily News,* January 10, 1986.
9. *New York Times,* April 28, 1986.
10. *New York Times,* May 18, 1986.
11. *New York Times,* June 1, 1986.
12. *The Nation,* April 26, 1986.
13. *Ibid.*